After Auschwitz

Eva Schloss

with Karen Bartlett

After Auschwitz

A Story of Heartbreak and Survival by the Stepsister of Anne Frank

HODDER &
STOUGHTON

First published in Great Britain in 2013 by Hodder & Stoughton
An Hachette UK company

4

Copyright © Eva Schloss and Karen Bartlett 2013

The right of Eva Schloss and Karen Bartlett to be identified as the Authors
of the Work has been asserted by them in accordance with the
Copyright, Designs and Patents Act 1988.

A CIP catalogue record for this title is available from the British Library

Hardback ISBN 978 1 4447 6068 2
Trade paperback ISBN 978 1 4447 6069 9
Ebook ISBN 978 1 4447 6070 5

Typeset in Sabon MT by Palimpsest Book Production Limited,
Falkirk, Stirlingshire

Printed and bound by
CPI Group (UK) Ltd, Croydon CR0 4YY

Hodder & Stoughton policy is to use papers that are natural,
renewable and recyclable products and made from wood grown in sustainable forests.
The logging and manufacturing processes are expected to conform to the
environmental regulations of the country of origin.

Hodder & Stoughton Ltd
338 Euston Road
London NW1 3BH

www.hodder.co.uk

This book is dedicated to the memory of the victims of the Holocaust and genocide who could not tell their own stories.

Eva Schloss

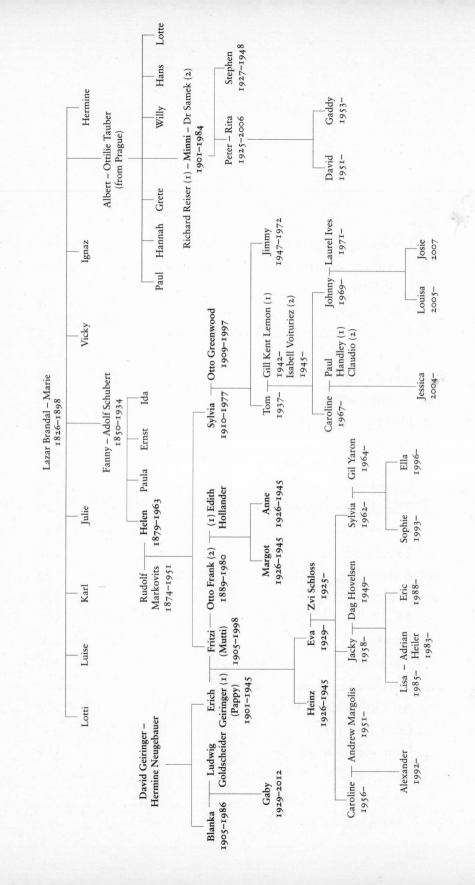

Contents

1. Leave Something Behind   1
2. A Viennese Family   7
3. Childhood   15
4. The Nazis are Coming   28
5. An Undesirable Little Girl   41
6. Amsterdam   52
7. Anne Frank   61
8. Occupation   66
9. Hiding   80
10. Betrayal   91
11. Auschwitz-Birkenau   104
12. Camp Life   115
13. The Bleakest Winter   126
14. Liberation   137
15. The Road Back   152
16. Amsterdam Again   169
17. A New Life   178
18. The Trial   194
19. London   200
20. Zvi's Story   208
21. The Wedding   217
22. An Unbroken Chain   225
23. Otto and Fritzi   237
24. New Beginnings   250

25. One Day in Spring   258
26. The Play   270
27. Mutti   283
28. Reaching Out   295
29. Going Back   303
30. Epilogue   310

Acknowledgments   315
Index   317

I

Leave Something Behind

'A nd now I know Eva will want to say a few words.'
The phrase echoed around the large hall, and filled
me with dread.

I was a quiet middle-aged woman, married to an investment banker, with three grown-up daughters. The man
who had spoken was Ken Livingstone, then still the fire-
brand leader of London's soon to be abolished Greater
London Council, and the biggest thorn in Prime Minister
Margaret Thatcher's side.

We had met earlier that day, and he was certainly not to
know that those few words would send me into turmoil.
Even I didn't know that this was the start of my long
journey towards coming to terms with the terrible events
of my childhood.

I was fifteen years old when I and thousands of others
rattled across Europe in a train made up of dark, cramped
cattle trucks and was dumped out at the gates of Auschwitz-
Birkenau concentration camp. More than forty years had
passed, but when Ken Livingstone asked me to speak a
feeling of total terror gripped my stomach. I wanted to
crawl under the table, and hide.

It was an early spring day in 1986, and we were at the
opening of the Anne Frank Travelling Exhibit at the Mall
Galleries, next to the Institute of Contemporary Arts in

London. More than three million people around the world have now seen that exhibit, but back then we were just beginning to tell the story of the Holocaust to a new generation through Anne's diary, and the photos of Anne and her family.

Those photos connected me to Anne in a way that neither of us could have imagined when we were young girls who used to play together in Amsterdam. We were very different characters, but Anne was one of my friends.

After the war, Anne's father, Otto Frank, returned to Holland and began a close relationship with my mother that was borne of their mutual loss and heartbreak. They married in 1953 and Otto became my stepfather. He gave me the Leica camera that he had used to take the pictures of Anne and her sister Margot, so that I could find my own way in the world and become a photographer. I used that camera for many years and I still have it today.

Anne's story is that of a young girl who has touched the whole world through the simple humanity of her diary. My story is different. I was also a victim of Nazi persecution and was sent to a concentration camp – but, unlike Anne, I survived.

By the spring of 1986 I had been living in London for nearly forty years and in that time the city had changed beyond recognition from a poor, bombed-out shell into a teeming and energetic multicultural metropolis. I wish I could say that I had undergone a similar transformation.

I had remade my life, and started my own family with a wonderful husband and children who meant everything to me. I was even running my own business. But a large part of me was missing. I was not myself, and the outgoing girl who once rode her bike, flipped handstands and never stopped chattering was locked away somewhere I couldn't reach.

At night I dreamed a big black hole would swallow me up. When my grandchildren asked about the tattoo on my arm that I had been branded with at Auschwitz, I told them it was just my telephone number. I did not talk about the past.

I could hardly refuse an invitation to speak at the opening of the Anne Frank Exhibition, though – especially when it was Otto and my mother's life's work.

At Ken Livingstone's urging I stood up and haltingly began to talk. Probably to the dismay of those in the audience who were hoping for a short introduction, I found that once I started I couldn't stop. The words tumbled out, and I talked on and on, recounting all the traumatic and painful experiences I had lived through. I was light-headed and terrified; I have no recollection of what I said.

My daughter Jacky, who was listening, says, 'It was very nerve-wracking. We hardly knew anything about Mum's experiences and suddenly she was on stage, finding it difficult to talk and breaking down in tears.'

My words may not have been coherent to anyone else, but it was a very big moment to me. I had reclaimed a small part of myself.

Despite such an unpromising start, after that event more and more people asked me to talk about what had happened during the war. At first I asked my husband to draft speeches for me, which I read out – badly. But gradually I found my own voice, and learned to tell my own story.

Many things have changed in the world since the end of

World War Two, but unfortunately prejudice and discrimination have not. From the Civil Rights movement in the United States to Apartheid South Africa, the war in the former Yugoslavia to those caught in ongoing conflicts in countries like the Democratic Republic of Congo, I saw people across the world struggling to be treated with equal human dignity and understanding. And as a Jewish person I saw that even the truth about the Holocaust had not woken the world up to the full horror of anti-Semitism. Today there are still many people who look for scapegoats based on the colour of someone's skin, their background, their sexuality − or their religion.

I wanted to talk to those people about the bitterness and anger that made them blame others. Like them, I knew just how hard and unfair life can sometimes seem. For many years I was full of hate, too.

As my world expanded I began to work with the Anne Frank House in Amsterdam and the Anne Frank Trust in the UK. Early on, I wrote a book about my experiences, pouring out raw memories of the Holocaust, and then, much later, an account of my life with my brother Heinz for younger children. I was astonished when other people also wanted to write about my story.

Eventually I found myself travelling the world and talking to people in the US, China, Australia and across Europe. Everywhere I spoke, the people I met touched me and changed me until I could honestly say that I was not a person driven by hatred and bitterness any more. Nothing can ever excuse the dreadful crimes the Nazis committed. Those acts will always be absolutely unforgivable and I hope that because of personal stories like mine they will always be remembered as such. But through my work in reaching out to people and telling my story I blossomed into a new person – maybe the person I always was inside – and that has been a gift for me and my family.

Talking to children in schools and people in prison has been perhaps the most meaningful part of my work. When I look out at an audience of small children from different backgrounds and countries, or men and women convicted of serious crimes, I can tell that they are wondering what on earth they will have in common with me – a small lady with a neat cardigan and an Austrian accent. Yet I know that by the end of our time together, we will have shared our feeling that sometimes we don't fit in, life has been tough and we don't know what the future will hold. We usually turn out to be not so different after all.

I want them to know what I have learned: that however deep your despair, there is always hope. Life is very precious and beautiful – and no one should waste it.

In this book I will tell you about my family and the long journey I undertook, literally and in spirit, with my mother. I will also tell you much more about my father, Erich, and my brother, Heinz. All I will say here is that I lost both of them and that, even if you met me now as an elderly woman, part of me is still the fifteen-year-old girl who loves and misses them desperately and thinks of them every day.

There is a particular memory from our time together as a family that has guided me through all the years since, and influenced my work.

It was May 1940 and we were gathered in our flat in Amsterdam. We had already fled our home in Vienna, and now the Nazis had invaded Holland – the worst possible news. I could usually rely on my big brother Heinz to reassure me and cheer me up but that night he was upset and at a loss for words. He told me he didn't know if our father could keep us safe any more, the Nazis were coming and taking Jews away. 'I'm really scared, Evi,' he said. 'I'm really afraid of dying.'

My father gathered us together on the sofa and wrapped us up in his arms. He told us that we were links in a chain, and that we would live on through our children.

'But what if we don't have any children?' Heinz asked.

'Children, I promise you this,' my father said. 'Everything you do leaves something behind; nothing gets lost. All the good you have accomplished will continue in the lives of the people you have touched. It will make a difference to someone, somewhere, sometime, and your achievements will be carried on. Everything is connected like a chain that cannot be broken.'

In this book I will tell you how I have tried my best to leave something important behind.

2

A Viennese Family

If you were young, ambitious and Jewish at the turn of the twentieth century there was only one place to be: Vienna.

My child's eyes took the city's majestic size and sophistication for granted; it was home, and I was a true *Wiener*. By the time I was born we were living in a spacious villa out in the leafy suburb of Hietzing, although my family had a long and sometimes turbulent history with the city.

Until the end of World War One, Vienna was the jewel in the Hapsburg crown, the seat of the vast and powerful Austro-Hungarian Empire that stretched from the Ukraine and Poland across Austria and Hungary and down to Sarajevo in the Balkans.

Pre-war Vienna was a commercial and cultural powerhouse; business was fuelled by trade from the River Danube while composers like Gustav Mahler, writers like Arthur Schnitzler and doctors like Sigmund Freud lit up the streets, opera houses and cafés with new ideas. It was almost impossible not to be caught up in the ferment of exciting people planning dramatic activities. Down at Café Central you could find Leon Trotsky playing chess and plotting revolution; over at Café Sperl, Egon Schiele and one of his models might be taking a break from painting his provocative nude portraits.

Those were exhilarating days. By 1910 the city's population had reached more than two million. The imperial boulevards of the Ringstrasse were surrounded by streets of new apartment buildings for a growing middle class of shopkeepers and merchants. These people formed the mass audience for Viennese culture – suddenly they were buying theatre tickets, eating out and going on tourist trips into the Vienna woods and hills.

A growing part of this middle class was a well-educated and successful Jewish community.

Of course Jewish people had been living in Vienna, on and off, for about 700 years; but a series of unsympathetic rulers meant that Jews were often driven out of the city, and the community had remained small and unsettled. It wasn't until Emperor Franz Josef's policy of religious tolerance and full civic equality in 1867 that the Jewish community really began to flourish. In the thirty years that followed, the Jewish population of Vienna shot up from less than 8,000 to more than 118,000 – and soon started to play a prominent role in Viennese life.

Some of these Jewish families were very rich and well known indeed. They bought palatial homes along the Ringstrasse and decorated them in marble and gold. Lower down the social scale were the middle-class professionals. By the beginning of the twentieth century nearly three quarters of all bankers and more than half of all doctors, lawyers and journalists were Jewish. There was even a hugely popular Jewish soccer team that was part of the Hakoah sports club.

Then an economic crisis and the collapse of the paraffin industry, which employed many Polish Jews, followed by unrest in the Balkans and eventually World War One, brought fresh waves of immigrants to Vienna. These newcomers were poorer, less educated Jewish families who arrived from areas further east, like Polish Galicia. They settled around Vienna's northern railway station in a part of the city called Leopoldstadt. These families seemed more religious, and less 'German' in their culture than the Jewish community that had already assimilated into Austrian life. Families like mine would never have met or mixed with these new immigrants, who were to become the focus of much deep anti-Semitic prejudice.

My father's background was typical of a well-established middle-class family. My grandfather, David Geiringer, was born in Hungary in 1869. After moving to Vienna he founded a shoe factory called Geiringer & Brown, and by the time my father Erich was born in November 1901, he was doing quite well for himself.

I only have one photo of my father's parents together. My grandfather looks businesslike with his moustache and bowler hat, while my father and aunt, small children, are dressed up in little sailor suits and solemnly staring at the camera. My grandmother, Hermine, is slim and elegant and made at least a foot taller by an enormous hat wreathed in layers of black lace and chiffon that was then the height of fashion. She had come to live in Vienna from Bohemia in what is now the Czech Republic.

Even with the demands for frigid stillness that photography required at the time, they seem a happy family, and that is how my father remembered it. Unfortunately soon afterwards my grandmother was diagnosed with cancer, and died in 1912 at the age of thirty-four. My grandfather remarried, to a woman who turned out to be an unsympathetic stepmother, and so my father left home when he was still a teenager and set out to forge his own way in the world. His first experience of a close family life had been brought to an abrupt and unhappy end – but he was about to meet the woman who would shape the rest of his life, my mother.

I have to say that my mother was beautiful. While my father was dark and dashing, my mother was blonde and blue-eyed, with wavy hair and a dazzling smile. Her name was Elfriede Markovits but everyone called her Fritzi, and she was full of life. One of my favourite photos of her was taken when she was only a young girl, laughing and feeding a horse. The circumstances were far from funny – she had gone to the country where my grandfather was stationed with the army to escape the worst of a famine; but she is still smiling. The photo might give you the impression that she was down-to-earth, practical and rustic in some way, but actually she was none of those things. At least not then.

Fritzi's mother, Helen, came from a very wealthy family who owned vineyards in what is now the Czech Republic, and a sulphuric spa near Vienna, in Baden bei Wien, which I hated visiting because it smelled like rotten eggs.

My grandmother's circumstances were considerably reduced when she married my grandfather, Rudolf Markovits, who represented Osram, a company that made light bulbs amongst other things. Although my grandfather was a good salesman and the family were far from poor, the end of World War One brought hard times to most Austrians.

Food had been severely rationed during the war, and the collapse of Hapsburg rule in 1918 left Austria in dire straits. The country faced crippling reparations under the 1919 Treaty of Versailles peace settlement, but the nation went bankrupt before the rate could be set.

What had once been the head of a vast empire was now a small country, minus its more profitable limbs. The industry and agriculture that had been the backbone of the Austro-Hungarian Empire was now holding up the economies of other countries, like Poland and the newly independent Czechoslovakia, Hungary and Yugoslavia. These new nations held Austria to ransom until border disputes were settled, and soon all of Europe was whispering that the citizens of Vienna were starving to death.

At one point the Markovits family were so hungry they killed and cooked their pet bird. My mother, who loved the bird, remembered crying over her plate but pulling the meat off the little bones and eating it all the same.

So it's true that by the time seventeen-year-old Erich Geiringer met fourteen-year-old Fritzi Markovits, both my parents were acquainted with hardship and uncertainty. But the knowledge that life could bring swiftly changing circumstances did not affect their *joie de vivre* in roaring-Twenties Vienna one bit. As this letter from 1921 shows, my father was determined that no one would stand in the way of their courtship – not even Fritzi's mother who had told him her daughter was too young for such a serious entanglement.

Vienna, 17 August 1921

Your honoured lady,

*I got your letter today from the 15th and at first I
was actually quite shocked – but then it ripened in
my conscience that your honoured lady must mean it
with good intentions. I am very grateful for the trust
that you give to Fritzi and myself. You are quite right
on many points, and I have to admit, though it is very
painful for me, that I rushed forward with our future
plans.*

*The idea ripened in my brain in a single moment, and
I didn't realise the resistance it would bring.*

*I'm sorry I can't accept the suggestion that your
honoured lady made to me to enjoy myself. My
dislike of those enjoyments is already deep and
long standing. From the moment I met Fritzi I was
under her spell, so I'm not interested in any other
enjoyments . . .*

*We were very serious about each other immediately,
otherwise we wouldn't have carried on with our deep
friendship . . .*

*Honoured lady, I hope you won't be too annoyed
when I tell Fritzi about your letter. I can't keep
something so important from her. I want to ask your
forgiveness when I deny that Fritzi is still the schoolgirl
that your honoured lady and husband believe – even*

*if she still goes to school she has much more maturity
than her age would suggest. An effect which your
honoured lady would have to admit.*

*I thank your honoured lady again for the good inten-
tions that you have shown me . . .*

Your very subdued,
Erich Geiringer

He was not subdued for long – they married in 1923, and
they were quite the young couple about town. If you'd
bumped into them parading down the Ringstrasse, hiking
in the mountains, or drinking with friends in one of the
city's famous 'new wine' gardens, this is how they might
have appeared.

My father was energetic and cheerful; warm and
charming. He had studied at the University of Vienna before
taking over the family shoe factory after my grandfather's
death in 1924. My mother lacked my father's fondness for
sports and outdoor pursuits, instead she loved listening to
music, playing the piano and spending time with all her
extended family.

They were both stylish. My father's suits had been impec-
cably tailored in Savile Row, and he took to wearing pink
shirts long before they became fashionable. My mother
always managed to look elegant, even with her hair cut in
the new short style, or wearing a tartan beret.

In all things, my father was the head of the family –
picking activities, leading expeditions, running his business
and furnishing the Geiringers' large new home in
Lautensackgasse with an impressive array of antiques,

including a marital bed that had once belonged to the Empress Zita. He was an indefatigable bundle of enthusiasm and ideas, for work and play, and my younger, more cautious mother followed in his wake.

They were young and in love, and felt lucky to have found each other.

3
Childhood

'Come on Heinz, I want to do it . . .'
I was a stubborn little girl with straight blonde hair and my chin often set forward in determination. My brother Heinz was tall and willowy, with long slim legs, dark hair and soulful eyes.

When the weather was nice I often wanted to pull our little hay wagon up to the top of the slope in our park-like back garden, jump in and then careen wildly down to the bottom again. This was one of my favourite games, and it was quite dangerous. We often incurred injuries, as the only way of controlling the wagon was by using a pole as a makeshift rudder. I suspect Heinz was significantly less enthusiastic about these joyrides than I was, but – as usual – he was humouring his little sister.

We were three years apart in age, and completely different in personality and looks.

Heinz was born in 1926, and my parents doted on him. The first trauma in his life occurred one spring day three years later when he was sent away without explanation, to my grandmother's house. A fretful week passed, still with no word of what had happened to my mother or father. Eventually he returned home to find my mother happily ensconced with a new baby bundled in her arms – me.

I was born on 11 May 1929 in Vienna's General Hospital,

and that first meeting with my brother might have caused a lifelong resentment. It seems amazing to me now that most adults thought it best not to introduce their children to the idea that a new baby was on the way, but that is how it was in those days.

Luckily for me Heinz did not bear a grudge, in fact he quickly became my staunchest supporter and the best big brother I could have hoped for. But the trauma of that week did leave one lasting impression on him. He developed a stutter that no doctors' visits, or remedies, could cure. My parents even took him to see Anna Freud, Sigmund Freud's daughter and the founder of child psychoanalysis – but to no avail. From the very beginning, he was a sensitive boy.

I wish I could say I was so delightful, but I inherited none of Heinz's easy-going temperament. In one family photo I sit frowning, squashed between my parents, Pappy and Mutti, looking slightly annoyed that they might want to pay attention to each other, or to Heinz.

I grew older, but no less wilful. I distinctly remember spending many evenings standing in the corner of a room, where I was supposed to reflect on some misdemeanour, and then apologise. There was a bentwood chair and I would walk round and round it, outlining the circle of the seat with my finger, and repeating that I would never say sorry.

These scenes were frequently brought on by disagreements over food. To put it mildly, I was a fussy eater, and I detested vegetables. I would usually be left alone at the table long after everyone else was finished, forbidden to leave until I had eaten everything on my plate. I often resorted to sticking peas to the underside of the table one by one.

One evening my parents said good night to us and left for an evening out, while Heinz and I ate dinner with our maid. The food consisted of a bony type of fish, and I hated pulling the sharp bones out of my mouth. In the middle of the meal my mother rang to find out how we were. 'They're fine,' the maid told her, before I ran to the phone and snatched it out of her startled hand and protested loudly to my mother, 'I'm not fine. We're eating fish, and it has lots of bones and I hate it.'

Naturally, my mother told me to go back, sit down and finish my dinner immediately. But I sometimes wonder if that streak of stubborn defiance kept me going in infinitely worse circumstances later on, when I really needed every ounce of flinty wilfulness not to give in.

For those first few years of my life our family home was the middle floor of a large nineteenth-century house in Hietzing. Hietzing was known as the greenest district in the city because of all of its parks and gardens. The Hapsburgs' summer home, Schönbrunn Palace, was around the corner, and famous architect Otto Wagner had built a personal subway stop nearby for the Emperor. (He used it twice.) Around the corner, Hietzing cemetery had a fearsome collection of dead Austrian aristocrats, making it one of the most upmarket spots in the city.

How well tended and comfortable the area must have looked to a down-on-his-luck and unpromising artist who had passed through Hietzing in the first decade of the twentieth century. Adolf Hitler came to study for entry to the prestigious Vienna Academy of Fine Arts but despite

the extra tuition, he failed his entry to the art academy
– twice.

Our house on the corner of Lautensackgasse looked
more like a castle than an ordinary suburban villa, with a
large turret and a big garden where we often had our
birthday parties.

I loved our busy home, and the people in it. We weren't
rich, but we lived in a comfortable warm house with double-
glazed windows that protected us from the harsh Vienna
winters. There was a maid who lived in the little room
behind the kitchen, and other women came by on a weekly
basis to help with washing and sewing.

If you'd dropped in to see us you might have found me
sitting at the little table I'd laid with a tea set in the alcove
of my bedroom, or all of us sitting down with Pappy in
our flowery wallpapered dining room to eat the main meal
of the day at lunchtime. At night people wandering past
would have heard Heinz whispering to me on the large
front porch while we looked up at the stars and he told
me some of his favourite Karl May Cowboy and Western
stories about Winnetou and Old Shatterhand.

Although there was a local synagogue very few Jewish
people lived in Hietzing, and Heinz and I really only became
aware of our religion and culture when we started going
to school. All Austrian children had compulsory religious
education. For the vast majority of the class this meant
receiving instruction in Roman Catholicism, but we were
sent for separate lessons three times a week – which meant
that everyone knew who the Jewish children were.

We enjoyed our religious lessons and we both became
quite enthusiastic about celebrating Jewish holidays and

traditions. My parents went along with our interest, and dutifully started lighting candles before the Sabbath meal on a Friday night. Friday nights became special occasions: Mutti would call to Heinz and me, and we would help her set the table for our Sabbath dinner. Laying out our best silver and china and putting the candles in the candlesticks was one of the highlights of my week, and I felt proud of growing up in a Jewish family.

Neither Pappy nor Mutti really had much interest in religion, though. My mother was quite unaware of a lot of Jewish traditions and my father was not observant, although he felt strongly about preserving our heritage and culture. On a day-to-day level that included having big family gatherings for Jewish holidays like Passover, and never allowing pork in the house. But there were times when our religion did rear its head in bigger ways.

Occasionally our Catholic maid and housekeeper took us to Mass. I think this was mainly so that she could go to church herself on Sundays, and I know lots of Jewish children had the same experience because most of the domestic servants in Vienna were farm girls from large Catholic families. I thoroughly enjoyed these outings, especially the ceremony, sights and smells of a Catholic communion. But when my father found out about these trips he was furious. He fired our maid immediately.

Later, my mother's sister and her family moved to England to escape the Nazis, and converted to Christianity. This upset my father deeply. He believed that if you were born Jewish you stayed Jewish. In his opinion, to convert because you feared persecution showed a remarkable lack of backbone.

As well as our Jewish traditions and culture, we partici-
pated in Viennese life in the same way as other middle-
class Austrians. Although we didn't celebrate Christmas
as such, we did welcome St Nicholas and his assistant
Black Peter on their feast day, which fell on 5 December.
For many years I longed for St Nicholas, the forebear of
Santa Claus, to bring me a little red car with pedals. I
dropped hints about it to my parents months in advance
and I would wake up early on the long awaited day and
look under my bed to see if it had arrived during the
night. It never did, but the first grown-up car I ever bought
was red.

Looking back, my parents may have thought we received
more than enough gifts and treats, because they sometimes
wrapped up presents they had given us in previous years,
and delivered them all over again.

It's true that we were not short of attention, or affection.
One of our daily outings was to visit my mother's parents
who lived in a smaller apartment down on Hietzinger
Haupstrasse. I say we visited my grandparents, but a major
part of these visits was seeing their maid, Hilda, who ran
the house like a martinet but spoiled us rotten. Hilda
was part of the family for forty years and although my
grandmother was nominally in charge and could be very
vocal on other occasions, she stayed quiet at home and
let Hilda run the house exactly as she saw fit. When my
grandparents were forced to flee the Nazis, Hilda looked
after the flat for them before eventually returning to her
own home village.

The only part of our daily visit that I did not enjoy was
having to say hello to my great-grandmother, who by then

was also living there. Great-Grandmother seemed to loom over me as a frightening figure, dressed head to toe in black. I told my mother that she was 'old and ugly', and I begged not to have to go and speak to her. No matter how much I protested, I was always pushed into her back bedroom where I would have to tiptoe over to the old lady and nervously give her a kiss on the cheek.

Luckily, the lure of spending time with my grandparents overcame my apprehension. In particular, I adored my grandfather. Grandfather Rudolf had special activities for each of us. He was very musical and Heinz would sit next to him on the piano stool where he would watch my grandfather draw a deep breath, close his eyes, and then let his hands fly up and down the keyboard. The music was always magnificent but my grandfather could only play by ear because as a young student he'd refused to learn to read sheet music.

I may have inherited his stubbornness, but I did not inherit my grandfather's musical talent. While Heinz spent hours practising the piano, and then the accordion and guitar, I occupied myself with more outgoing activities.

On Sunday mornings my grandfather took me to his local tavern next to the railway crossing where he had beer and I had soup. Taverns in Austria were more like cafés and wine gardens than pubs or bars; they were places men gathered at their regular tables for a convivial chat. The best part of this Sunday ritual was sitting next to my grandfather at our place on the table, while the waitress brought us goulash soup. The goulash was kept hot in a large stainless steel cup, and the waitress would carry over the cup and then pour it into our soup platters, while I watched wide eyed, counting out how many pieces of beef fell onto my plate. I was the centre of attention. My grandfather's friends listened with great interest to my accounts of what I'd done that week, or my latest hobbies. It was heaven.

In the city our lives revolved around family, home and school. Our maid encouraged us to let off steam by taking us to play in the park by Schönbrunn Palace, or to a Shirley Temple film, and occasionally the famous Vienna amusement park, the Prater, for a treat. More often we visited my parents' relatives, my father's sister Blanca and my cousin Gaby, who was also my best friend. My mother's sister, Sylvi, and her husband Otto lived nearby too, and I could go and play with their new baby, Tom.

I've always loved children and looking after babies, and I was fascinated by my new little cousin. After I saw Aunt Sylvi breastfeeding him I even tried this myself at home with my friend Martin. Martin and I were still both small children, and I had no breasts of course, but Martin's mother found us and caused an enormous fuss. I was extremely upset when she refused to allow him to come and play with me for a while. I felt confused, and perhaps for the first time, ashamed.

At school I laboured over my reading but didn't mind sums. In the afternoons we spent hours writing out words and letters from the gothic alphabet on a slate.

It was outdoors that I really came alive. I wanted to be just like Pappy; diving, swimming, running and climbing.

'You must never be afraid,' Pappy would shout, usually

before hurling us into some dangerous pursuit that thrilled me, and appalled Heinz.

He began training me to be fearless by encouraging me to jump off the tall wardrobe in my bedroom into his arms, and this progressed to dropping me into the deep end of the swimming pool. My mother would look on in alarm at these activities and Heinz would smile and say, 'No thank you, Pappy,' before returning to reading one of his favourite Jules Verne stories. But I trusted Pappy never to put me in any real danger, and I was sure his big arms would always be there to catch me.

Heinz found some of my hero worship highly amusing, and laughed at me when I decided to sleep on a stone pillow because Pappy said a soft mattress caused bad posture. During our mountain expeditions, Heinz would often wait with Mutti at the bottom, while I climbed crevasses, scampered barefoot up rocky paths and swung on ropes.

I even looked like a skinny little monkey. I was still a fussy eater and a disastrous trip to a sanatorium combined with lashings of cod liver oil had not filled me out. So I dangled on long skinny arms, with my ribs sticking out like the ridges on a washboard.

Every Sunday we headed off on these family adventures and for holidays we travelled further, up into the Austrian Tirol and Alps, staying in homely wooden chalets and wearing traditional Austrian lederhosen and Tirolean dresses.

These trips became even more enjoyable once Pappy drove home one day in our very first car. Pappy of course liked to drive very fast, squealing around the hairpin bends on high mountain passes so that we lurched to the side of the car looking straight down into the tiny homes of the villages below. Mutti sat next to him in the front, screaming, while Heinz and I were jammed in the back, clutching each other so tightly I thought our bones might break.

In the hot summer my mother took us out of the city on long holidays, usually accompanied by my Aunt Blanca and cousin Gaby. We would head down to the Adriatic coast in Italy where we could swim and play on the beach. Heinz worried about the jellyfish but I loved to bury myself in the fine sand and then run into the sea.

We were too young to understand the purpose of these trips, but my mother was visiting her Italian boyfriend and sometimes we stayed for three months at a time. Gino was very dapper and charming with smart white flannel trousers and gleaming dark hair. Although my mother may have had other boyfriends as well, Gino was an enduring and serious presence in her life. At one point he travelled to Vienna and demanded she get divorced and marry him. They kept up a long correspondence, even after my mother discovered he too was married to someone else.

At the time Vienna was well known for having a fairly accommodating attitude towards marriage, and my father also had numerous female admirers to keep him amused while he spent the summer working at his factory. That was the spirit of the era, but we were a very happy family nonetheless. Our contrasting personalities – daring and outgoing in the case of my father and me, creative and gentle in the case of my brother and my mother – complemented each other perfectly.

My parents shared a deep love of classical music and sometimes, instead of bedtime stories, my father would start the gramophone and play us the Trout Quintet by Franz Schubert. Then the four of us would lie on the floor of our big living room and drift away to the sounds of what we called the 'sleeping music'.

To me, those days and the sprightly tones of the Trout Quintet made the world seem innocent and carefree but in actual fact ominous events were clouding the horizon. Many of them emerged in one momentous year, 1933.

When he was seven Heinz developed a serious infection and lay in bed with a raging fever, staring at the walls.

I crept in to see him and peeped over the top of his bed.

'Do you want to read any of your stories?' I whispered, thinking that would make him feel better. 'What about Old Shatterhand?'

But Heinz shook his head. He was too ill even to read.

'He's not getting any better,' my mother fretted anxiously. 'Why can't they find out what's wrong with him?'

Doctors came and went, but none seemed to know what was wrong.

'I'll find another doctor,' Pappy said, trying to sound reassuring. 'Don't worry – we'll get to the bottom of it and he'll be fine.' But even Pappy sounded very worried.

After many consultations with different doctors my parents finally found a specialist who correctly diagnosed the problem, and removed Heinz's tonsils. He began to recover but by then the infection had already affected his eyesight, and he went blind in one eye. Of course, this made my parents frantically anxious. And Heinz was terrified too. 'Pappy, what if I can never read my books again?'

All I could do was fret, beside his bed, unable to do a thing. 'Are you feeling any better today, Heinz?' I would ask him, terrified to see my big brother so weak and helpless.

It was a terrible ordeal for all of us. Heinz never really recovered from the fear of losing his sight, while my father worried that Heinz's newly developed anxieties would stop him making his way in the world.

As a family we were about to undergo another wrench. The Great Depression and raging inflation were causing immense hardship in Austria, and Pappy's business was failing. A tram ride that had cost half a Krone in 1918 now cost the equivalent of more than 1,500 Kronen in Schillings, the currency that had replaced the old Kronen in 1924. A one-Krone dinner was more than 30,000 Kronen.

There was no future for our factory, Geiringer & Brown, but Pappy was inventive and entrepreneurial, and he began employing women to work from home making moccasins. Until he could rebuild the family business, however, we had to move into more modest surroundings. 'Our new apartment is a bit smaller, but it's very nice,' Mutti told us, trying to sound cheerful, 'and just think how much nearer we'll be to Grandma Helen and Grandpa Rudolf.' But not even that could compensate for my feeling of loss.

'It will all work out, Evi,' Pappy told me, but I could hear a catch in his voice that told me how sad he was to be leaving our house in Lautensackgasse.

A happy family home is about much more than four walls, but I knew that we were shutting the door on our earliest memories together of laughter, quarrels, growing up, meals and birthday parties. A new stage in our lives had begun.

With all these family traumas and upheavals to occupy

my thoughts, I suppose it's little wonder that I can remember only the vaguest whisperings about bigger world events. Occasionally I would see an aunt or uncle furrow their brow, or I would hear a note of worry in my parents' voices as they listened to a radio broadcast. It was 1933, and in Germany Adolf Hitler had just come to power.

4
The Nazis are Coming

The Austrians were well known for being charming and laid-back people. As I was to discover, they were 'charming Nazis' – smiling and pleasant as they cheered Hitler back over the border after the Anschluss between Germany and Austria in 1938.

My mostly carefree childhood years of the 1930s had been turbulent ones in Vienna, and the culmination of decades of violent strife.

As the Austro-Hungarian Empire disintegrated the city witnessed scenes of virtual civil war. Different nationalities and ethnic groups had been pulling the Empire apart from the turn of the century. While politicians shouted at each other in different languages across the floor of the parliament, outside on the Ringstrasse, poverty-stricken workers took to the streets in protest over high food prices, overcrowded accommodation and a flood of immigrants making it harder, they believed, to find work.

Vienna was wonderful and exciting if you were wealthy but a tough place to live if you were not.

An extremely popular mayor, Karl Lueger, had transformed the turn-of-the-century city with electric lighting, a tram system, clean water for hospitals and even public swimming pools. But he had also overseen a dramatic rise in homelessness, with people sleeping in cots under the tram shelters, queuing all day for entrance to overnight hostels, and finding themselves unable to afford to buy food. While rich Vienna gathered in cafés to discuss ideas, poor Vienna visited 'warming rooms' to fend off the cold, read the newspapers and have a bowl of soup.

Those newspapers often told them that their problems had a single cause – the Jews. Mayor Lueger was famously anti-Semitic, knowing that he could always raise an easy cheer by blaming hard conditions – untruthfully – on Jewish businessmen. 'Nothing but Jews' was how he once dismissed the city.

Not everyone liked the idea that Vienna was a multi-ethnic melting pot, drawing in a wide range of people from across the empire. Some writers and politicians began to agitate for a Pan-German movement, harking back to ancient myths of an Aryan people coming from northern Europe who were superior to other people from the Empire, particularly Czechs, Slavs and Jews. Men such as parliamentarian Georg von Schönerer wanted to claim 'Germany for the Germans' – including a reunion of Germany and Austria – but while Emperor Franz Josef remained on the throne they were one voice amongst many in the throng of ideas and debates of the time.

Without World War One and the fall of the Hapsburg Empire perhaps few would have taken the idea of a 'Pan-German master race' seriously, but this rag-bag of populist slogans and re-invented myths and traditions strongly influenced Adolf Hitler, who between 1908 and 1913 was a failing artist living in a Vienna men's hostel.

Hitler, a customs officer's son from the provincial Austrian city of Linz, hated Vienna's internationalism – its modern art and music, liberal sexuality and sometimes chaotic politics, that excluded him at all levels. Hitler was like a poor boy with his face pressed up against the window of the sweet shop, while inside exclusive Vienna society and intelligentsia ignored him.

When the war came, it brought hardship, famine, financial collapse and ultimate humiliation in 1918. While the rest of Austria remained ruled by conservative government and the Catholic church, the citizens of Vienna rebelled, and from 1919 to 1934 the city's administration was socialist, with progressive thinking on social housing and public health care. Once again, Vienna was at the crux of a bitter and violent battle between rival political ideologies.

In 1934 'Red Vienna' came to a crashing end when the Christian Socialist chancellor Engelbert Dollfuss swept Austrian democracy to one side, and set up a one-party fascist regime. Although it seems paradoxical, Dollfuss was opposed to the Nazis or the prospect of Austria becoming annexed with Germany, and he tried to protect Jews by banning anti-Semitic propaganda and discrimination against Jewish students. When Dollfuss was assassinated by Austrian Nazis in 1934 another member of his government, Kurt von Schuschnigg, took his place – and he also tried to keep Hitler at bay.

For three years he succeeded, but there was no way that Hitler would allow Austria to vote in a free referendum on the question of unification with Germany, especially when it was predicted that two thirds of the Austrian people favoured maintaining independence. On 9 March 1938 German troops silently rolled over the border into Austria, meeting no opposition. One month later Hitler ordered the Austrian people to vote in his referendum on Austria's future. The official result recorded that 99.75 per cent voted in favour of union with Germany.

I will never forget the fear and foreboding that I felt the night the Nazis arrived in Vienna. German soldiers were welcomed into the city with ringing church bells and cheering crowds, while gigantic red flags with black swastikas were unfurled from every window and building, blooming across the city like a swathe of poisonous flowers.

My family gathered together at my grandparents' apartment and anxiously listened to the news. I played together with my cousins and Heinz, but I could tell that something was very wrong.

'We have lived here for our entire lives,' I heard my grandfather say, 'and Austria has been our homeland for generations.'

Someone tried to reassure him. 'It can't possibly get so bad, our non-Jewish friends won't allow it.'

'What do you think is going on?' I whispered to Heinz, but he put his finger up to his mouth and widened his eyes to shh me, meaning we would talk about it later.

We walked home in silence and when Mutti and Pappy put us to bed, Mutti kissed our heads and said, 'Tomorrow will be a better day.'

That night her words of reassurance made me sleep easier, but I believe she knew in her heart that the fate of Vienna's Jews had been sealed.

Hitler appeared on the balcony of the Neue Hofburg Palace in front of the huge Imperial Square, Heldenplatz, on 15 March 1938. He spoke to the teeming crowds of Austrian people in front of the chiselled gold slogan that had been erected for Emperor Franz Josef: Justice is the foundation of governments.

'This country is German,' he said. 'I can report to the German people the greatest accomplishment of my life. I am announcing to history my homeland's entrance into the German Reich.'

The city that had snubbed him for so long was welcoming him back with open arms and his first priority, he confided to Nazi propaganda chief Josef Goebbels, was to cleanse it of 'filth and roaches' – he meant the Jews.

In that first week of Nazi rule everyone's worst fears were confirmed. Austrian Nazis were allowed to run riot, beating up Jews, looting Jewish property, forcing Jews to call each other insulting names in the street and ripping the World War One medals off the chests of Jewish former army officers and soldiers.

Suddenly the easy-going friends of my childhood were gone. I wondered who these new people were. The ordinary shopkeepers, tram conductors and building supervisors whom I thought I knew were now making Jewish people get down on their knees to scrub pro-democracy statements off the pavements.

Surely these were not the same people that my family had lived side-by-side with for so long?

Even if you were not interested in politics, you could not be oblivious to the anti-Semitism that had existed in Vienna for so many years. You didn't have to read a Pan-German newspaper to know that a Jewish-looking man could get his hat knocked off walking down the Ringstrasse, or that students had been sent fleeing from Vienna University to jeers of 'Jews out'.

In the years leading up to the Anschluss, all the major political parties had anti-Semitic statements in their manifestos, and even the Dollfuss-Schuschnigg government, which purported to protect Jews, had many anti-Semites in its cabinet. This prejudice was a deep, long-standing undercurrent in Jewish life but only now did it start to encroach upon my sheltered existence.

My first encounter with these new Austrian Nazis shocked me.

'We don't have to bother with your kind any more,' my friend's mother told me, slamming her front door in my face.

I ran home, bewildered and crying.

'Well, this is what it's going to be like for Jewish people from now on,' my mother explained, wearily.

Black Nazi swastikas appeared everywhere and laughing Austrian men, wearing the national costume of neat felt hats and trousers tucked into their socks, forced small children to paint *Jude* across the windows of their parents' shops.

When we peered out through our living-room shutters we saw rows of Nazi soldiers marching down the street, their boots cracking in chilling unison on the road. One day we went to visit the small garden that belonged to my grandparents' apartment building, only to be told 'No Jews allowed!' by the block supervisor, a woman who appeared to have become an ardent Nazi overnight.

New laws, written with exquisite bureaucratic logic, demanded that all Austrians swear an oath of allegiance to Hitler and the Nazis. Since, this law reasoned, Jews could not be expected to swear such an oath, they would automatically be banned from all government or professional jobs. Jewish teachers could no longer work in schools and Jewish doctors were forbidden from treating non-Jewish patients.

Austrian Jews began running from one foreign embassy to another, desperate for a visa that would allow them to escape. Unfortunately, most countries would not let them in.

My own family quickly began making plans to leave. All Jewish people now had to carry identification papers with them at all times. We were frequently stopped in the street and told to show our papers, or risk being turned over to the authorities.

Aunty Sylvi's husband Otto was an expert in Bakelite plastic manufacturing, and they quickly got visas for the UK, settling in a small town in Lancashire with my cousin Tom. Sylvi and Otto converted to Christianity almost as soon as they arrived, and Otto worked for a company that made Bakelite umbrella handles. They managed to take a shipping container full of treasured family possessions including family photo albums, so unlike many Jewish families, we still have some of these precious items today.

Other members of my family also departed for England. Pappy's sister Blanca was married to an art historian who worked for Phaidon Press, and they fled to London with my cousin Gaby. I remember sitting on Uncle Ludwig's knee a few days before they left, while he showed me my favourite prints in his big heavy art books. I was just nine years old, but I could feel that there were worse things to come even than humiliation in the street or losing my old friends. The palpable tension of the adults around me had filled me with anxiety. I wondered if I would see those pictures again.

Another of my mother's cousins, Litty Kloss, left for England. She was married to a Catholic who was quite a well-known artist, but he deserted her on the day the Nazis arrived.

Litty managed to get to London on a domestic service visa. Although the Kindertransport for ten thousand Jewish children has become more famous, by far the largest number of Jews who arrived in the UK did so as domestic servants. Most of the 20,000 women who got domestic servant visas were completely unused to hard domestic labour and struggled with the long hours and backbreaking work. Litty hated being a servant and lived in hope that, when the war was over, her husband would take her back. By then he already had another girlfriend, and he never showed the slightest interest in her welfare.

Even Grandpa Rudolf and Grandma Helen were hoping to move to England.

'Since Sylvi and Otto are there, I hope that we can get visas too,' I heard Grandma Helen tell Mutti.

'It takes such a long time though,' Grandpa Rudolf fretted.

'I'm sure the visas will come through,' Mutti reassured them.

Secretly I wished we could join them and move to England along with the rest of our family, but it was not to be.

Pappy knew the Nazis were dangerous from the moment Hitler came to power in Germany in 1933. He never talked to us about it, but he'd been searching for a safe place for us to live, should we need it, ever since. As a shoe exporter

35

he travelled frequently and had contact with lots of foreign firms. When a factory in the Netherlands was going out of business, Pappy decided to invest in the firm and keep some of our family capital there in case we needed to leave Austria. It seemed like a good idea: southern Holland was the centre of the European shoe industry, and the Netherlands had remained neutral in World War One. My parents hoped it would remain so in the event of another war. But even if things didn't escalate to that level, it was clear that our lives in Austria had changed for ever. They decided the time had come for us to leave.

'Austria isn't a nice place for us to live any more,' Pappy told us, 'but Holland is a wonderful country. Just think, Evi – we'll be near the sea and there'll be lots of lakes and rivers to sail boats on.'

I found this idea quite tempting. Austria was a landlocked country and Heinz and I loved going to the seaside.

'But why do you have to go without us?' I asked him, trying to hold back the tears in my voice.

Leaving our home was going to be hard, but it was even more upsetting when I found out that we could not all go together. Only Pappy could get a work and resident's visa. Mutti, Heinz and I could only stay with him as visitors for a short time.

'We won't be apart for long,' Pappy said. 'I'm going to be very busy with the new factory, but when we see each other we'll do all the things that you like.'

Mutti told us that until we could all get visas we would be going to live in Brussels, and that Pappy would be working over the Dutch border in a small town called Breda and visiting us at weekends.

I tried not to show Mutti how scared and confused I was. Pappy told us to be good and well behaved and that he would see us soon. Giving us a kiss and a hug, he said time would fly past until we were all together again – and then he left.

As I later found out, it was in the nick of time. Soon after, in September 1938, the Nazi authorities wrote to us demanding that he appear before them in Vienna to account for his assets and hand them over, but by then he was gone.

Mutti had worries of her own. The Nazis were imposing restrictions on the amount of money and goods Jews could take with them when they were leaving the country. I watched as all of the belongings that had meant so much to our family were sold off, one by one. One day our marble-topped table was gone, the next day it was the few heirlooms Pappy had inherited from his own father. Some of these items were valuable but Mutti could never get a fair price for them. Everyone knew that Jews were selling all their possessions and having to accept the lowest bids.

The Nazis had already altered our family life for ever. I saw a change come over my parents' personalities. My carefree mother, who had never cooked a meal, cleaned a floor or made an important decision, was suddenly trans-formed. Her family nickname had always been 'Lamb' but from the moment my father left she was in sole charge of Heinz and me, our home and our future. She truly rose to the occasion, showing us what a strong-minded, practical and mature woman she had been all along.

One of the first things she did was set about learning a new skill so that we would have something to fall back on. Giving it some thought, she decided to do a six-week beautician's course, and before long, various creams and implements appeared in our house. Mutti proved to be quite adept at making up the creams and lotions – but less so at applying them. Eyebrow waxing was her nemesis; she dreaded the thought of pasting hot wax onto someone's face and then violently ripping it off, and many of her friends left our apartment with one eyebrow thinner than the other, or unnaturally arched in perpetual surprise.

One day, we clashed. Mutti had told me that we could only take a few clothes, whatever we could stuff into a small suitcase, and we had planned exactly what to take. I needed a new winter coat and so hand in hand we headed off to Bitman's department store to choose one. I had never been asked for my opinion on what clothes I wore, and Mutti showed no sign of consulting me now. She discussed the matter with the sales assistant, who then presented me with a bright orange coat and a matching plaid hat.

My wilfulness had not deserted me. I detested it. 'That is dreadful,' I told them. 'I'm not going to wear it!'

Mutti tried to persuade me that this outfit was the height of fashion in Belgium, and I tried to persuade her that it didn't fit. We both got our way; we left the store with the coat and hat, and I swore that I would never put them on. Eventually we reached a compromise, but only once Mutti had the coat dyed navy blue.

It's only looking back as a mother and grandmother that I realise how difficult this time must have been for Mutti. Her worries only got worse when Heinz came home from school one day with a bloody and beaten face. Some boys had started taunting him in class because he was Jewish. Then they hit and punched him and gashed his healthy eye. His teachers stood by and let those boys beat him up. Vicious mob rule was taking over in Austria, and Heinz was one of the helpless victims.

Together we tried to soothe him; Mutti cleaned his face while I held his hand and listened as he sobbed inconsolably. My parents decided it was better for Heinz to leave as soon as possible, and a few days later we took him to the train station to see him off. We knew that Pappy would be collecting him at the other end, but my twelve-year-old brother looked very young and uncertain that day as he made his way down the thronged platform holding only a small suitcase and a satchel full of books. He seemed far too young to be heading out on his own across Europe, but there were a lot of Jewish children embarking upon the same journey into the unknown.

Mutti and I stayed behind for a few more weeks while she tried to sell our final possessions, but eventually the day came for us to leave, too. I felt afraid, confused and even childishly excited. For a nine-year-old it was like embarking on a big, nightmarish adventure.

We said goodbye to Grandma Helen and Grandpa Rudolf, who were still waiting for their visas to England. At the railway station we took a deep breath as we prepared to leave behind everything we had known, and Mutti held my hand tightly as we boarded the train for the longest, most nerve-wracking journey of our lives.

The hesitant, jerky train ride went on and on. We rattled across Europe, crammed in our small compartment and taking care not to make too much eye contact with our fellow passengers. We watched as first Austria and then Germany passed by in a blur outside the steamy windows.

I itched uncomfortably in all the extra layers of clothes that Mutti had made me wear because there was no more room in our suitcases. My hands trembled every time we were forced off the train to show our papers and my eyes widened at all the soldiers we saw, the men with the hard faces, and the guns.

After what felt like days, the train pulled to a stop and I literally wilted with relief and exhaustion when I saw Pappy and Heinz on the platform. They embraced us and I began to chatter eagerly to Heinz about everything we had seen along the way – and how much I hated my horrible orange coat.

We'd escaped just in time; only a few weeks later, in June 1938, many countries closed their borders to Jewish refugees.

5

An Undesirable Little Girl

The first few weeks of our new life felt like being on a long, strange holiday. It was June 1938; we were staying with Pappy in Holland, going for long walks and cycling across the Dutch heather moors that surrounded the town of Breda. After all those tense weeks waiting in Vienna for our visas I basked in the relief of breathing fresh air and chatting to Pappy and Heinz, even though most of what I had to say was about how awful things had become back in Austria.

All too soon, though, our Dutch visitors' visas ran out and we had to cross back over the border into Belgium. I began the seemingly endless task of counting the days until the weekends, when Pappy could visit and we could all be together again.

There were many Jewish families arriving in Belgium in 1938, looking for a safe haven from Hitler's Third Reich – but the welcome we received was often far from friendly.

Following the German annexation of Austria, the Belgian Justice Minister, Charles du Bus de Warnaffe, had ordered the Belgian embassy in Vienna to deny visas to Jews telling Parliament that the Jews had 'for centuries constituted a problem in Europe'. He then wrote an article calling Jewish people 'extremely unreliable', with no sense of honour. From our point of view it seemed that the reverse was true: in 1930s Europe 'honour' was in short supply.

The magnitude of the changes in my life made my head spin. Only a few months earlier I had been a little girl, secure in my Austrian upbringing, surrounded by a big family of grandparents, aunts, uncles and cousins, and going to school with my friends.

'I want to go home to Austria,' I cried to Heinz.

But we knew we could not return. A lot of my relatives and friends were trapped, but others had fled to countries I'd only ever heard of. Grandpa Rudolf and Grandma Helen were still waiting anxiously in Vienna for permission to travel to England. Even our own tight-knit family of four had been broken up. How could we ever call a new place home without Pappy?

After the elegant boulevards, Linden trees and cafés of Vienna, the dark, damp cobbled streets of Brussels depressed me. Grey skies pressed down on us through the drizzle; it hardly felt like freedom.

Mutti, Heinz and I moved into two small rooms in a boarding house on Rue de L'Ecosse. When I looked around our new living quarters my heart sank. I imagined my bedroom back in Vienna, but of course the truth was that another Austrian family would have moved in to our house and be living there by now. I longed for our own furniture instead of the shabby careworn chairs and beds – but then I remembered that Mutti had been forced to sell all of our belongings.

We were truly 'stateless' people, and not welcome anywhere.

Living in Brussels would be a traumatic experience for

me, and a hard adjustment – for one thing I did not speak French. While Heinz ran home from school every day to lie on his bed and pore over his new textbooks, I struggled. In school I grew red-faced with shame at my inability to complete even the simplest task, or answer any of the teacher's questions. The other children happily chanted their answers, which swirled around me in a wall of sounds. Although I was sporty and loved to be outdoors, back in Vienna I'd also been a good student. Now I was the class dunce.

'Eva . . . why can't you learn this verb?' my mother would say in exasperation as she tried to give me extra language lessons. Mutti had been a French tutor back in Austria, although we used to tease her that she was so bad, her one and only student had committed suicide. She may not have been *that* bad (she actually had a diploma from the University of Vienna) but her French language teaching certainly passed right over my head.

One of the few good things to emerge from our stay in Belgium was that I made friends with Jacky, the young son of Madame Le Blanc who owned the boarding house. I'd always found it easy to make friends with boys, like Martin back in Vienna, and Jacky and I got along very well despite having virtually no language in common.

We decided to play a trick on one of the other residents; a middle-aged man called Mr Dubois who lived permanently at Madame Le Blanc's having retired from a career as a civil servant in the Congo. He seemed to exude a dour intensity, and we circled him cautiously whenever we passed in the hallways. One day, after breakfast Jacky and I crept into his bedroom and waited for him to return.

The wall behind the bed was covered in spears and all sorts of menacing souvenirs from his time in Africa. Giggling, we climbed behind the bed and crouched down. After what felt like an eternity we heard the door handle jiggle and his heavy footsteps. Then Jacky and I screamed. With a bellow Mr Dubois leapt up on the bed and grabbed a spear – ready to stick it straight through us. Squealing, we crawled out from behind the bed and ran breathlessly from the room.

Jacky and I vowed not to go near Mr Dubois again; he radiated a dark and heavy anger that we found scary. I wanted to avoid him at all costs, but a few days later, when I was alone, he cornered me in the hallway. 'Do you like my spears?' he asked me. I didn't like them at all, but I muttered something polite. Why didn't we look at his collection together, he said, and then I wouldn't get into any trouble over the trick I'd played on him – he'd never tell anyone. He ushered me into his bedroom, telling me he wanted to show me more pictures from the Congo.

I stood reluctantly beside him while he sat at his desk and leafed through sepia photograph albums. The seconds and minutes ticked by in slow motion. Finally it seemed our session was at an end, and I breathed a sigh of relief to be able to leave and go back to the room I shared with Heinz.

But a few days later, Mr Dubois cornered me again. As before, we went to his room and I stood, mutely, while he pored over his old photos. His silent tension and shallow breathing seemed to fill the room with a strange energy, but when he finished showing me his photos, I once again made my escape, full of relief. Maybe I wouldn't have to see Mr Dubois any more.

These afternoon sessions were so fraught that I hoped Mr Dubois would lose interest in them, but he came looking for me the next day, and a few days after that.

As the weeks passed, he started lifting me onto his knee while we stared at the pages of the album. I liked this even less than standing next to him, but I sat still and waited until I could go back to Mutti, who had no idea what was going on. After a few times of sitting on his knee I noticed that he was fondling himself. Although I didn't understand what he was doing I knew that it felt wrong, and I was frozen stiff with fear.

This was our secret, he told me. I mustn't tell anyone or I would get into terrible trouble. He could take one of those old spears off the wall, and kill me with it.

Soon Mr Dubois made me fondle him too, and I hated touching him down there.

Mutti and Heinz started to notice that I was becoming very withdrawn, but they didn't know what was wrong. I was already sad that I was living in a foreign country, away from Pappy. Now I hardly spoke any more, and my self-confidence seemed to have drained away.

The horrible sessions continued, until one day Mr Dubois' abuse intensified into such a frenzy that he ejaculated into a handkerchief.

I was so horrified and overwhelmed that I ran out of the room, straight into the path of Mutti. Seeing how upset I was, she grilled me about what was going on, and I broke down and told her the truth.

Mutti went to find Madame Le Blanc and together they went to Mr Dubois' bedroom to confront him. Of course he denied it, but there was proof – his dirty handkerchief in the waste paper basket. Seeing that there was no point in continuing to lie, he confessed, and made up some excuse about what had happened.

Mutti was outraged and demanded that Madame Le Blanc ask him to leave the boarding house immediately. Much to Mutti's surprise, Madame Le Blanc refused. We were only temporary residents, she told Mutti – Mr Dubois was a permanent boarder and he would be there, paying his rent, long after we left.

It was hard to believe that anyone could say such a thing, and a sense of shock settled over Mutti, and Pappy and Heinz when she told them. But there seemed to be nothing we could do. We were poor refugees in a strange country, waiting for our visas so that we could be a family again.

Mutti told me never to speak to Mr Dubois again, and she did everything she could to protect me – sitting in our room beside my bed every night while I went to sleep. But for months we would pass him in the hallways and had to sit in silence in the dining room while the man who had molested me carried on with his daily life undisturbed. That was almost the worst part of the experience. In fact he looked at me as if I were the one who had committed the crime – against him.

It felt as if the strongest pillars of security in my life were crumbling around me. Only a short time before I'd been a bright happy little girl who'd jumped blind from the top of the wardrobe, knowing that Pappy would always be there to catch me. Now I saw that, despite their reassurances, my parents were powerless to protect us from the evil in the world. They'd been unable to keep us safe from the Nazis, and we'd had to flee from our home. And now they couldn't even protect me from a man who had hurt me in the worst possible way.

How awful it must have been for them, and how awful it was for me.

Until now my memory of being sexually abused was so deeply shameful and painful that I have never discussed it, even though I've often spoken about far worse experiences that we were to go through as a family.

The remainder of our stay in Belgium was bleak and anxiety ridden. I withdrew into my shell, with only a few bright moments to draw me out. There were few other people to make friends with at the boarding house. As I looked around the dining room I saw the faces of other solemn and uprooted Jewish families from across the continent, each just as miserable as us. But there was one childless couple, Herr and Frau Deutsch, whom I started to call Aunty and Uncle. They were well-to-do Jewish refugees from Germany, waiting for visas to go to America.

As a treat they gave me bars of Côte d'Or chocolate, which came with a postcard of a member of the Belgian Royal family. I soon became fanatical about collecting these postcards. I memorised every member of the Royal household as a way of trying to crawl inside their seemingly perfect lives. Heinz sometimes helped me to acquire the precious photos by trading them with his friends – usually making me pay for the privilege by getting me to clean his shoes, or arrange his books. One day Aunty and Uncle even gave me a kite, and they sometimes took us to the seaside in their car. Later I learned that their visas never arrived, and they were deported to concentration camps.

In Belgium anti-Semitic sentiment was intensifying. The

Nazi campaign against the Jews was widely reported in the Belgian press. Maybe the Jews really were the cause of all the problems in Europe, some wondered, and perhaps, the Belgians thought, those problems were inching closer and closer to their own doorstep.

For my tenth birthday in May 1939 I begged Mutti to make me a cake with ten candles, and I proudly handed out invitations to my friends at school. They were all delighted, and we chatted happily about what sorts of presents I'd like.

The next day I arrived at school eager to talk to them about more exciting ideas for my party – but each one in turn told me that they wouldn't be able to come after all. Their parents wouldn't let them.

'It's because we're Jewish,' Heinz told me, sadly.

I was ten years old, and 'undesirable' to know.

I didn't know if everything we heard about what was happening to Jews in Germany was true, but I did know that Pappy was finding it harder to visit us at the weekends. Every page in his passport was filling up with stamps from making the awkward border crossing between Holland and Brussels to see us, and soon he would need a new one. Mutti was working hard with the Centre for Refugees to get us Dutch visas, but we waited and waited and heard nothing. I didn't realise that she was also trying to find any other safe country to take us in – but that her search was in vain.

'*Bad news,*' she wrote to my Aunt and Uncle in England, '*our application to emigrate to Australia has been denied . . .*'

It's almost unbearable to think how much that denied visa application changed our lives.

By September 1939 the tension had reached fever pitch, but at the last moment, we had one piece of good news.

I was almost overcome with excitement when I heard that we would be seeing Grandpa Rudolf and Grandma Helen. They had finally been granted their visas, after a gruelling procedure that had seen them leave Austria with permission to settle in the UK, only to be turned back at the Belgian border because they didn't have a Belgian transit visa. They had to go all the way back to Austria, apply for the Belgian visa and then wait anxiously for word that it had been granted – before fleeing at the very last moment.

I wasn't aware of any of that. All I knew was that seeing Grandma and Grandpa again after all that I had been through was like a wonderful dream. They weren't just figures of my imagination, left behind with all our other memories and possessions in Austria – they were real.

On the day that they arrived my feet seemed to float above the dreary streets of Brussels as we rushed to meet them at the Centre for Refugees. The Centre was always crowded. There were long rows of tables at which officials sat, sorting through endless index cards, trying to reunite families, arrange visas and pass on snippets of news. I usually found it overwhelming, but that day I was so excited I could hardly stand still.

'Grandma! Grandpa!' I shouted as soon as I saw them, not noticing how thin Grandpa had become, or how Grandma looked over her shoulder nervously all the time. I hugged them, grabbing their arms as I said, 'Wait until I tell you about my new school, I have been learning French – although Mutti says I'm not good at it – and in the boarding house where we live I've got a new friend called

Jacky . . .' My words of delight tripped over each other as I tried to tell them in a garbled rush all about what had happened to us since we left Austria.

The days we spent together passed so quickly, it hardly seemed like any time until Grandpa and Grandma had to board the boat for England. Although they tried to talk quietly with my mother, I overheard snatches of conversations about what sounded like incomprehensible developments. Grandma and Grandpa brought whispered news of new, terrible things that were happening to the Jews: ghettos in Poland, and a *Kristallnacht* in which many German synagogues were set ablaze and Jewish shops looted.

A week after my grandparents left for safety Germany invaded Czechoslovakia, allegedly to protect the German people of the Sudetenland and reunite them with their Fatherland. Germany also signed the Pact of Steel with Italy. Then Germany invaded Poland – and France, England and all the countries of the Commonwealth: Australia, New Zealand and Canada, declared that the time for appeasement was over.

'I am speaking to you from the Cabinet Room at 10 Downing Street,' British Prime Minister Neville Chamberlain began his famous radio broadcast on 3 September 1939. 'This morning the British Ambassador in Berlin handed the German government a final note, stating that unless we heard from them by 11 o'clock that they were prepared at once to withdraw their troops from Poland, a state of war would exist between us. I have to tell you now that no such undertaking has been received, and that consequently this country is at war with Germany.'

He ended his announcement by saying, 'It is the evil things that we shall be fighting against – brute force, bad faith, injustice, oppression and persecution; and against them I am certain that right will prevail.'

World War Two had begun.

It was news that had seemed unavoidable for so long but when it came, a strange sense of restlessness and uncertainty gripped us. My parents were distracted, and seemed lost in their own thoughts.

Outside, on the streets and in school, an eerie calm fell over Belgium, as though people knew that change was coming but not what it would bring.

There were moments when it seemed as if we were pulled as tight as elastic and that we couldn't endure another moment of that unnatural calm, but we had to nervously measure out every long, anxious day for another six months.

Finally, in February 1940, we got the news we were waiting for. We had been granted Dutch visas and could travel to Amsterdam to live with Pappy.

My time in Belgium had changed my life in more ways than I could possibly have imagined. Despite their outer displays of confidence, I knew my parents were deeply shaken – and I was a very different little girl to the one who had boarded the train back in Vienna. This time I began our trip withdrawn and quiet, with little sense of adventure, only relief. My eyes had been opened to some of the unpleasant things in life, and I could only be glad that, whatever Amsterdam had in store, it was the next stage in our journey together.

6

Amsterdam

Life in exile was undoubtedly an anxious strain for my parents, but I was about to enjoy two very happy years of my life.

During the time that we lived in Amsterdam we formed deep family bonds. Heinz and I were growing older, going through the same emotional and physical growing pains as all other adolescents. We made new friends and went on daring adventures, sailing across the Dutch lakes and canals in small wooden boats. And we took our first steps towards tentative romances with members of the opposite sex (or not, in my case). With no servants to look after us, and later, a Nazi-imposed curfew to keep us at home in the evenings, the four of us knitted together into the closest of family units.

After the trauma of life in Brussels I was entranced by our new home, which was utterly unlike what we had left behind. Austria was rugged and earthy, with a people who were rooted in the shadows of deep mountains, and glacial lakes of icy cold and impenetrable depths. With unhappy hindsight, my homeland had seemed to make us cower beneath its dark forests and mountain peaks, while Holland floated by in a hazy watery landscape.

I could ride my bike alongside the miles of rural dykes that wove across the small country, watching the cattle grazing by the grassy water's edge while the windmills slowly, silently turned in the breeze.

The Netherlands had remained neutral in World War One, and expected to do so again, hoping that, if absolutely necessary, the country's network of waterways could be flooded to stop a Nazi invasion.

In April 1939 Hitler had promised to respect the neutrality of the Low Countries, but following Germany's invasion of Poland it had become apparent that such promises were worthless. A panicked Dutch government mobilised the unprepared army, but the largely pacifist population and politicians were unable to comprehend the scale of the threat they faced.

By the beginning of 1940 most of Europe was in turmoil but the Dutch maintained an air of tranquil innocence, still untouched by the bloodshed of the twentieth century and as yet unaffected by the modern war machine massing on the German border.

On Sundays country farmers still walked to church wearing wooden shoes. Their trim square houses were painted neatly in bright colours, with windows outlined in white. Although electricity had been widely introduced to cities like Amsterdam, in some places lamplighters still walked the streets at dusk. The country was holding on to the last vestiges of old Europe, praying for the best.

We arrived at Amsterdam Central Station on a cold morning in February 1940. Pappy met us with a huge smile on his face, and we climbed on board Tram 25 to take us to our new apartment. Along the way he pointed out the canals, and the tall merchants' houses that signified the wealth and success of the Dutch trading empire. He told me, in a whisper, that the wooden bridges had gaps in the planks so that you could the see the water and boats underneath – knowing that probably only I would appreciate that detail.

The tram took us south across the city, through the working-class neighbourhood of De Pijp and across into South Amsterdam and an area called the River Quarter. A building that looked to me like a tall skyscraper loomed on the horizon. The River Quarter was so-called because its poplar-lined streets were named for the various rivers that flowed through the Netherlands into the sea – including the Rhine, the Maas, the Schelde and the Jeker. In the 1920s socially progressive companies had built new blocks of flats for their workers with government assistance. A lot of the buildings were made from dark brick with orange roofs, but each large window usually had a flower box with its own display, framed delicately by a lace curtain. At night the Dutch would put lamps in these windows, and you could see families eating meals, doing homework and reading books. The apartments were small but comfortable, with indoor plumbing and there were communal gardens for children to play in.

The Great Depression had ended the building boom and many apartments remained uninhabited, including those of the twelve-storey building I had noticed as we arrived. The skyscraper towered, empty, over the city streets for years. Now an influx of Jewish refugees like us were renting in the skyscraper and the apartment buildings around the large open square called Merwedeplein. For years the tower was our anchor. Wherever we were in the city, all we had to do was look up, see its looming presence in the distance, and head for home.

Our new apartment was 46 Merwedeplein, in one of long buildings that faced onto the square.

The triangular open space of the plaza seemed irresistible that first day, and I jumped off the tram and ran across the grass, turning cartwheels. Heinz ran past me, and together we raced up the steps to our apartment on the first floor.

'Oh, Erich,' my mother gasped as she set foot inside. There, in the middle of the living room, was a baby grand piano.

Our apartment was beautifully furnished and highly sought after, but Pappy had managed to charm the Christian lady who owned it into renting it to us. He asked her to keep it in her name, anticipating the problems Jewish people might have if events took another turn for the worse.

The moment she saw the piano, Mutti left her belongings in the doorway and sat down immediately to play a piece by Johann Strauss that we had all loved listening to in Vienna.

Then my father motioned us into the kitchen, where we observed the stove and table and tidy workbenches. 'Well, Fritzi,' he said with mock solemnity, 'I believe cooking will be a new venture for you.'

Indeed it was. My father was a lovely man but he was just as demanding as most other husbands of that era. After a hard day at work he expected to sit down to the kind of three-course dinner our maid would have laboriously prepared for us. Now that task fell on my mother's shoulders.

At first she struggled. Until that day I suspect my mother had never even boiled an egg. Now she had to search for ingredients and concoct heavy, time-consuming Austrian dishes with noodles, and puddings such as sweet dumplings filled with stewed plums. With time and the help of an Austrian lady called Mrs Rosenbaum who was married to a German lawyer who was a friend of my father, she became a good cook, although never a great chef. And she always preferred playing a symphony to stirring saucepans. Who could blame her?

She certainly intended to take full advantage of the piano. As soon as we had settled in my mother began looking for a music teacher for Heinz, and she set up a small group of Jewish musicians to hold evening recitals.

This was often more than my father, who loved music, could bear since some members of the group were more enthusiastic than accomplished. At first Pappy would sit tensely behind his newspaper. Then as the violinist warmed up, drawing his bow discordantly across the strings, the newspaper would twitch and my father's knuckles would whiten, until he announced tersely that it was time for him to take his evening stroll with Mr Rosenbaum.

'I just can't listen to that screeching!' Pappy would tell my mother when he returned and the recital was over.

I preferred to be outdoors too – and not just to escape the music.

In Amsterdam I felt a renewed sense of freedom; I made new friends and found I particularly liked a girl called Janny Koord. Janny's parents were both doctors, and she was rather stolid and clever and good hearted, going out of her way to be nice to me and help me learn Dutch. Soon

Janny and I were visiting the young mothers in the square, helping them with their babies. I also began to ride my second-hand black bike and play hopscotch and marbles in the street, as if I'd lived there all my life.

I carried a heavy bag of marbles with me and challenged other children to play. When no one was around, I spent hours skipping and practising the gymnastic exercises I'd been so good at in Austria, hanging off an iron rail on the steps to the apartment building.

'*How I would have liked a sweet gentle daughter, instead I've got a wild tomboy . . .*' Pappy wrote to my grandparents in England, adding, '*Whenever Evi and Mutti armwrestle, Mutti always has to ask for an armistice!*'

Soon the other children in Merwedeplein started to realise that I was athletic and good at games. In no time at all I was being picked first for the rounders team, cracking the ball far off into the distance and speeding from base to base. We played out there in the square for hours and hours until late evening when it was pitch black, when Pappy would come and call me in.

Most of the other children in the square were from different places too, and a lot were Jewish. It was the first time I had ever lived in a predominantly Jewish community, and we had a lot to learn from each other. At first, of course, I hardly spoke any Dutch – another frustration. I had just mastered French!

Soon I was enrolled in yet another new school, facing what were becoming familiar hurdles: new language, new teachers to impress – and new gangs of girls to somehow become a part of.

At home my parents still spoke to each other mostly in

German, while Heinz and I took to speaking a strange hybrid of French and Dutch. We were rapidly becoming a mixed-up family, with our experience as refugees leaving traces in all areas of our lives.

Although I enjoyed everything the city had to offer, none of us could ignore the circumstances that had brought us to Holland, and the looming crisis.

At school we practised air raid drills, and people greeted each other with a nervous edge in the streets, asking after friends and family.

The Amsterdamers I met were almost all warm and friendly but Dutch society was deeply divided into different political, social and religious 'pillars'. Each had its own political party, and which 'pillar' you belonged to determined the newspaper you read, the clubs you joined and the schools you sent your children to.

There was also a party of National Socialists, called the NSB, who emulated Hitler and carried out gang raids. They attacked a Jewish ice-cream parlour and smashed the windows of the Committee for Jewish Interests. The NSB was never a very large party, at its height in the mid-1930s there were only 38,000 members and most Dutch people treated the NSB with contempt. Leader Anton Mussert was often ridiculed for marrying his aunt, a woman eighteen years his senior.

As the late winter and early spring of 1940 wore on we became accustomed to hearing the heavy drone of German bomber planes flying overhead on their way to bomb Allied strategic targets, such as the Scarpa Flow naval base in Scotland.

I lay in bed at night imagining plane after plane flying

out over the North Sea, heading towards Grandma Helen and Grandpa Rudolf and my aunts and uncles and cousins. I knew that Grandpa Rudolf had not liked England at first, and refused to speak a word of this new, strange language. He had, after all, served with the Austro-Hungarian army in World War One, and some lingering wariness remained.

Then one evening he went to the pub in the small Lancashire town where they had settled and sat down to play the piano. Instantly he found himself the centre of attention. He won over many new friends, who treated him to a pint of beer when they discovered that he had arrived in his new country virtually penniless.

I hoped that he was thinking of me in the same way that I was thinking about him, and remembering our Sunday outings to the tavern back home in Vienna.

On 9 April 1940 events in Europe took a further turn for the worse. Germany invaded Denmark and Norway – claiming they had come to protect the two countries from 'Franco-British aggression'.

The invasion of Demark was the shortest campaign conducted by the Germans during the war; Denmark's small army was defeated, and the government surrendered, in only six hours.

In Norway the campaign was of a different order. Norway was strategically important to Germany both as a conduit for Swedish iron ore and as a base for the U-boat operations with which Hitler hoped to sink British shipping, and starve the UK into surrender. But the Norwegians did not give up easily in the face of German aggression, fighting on for sixty-two days across mountainous terrain.

None of this bode well for the Netherlands, with its

ill-equipped armed forces and largely pacifist government of national unity. But the Dutch people still maintained an attitude of denial, whistling into the wind with 'an atmosphere of cheerful disbelief and deliberate self-deception,' as one Dutch historian later put it.

My parents followed events closely on the radio and spoke quietly to each other when they thought we were out of earshot – but if they still feared for the future (as they must have done) or realised, with a lurch in their stomachs, that our new home had brought us only the shortest of reprieves, they never let it show.

On a deeper level these changes and uncertainties must have affected me, and I remember an incident from that time which left me distraught. Our move from Brussels had once again been hurried, and it was only after we arrived in Amsterdam that I realised I had lost my collection of Côte d'Or postcards of the Belgian Royal family. No matter how hard we looked it was nowhere to be found, and I was anguished. I felt that this small incident somehow magnified all the darkness and loss in the world.

We were four very different people from the ones who had left Vienna.

A few months after our arrival in Holland my mother stood Heinz and me up against the bedroom wall and marked off our height with the dash of a pencil. My father had made the first marks when we arrived, to inaugurate our new home. It had only been a matter of weeks, but we had both grown.

7
Anne Frank

I made many new friends in Amsterdam, especially with the girls and boys from the families settling in Merwedeplein, but one in particular was to become known to millions of people around the world.

If you are one of those millions who have read *The Diary of Anne Frank* you may believe that you already know a lot about her.

You would certainly recognise the iconic image of her that was taken by her father Otto and adorns countless posters and book covers; dark hair curled to one side, shy and cheeky smile.

If you read the diary when you were young, you may well have seen yourself in her descriptions of growing up, arguing with her parents, yearning for attention from a boy and wondering what the future holds. Like me, you will probably have been saddened to read about her hopes and dreams, and know that none of them came to fruition. Or that if they did, as is the case with her wish to be a famous writer, not in the way that she envisaged.

I did not know this Anne Frank of course, the soulful writer with sensitivities and depths that she explored only on the pages of her diary. But I can tell you about the Anne I met on Merwedeplein, and the brief friendship that began then. Later that friendship was to bring together our two families in a way that had a deep impact on my life.

On the day that I met Anne I came face to face, less with my mirror image, and more with my mirror opposite. I was a blonde-haired tomboy, sunburned from the hours spent outside, my clothes dishevelled from bike riding, marble playing and somersaults in the square. Anne was a month younger than me but she seemed dark and mysterious – peeping out from under her carefully coiffed hair. She was always immaculate in blouses and skirts with white socks and shiny patent shoes We lived directly across the square from each other, but we were so different.

If I made friends it was because people liked my sometimes blunt, straightforward enthusiasm for life. Anne drew people towards her, weaving a web of funny stories, whispered asides and the suggestion that she was just a little bit more knowing than the rest of us. She talked so much we called her 'Mrs Quack' and in my memory there was always a gaggle of girls around her, laughing and giggling at her latest observations and experiences. While I still happily played hopscotch, Anne read movie magazines and accompanied her friends to cafés where they ate ice-cream sundaes and conversed like the worldly ladies they wished to become.

One afternoon I was sitting at the dressmaker's, kicking my heels and idly waiting for Mutti so that we could get my coat altered. Behind the curtain I could hear a shopper critiquing her new outfit with the dressmaker's assistant. What did she think of the length of the hem? Would it look more stylish with big shoulder pads? To my amazement the curtain was pulled back and there was Anne, swishing her new peach outfit with green trim as she surveyed herself in the mirror, contemplating the latest fashion trends from Paris.

Anne had moved to Amsterdam from Frankfurt in Germany with her sister Margot and her parents, in 1933. Her father Otto ran a business, Opekta, making an ingredient called pectin used in jam. He was also a keen photographer, using his Leica camera with its razor-sharp Carl Zeiss lens to snap hundreds of images of his young daughters as they went about every aspect of their lives.

Like us, the Franks were Jewish refugees. Anne's mother Edith was always very quiet, and I found her almost timid. Otto was a tall, lean man with a small moustache and friendly eyes. He looked older than Mutti and Pappy, and I knew that he had married later and had Anne and Margot in his mid-thirties.

My first impression of Otto was of his kindness. After a few pre-emptive discussions at the Franks' apartment, Otto realised that I still spoke little Dutch. From then on he went out of his way to form a bond with me and make me feel at home by speaking German. I knew him for many years and, despite all that we went through, I never changed my opinion that he was warm and empathetic – a true gentleman.

I often visited the Franks' apartment and sat in the kitchen drinking homemade lemonade while I cuddled and fussed over their cat, Moortje.

When we had first arrived in Merwedeplein I'd found a little kitten near our apartment and carried her home. I whispered to her that she had a new family now, and Pappy gave Mutti and Heinz a wink and said we could keep her. I loved having something that belonged to me, and I was utterly inconsolable when I woke up one day and found that she had gone. I never knew what happened to my kitten, and I made everyone miserable as the days of hunting – fruitlessly – for her went on. I wished that Mutti would allow us to have another pet but, as that seemed unlikely, I had to be content playing with the Franks' cat instead.

Under normal circumstances my friendship with Anne would probably have been a passing acquaintance. As it was, the strongest connection between us at that stage was through another of my friends, Susanne Lederman.

Susanne had a clear complexion, blue eyes and thick dark plaits, and I worshipped her with girlish intensity. We used to send coded messages back and forth from our bedroom windows, which looked onto each other across a small back garden. Susanne made up a fearsome trio with Anne and another girl called Hanne, and they spent quite a lot of time discussing boys and potential boyfriends, which I thought was a complete waste of time.

Even Heinz was now attracting the attention of several girls in Merwedeplein, and he had fallen in love with a girl called Ellen. He was growing into a tall, handsome young man but his teenage crushes made me laugh. Romantic entanglements with boys were still beyond me. One afternoon Heinz announced that one of his friends, Herman, wanted to see me and I was mortified when this boy appeared in the doorway to my room and shyly presented me with a bunch of flowers. Under the pressure of the moment I reluctantly agreed to be Herman's 'girlfriend' but really, the kind of boy-girl attractions that Heinz, Anne and Susanne were increasingly interested in could not have been further from my mind.

We were all friends but we moved in different groups – and I was very upset when I discovered that Susanne had not invited me, or Janny, to her birthday party with Anne and some of the others. In an act of spite I took a box of chocolates and carefully unwrapped them, replacing each chocolate with a piece of carrot or turnip – before rewrapping each one in its silver foil. Then I gave the box to Susanne and wished her a happy birthday. Later Susanne's sister Barbara told me that Susanne had unwrapped every single one. 'Oh Eva,' she said, 'if only you'd left her one chocolate, just one.'

I still remember that I was very envious of Anne going to Susanne's birthday party, and how I wished that we'd all been closer friends so that I could go, too.

World events beyond our control meant that we would go on to have remarkable, and sometimes tragic, life stories – but at the time we were all just ordinary boys and girls, with the same jealousies, worries, aspirations, friendships and rivalries.

8

Occupation

During the night of 10 May 1940 the German planes flew over Holland as usual, but somewhere over the North Sea, they circled and turned back. We were woken from our sleep with the noise of low-flying planes, and shooting. By the time Pappy turned on the radio and heard the news, 4,000 German troops were already parachuting into Dutch airbases at Valkenburg, Ockenburg and Ypenburg. Later, thousands more landed in an even more formidable assault on other Dutch cities, including Rotterdam, while the German Fourth Panzer division launched a ground attack across the southern border.

It was the day before my eleventh birthday, and I had just written to my grandparents to tell them about a party I'd had the previous weekend.

Dear Grandma!

Thank you for your lovely letter and thank Grandpa for his pictures. My birthday party was very nice and I have put on 20 kilos. I'm wishing you a nice mother's day again. I have no time to write to Grandpa.

A hundred million kisses,

Eva xxxxxxxxxx
(Your birthday girl)

Now our worst nightmare had occurred. We were immediately flooded with a sense of panic and, like many other Jewish families, we gathered together a few belongings and rushed through the city streets to see if we could find a way onto a boat to England. The city was in a state of pandemonium with people running this way and that, trying to find their loved ones – or a way to escape.

We anxiously hustled from place to place for hours, getting increasingly tired and sore and upset, while Pappy tried to book us on any boat that was leaving. It was hopeless. The last boat had left, and there was no way we could have got on board.

Hand in hand, we made the long slow walk back to Merwedeplein in a silence as thick as the one that had engulfed us on the night the Nazis swept into Vienna.

The Dutch army put up a short, spirited resistance for five days but its unskilled troops and tiny air power were little match for the German war machine. The country's network of dykes that was supposed to provide a crucial line of defence was never flooded, as the bridges also provided a vital link between Dutch regiments. German tanks simply rolled across the Maas river and seized control.

The so-called 'phony war' that had lasted since September 1939 was over (although it was never 'phony' if you were Jewish, or living on the Eastern Front in countries like Poland).

In Britain Neville Chamberlain resigned as Prime Minster and was replaced by Winston Churchill, while in Poland a Nazi officer called Rudolf Höss was celebrating being made the first Kommandant of a new concentration camp called

Auschwitz. With chilling prescience, Höss announced that the empty lice-ridden Polish barracks would soon be transformed into the most 'efficient' concentration camp in the whole of the Third Reich.

Two days after the German assault on Holland began, Queen Wilhelmina fled to England on a British destroyer, with Crown Princess Juliana and Prince Bernhard and their children, and established a Dutch government-in-exile.

After four days of fighting, German planes bombed the centre of Rotterdam and reduced it to blazing rubble, killing 1,000 people and making nearly 80,000 homeless. The Dutch army had already surrendered, in order to spare the people of Rotterdam, but the Nazis claimed not to have received that information in time to halt the bombing. It was reported on the news that one little boy in the burning city said, 'Mummy, is it the end of the world?' With Amsterdam and other cities facing a similar threat, the Netherlands surrendered to Germany.

Our worst fears had come to pass. As of 15 May 1940 we were living under Nazi occupation, and we had nowhere else to go.

Once again, life changed in an instant. On that Wednesday German troops crossed the Berlarge bridge and entered Amsterdam. Some passers-by gave them a warm welcome on the Rokin, waving and reaching out their hands as the Germans swept through the streets. Most ordinary citizens reacted with horror and uncertainty. They deeply wanted to retain their Dutch independence, but also had to be prepared to go along with the new situation if that meant safety for themselves and their families.

Hoping to keep Anton Mussert's National Socialist party

out of power, a new political organisation, the Nederlandse Unie, was founded in July 1940. The NU advocated a 'sensible policy' of cooperating with the Nazis, and even discussed the 'Jewish problem'. This 'sensible cooperation' won many supporters and within months the NU had more than 800,000 members, with men and women lining up around the block to join.

After our experiences in Vienna and the reports we'd heard from the rest of Europe, we knew what was coming. The head of the new Nazi-appointed regime was Dr Arthur Seyss-Inquart, the former Austrian Chancellor who'd been responsible for allowing the Anschluss with Germany in 1938. But the Nazis proceeded cautiously at first, not wanting to alienate the majority of the Dutch population, and so we waited in our apartment in Merwedeplein, keeping each other cheerful but deeply afraid for the future.

That summer we managed to have one last family holiday together – a two-week break at the seaside in a town called Zandvoort, just an hour north of Amsterdam.

We posed for photos on the long beaches that sloped sedately down into the small stretch of the North Sea that separated us from England, but might as well have been as wide as the Atlantic Ocean. And we rode bikes together across the grassy flat lands, laughing as Mutti careened across the road and back again with her terrible sense of coordination. She never got the hang of bikes or cars – her one experience of driving led to her crashing into a tree.

The four of us talked and giggled and teased each other as if we had no cares or troubles. But in reality nothing could have been further from the truth.

In August 1940 the Nazis began to introduce laws against the Jews in the Netherlands. The first law prohibited butchers from killing animals by bleeding, as Kosher practice demanded, allegedly to 'cleanse Dutch national honour' of 'cruelty to animals'.

Then in September the Nazis banned Jewish merchants and traders from selling their goods in the streets. Next, Jews were banned from government and civil service jobs, and then universities. By October 1940 all Jewish businesses were required to register with the Nazis.

In January 1941 the Nazi regime demanded a full registration of the entire Jewish population of 130,000 people and in July, adults were issued with identity cards with a large J for Jew stamped on them. Jews could expect to be stopped and asked to produce them on any street, bus or tram, and if they made the mistake of leaving them at home the Nazis would arrest them on the spot. It seems incredible that the Nazis believed they could reduce thousands of men and women who had full, complicated personalities and lives to nothing but a giant J.

Mutti and Pappy had already had their Austrian passports stamped with a J, before they were taken away after the Anschluss and replaced with worthless German passports – also stamped with a J. Then those had also been withdrawn, leaving us all stateless. Even Mutti's Belgian visa inserted the word 'Sara' in her name so that authorities would know she was Jewish. (Jewish women were called 'Sara', and men had 'Israel' added to their names.)

Our lives were getting more and more restricted. As a Jewish business owner Pappy was forced to hand over the shoe factory in Breda to a Christian – although I believe he had an arrangement whereby he still received income from it. New travel restrictions meant that he wouldn't have been able to commute to work, anyway. Always an excellent businessman, Pappy started employing other Jewish people to make snake leather handbags from home.

We started to see signs going up on theatres and cafés and other public buildings – *Verboden voor Joden*. Forbidden for Jews. Even worse for Mutti and Heinz, everyone was forced to hand in their radios in case they were picking up news broadcasts from London. Pappy missed listening to heartening news about our English allies, and Mutti and Heinz pined for the music of the London Philharmonic.

In February 1941 hundreds of thousands of Dutch citizens brought Amsterdam to a standstill with a four-day general strike. The strike arose in protest at German brutalities against Jews following a fight outside an ice-cream parlour. It was the first sign of organised resistance from the Dutch people, and it took the Nazi regime by surprise. Until now Nazi policy had been to treat the Dutch leniently as part of their 'Aryan' race, releasing prisoners of war and turning a blind eye to ordinary people wearing orange ribbons or other symbols of resistance on the street. Now the strike ringleaders were rounded up and shot – a shocking development for the Dutch, and the first time the Nazis had revealed their true face in public. The general strike of February 1941 changed everything; it was the first turning point in the Occupation.

The Nazi Reichskommissar, Arthur Seyss-Inquart, told

the Dutch that supporting the Jews was unacceptable. 'We Nazis do not consider the Jews a part of the Netherlands people. They are our enemies.'

In case they didn't get the point, Dutch cinemas were instructed to show the most hateful kind of Nazi propaganda, including a crude film called *The Eternal Jew*. The film was a fake documentary intended to show that Jews were filthy and verminous, in fact barely human, and cut from footage showing Jewish 'parasites' on a crowded street in a Polish ghetto, to shots of rats swarming out of a sewer.

I usually loved the long warm spring evenings, but as the summer of 1941 blossomed we could hardly go anywhere or do anything. Even more restrictive laws had been passed: Jewish people weren't allowed in the Stock Exchange, Jewish doctors could only treat Jewish patients and Jewish musicians weren't allowed to play in orchestras.

For Heinz and me, and the other children in Merwedeplein, it meant we couldn't go the park, walk by the beach, ride on the tram, visit the zoo, cool off at the swimming pool or go to the cinema.

'All I want to do is see the Shirley Temple film,' I sighed to Heinz, one hot afternoon.

'What has Shirley got that I haven't got?' he asked me, jumping up from the bed where he was reading his book and starting to do a little tap dance on the floor.

'Isn't this as good as seeing the film?'

'The dancing isn't bad,' I replied, laughing, 'but you're not nearly as sweet as Shirley.'

As of September, we learned that we would have to go to separate 'Jewish' schools. Heinz was forced to leave the lyceum. At his new school he became quite good friends with Margot Frank. They were both academically minded and they sometimes ended up doing their homework together.

Mutti and Pappy decided that my Dutch was still not good enough for me to go to school, so they arranged for me to have private classes with ten other children. Mutti even went over to introduce herself to the Franks and ask if Anne would like to join us but Anne's Dutch was very good and her parents decided she could go to the proper school.

Our tutor, Mr Mendoza, was a middle-aged bachelor who gave us daily lessons in his apartment while his mother prepared our lunch in the kitchen. The Mendozas were part of the large community of Sephardic Jews who had fled persecution in Spain and Portugal hundreds of years earlier, and had built Amsterdam's magnificent Portuguese Synagogue. I believe that, like most of my other friends and acquaintances from Amsterdam, Mr Mendoza and his mother were deported to concentration camps and never returned.

As the end of our studies approached, my classmates agreed to buy Mr Mendoza a gift: two budgies in a cage. We kept the birds in my apartment and after lessons finished, the other children would come over and help me feed them.

Then one morning I woke up and found one of the budgies lying soft and pretty, and dead, at the bottom of the cage. None of my classmates seemed to be as upset about this as I was, and Mutti bought another bird to replace it. But I just couldn't forget about the bird that had died. I clenched my fists and wished and wished that I could turn back time, and bring the bird back to life – but there was no magic to make my wishes come true.

Now that the law stated that Jews had to be at home by 8.00 every evening, Pappy and Mutti improvised some entertainments for us to make it more bearable. Every evening the four of us would sit down and play bridge together. This was an unusual activity for teenagers, but bridge is a compulsive game and we quickly became embroiled in learning the complicated rules and strategies. I can't prove it, but we played so much I believe I became one of the most outstanding, and committed, child bridge players in the whole of Europe.

Even bridge games couldn't consume all our evenings, though. Sometimes we invited friends over in the afternoon and played Monopoly, and then later Heinz would sit at the piano and we'd listen as he played Chopin and Schubert, and his favourite – George Gershwin.

One day Heinz came home with cardboard and crayons and started a project in the living room. 'Don't come in,' he shouted to me, 'stay in your room until I call you.' It seemed to take for ever, but eventually he came and got me. 'Close your eyes,' he said as he led me into the living room. We were all required to have blackout blinds over the windows because of air raids, and when I opened my eyes I could see that the blinds were drawn and the room was dark. Suddenly Heinz flicked on a torch and shone the bright beam directly at the blinds, with each circle of light revealing a character from *Snow White and the Seven Dwarfs*.

'I know you were upset because you couldn't see the

film,' he said, but now you're going to have a show all to yourself . . .'

He had drawn all the characters of *Snow White*, bringing each to life with every touch of his crayon. He told me the whole story, lingering over every character and twist in the plot as if it were a film or a play. Mutti and Pappy sat watching him proudly, knowing he'd done all of that just to make me feel a little bit better.

'That was the best *Snow White* ever,' I said at the end.

Like all siblings, sometimes we argued and bickered, but I knew at that moment I could not have asked for a more thoughtful brother.

If only closing the curtains and pulling the blinds really could have kept the world out.

Unbeknownst to us, while we watched make-believe fairytale battles between good and evil, top Nazi officers had met in a villa outside Berlin and deliberated on the fate of the Jews. It was already Nazi policy to 'free up' German land and homes by transporting Jews to the east, but even that was proving problematic as ghettos in towns and cities were quickly filled.

At the Wannsee Conference on 20 January 1942 SS-Lieutenant General Reinhard Heydrich, Chief of the Security Police and Security Service, unveiled the 'Final Solution to the Jewish question': all European Jews were to be transported to camps in the east, and either worked to death or murdered.

Soon afterwards Amsterdam began to fill up with Jews from other parts of Holland who had been forcibly 'resettled'. They stayed wherever they could find a place, unaware that they were on the first stage of their gruesome journey. The Nazis always couched their atrocities in false words like 'resettlement' and 'Final Solution'. This was perfected of course in concentration camps, like Auschwitz, where people entered under the slogan 'Work makes you free' and were told they were going for 'showers' as they were marched straight into the gas chambers where they were killed.

In May of that year I found Mutti sewing a yellow Star of David onto my clothes. I must never take it off she told me, or hide it by hanging my coat over my arm. 'If any Jew is stopped and is not showing the star the Germans will arrest them,' she told me.

'We are like outcasts!' I shouted at her, with my fears and frustrations boiling over into hot angry tears.

'No, Evi,' she said. 'We hate wearing this badge but we are still proud of being Jewish. The Nazis might think that this is a badge of shame – but we can hold our heads up and know that it is a badge of honour.'

From then on we all wore a Star of David on our clothes, with the word *Jood* written on it.

As the weeks passed we became more aware of the growing danger in Amsterdam. One of Heinz's friends, Walter, was caught by the Nazis without his yellow star and arrested. Around the same time, I was walking down the street one afternoon when I saw Nazi soldiers catching a man who looked like Pappy and beating him furiously before throwing him onto the back of a truck and driving away. It was terrifying.

When Pappy heard about the Nazis rounding up men and boys and sending them to 'work' camps in Germany he managed to get Heinz admitted to hospital under false pretenses, but the news from the Dutch underground network was grim. By then rumours were filtering back that the Jews being deported were being murdered by the thousand in concentration camps. Although no one could bring themselves to fully believe this horror, Pappy realised that the net was closing in, and he would have to take more drastic action to try and save us.

His first move was to stockpile food, and hide it, so that we could survive during an emergency. By that time we were living on rations and saving food was not easy – but we gradually managed to put enough by.

I remember the sunny Sunday morning we set off across town with our first load, each of us carrying a bag or satchel containing tins of tomatoes, rice, olive oil, cocoa and condensed milk. The journey was heart-stopping; I was terrified that a soldier would stop us and demand to see what was in our satchels. At one stage I bent over to tie my shoelace and all my cans clanked loudly.

Finally we reached the warehouse next to the canal on Singel where Pappy had rented some storage space, and with a huge sigh of relief, we piled our food supplies into a large trunk.

After four of these trips the trunk was full and Pappy sprinkled mothballs on the top and closed it. We never did benefit from those supplies, but later on they did sustain another family through the war.

It turned out that Pappy's sense of urgency was well founded. Shortly afterwards, on 6 July 1942, Heinz received a letter telling him to report for deportation to a German 'work camp'.

I knew how scared Heinz was, it was the realisation of

his worst nightmares – but he blinked the news away bravely.

'I'll go,' he told Mutti. 'My friends will be there, and even Margot Frank has been sent a letter. I'm sure the Nazis will not harm me if I work hard.'

Luckily Pappy would hear none of it. 'I think it's time for us to disappear.'

At that moment I don't think any of us really knew what those words meant. We were heartened that the Americans had joined the war a year earlier and we hoped, and believed, that it would all be over soon. When I heard Pappy saying that we would have to 'disappear' I thought he meant for a few weeks – until the immediate crisis of Heinz's call-up had passed.

Before we went into hiding there was one more unpleasant hurdle to overcome; I had to have my tonsils removed.

I'd been absent from my school lessons with an infection, hoping that it would get better, but we couldn't go into hiding if I was ill. That would put all of us, and the people who sheltered us, in more danger. I couldn't go to hospital either, though; the Nazis were now arresting Jewish patients. The only option was to have my tonsils removed somewhere else, and eventually Pappy found a doctor who was willing to operate on me.

The thought of having an operation without the proper nurses and equipment was daunting, and I was gripped with a stomach-churning terror when the doctor took me into his small surgery and brusquely tied my arms and legs down to the table.

He held laughing gas over my mouth until I drifted off into a strange netherworld full of drugged dreams. As the operation progressed I dreamed that I was lying strapped to the table while the surgery caught fire, and blazing flames burned up everything around me, even the air caught fire as I struggled and fought against the straps on my arms and legs, screaming, screaming with white hot terror, but unable to get free.

9
Hiding

It's hard to imagine a life in hiding, restricted to the smallest, quietest space.

People often ask me how I coped, trapped in a small room, day after day.

When I look back at the boisterous, outdoorsy girl I was, I wonder too. I was a do-er, not a thinker like Heinz, but in hiding there was no space to turn cartwheels, and there could be no noisy household tasks such as putting up shelves, to distract me.

I coped because I had to cope. Remember, the choice was stark: hide, or die. And I coped because when you are hiding you tell yourself that it is not for ever. The prospect of for ever really would be unbearable, so you hide until tomorrow, and then until the next week, or even the next month. You wait one more day because you think freedom will surely follow the day after that.

'Be brave, Evi,' Pappy said, holding my shoulders. 'It will only be for a little while. Now that the Americans are in the war it will all be over soon.'

We were standing in the living room in Merwedeplein early on a Sunday morning, and Mutti and I had a small bag packed and ready to go.

'I know,' I said, 'but I don't understand why we can't go together, Pappy.'

'Now, don't get upset,' my father told me. He was trying to downplay what was happening as much as possible, and keep us all calm. My father had decided that it was safer and easier for us to split up, but I'd been very upset when he told me I would have to go with Mutti while he left with Heinz.

'Just think,' he said, 'while you are with Mutti, Heinz and I will be just across town – and we'll meet up as often as we can.'

'That's right,' Heinz said, 'and I'll try and write and tell you everything that we've been doing. I bet I get a lot more writing and painting done without my noisy little sister nattering away.' He grinned at me and I tried to smile back.

Then Pappy and Heinz hugged Mutti and me, and Mutti took my hand and led me out of the flat and down the steps quickly before I started to cry.

Everyone was putting on a brave face, but we all realised that our parting was momentous. We were crossing into uncharted waters; we hoped we would be together again, but we knew that anything could happen.

The square was still empty at that time of the day, and as we crossed it I could hear the echoes of all the ball games we'd played, marbles I'd rolled and arguments, dramas and parties that had been acted out. The only familiar face was our local milkman who usually had a few words and friendly smile for us. That morning he turned away and pretended that he hadn't seen us.

When the residents of Merwedeplein woke up no one would know that we had vanished. I looked up at Anne Frank's flat and wondered if they would have to leave too.

Thousands of other Jews were suddenly going on journeys to unknown destinations.

Mutti and I were each carrying a small bag, as if we were going on an ordinary outing. Unlike Otto Frank, my father hadn't planned for us to go into hiding and he had no contacts with the Resistance, but when Heinz's Nazi call-up papers arrived he had frantically asked around until he found a Christian friend, Frieda, who said that her sister would take us in and they could arrange a false identity for us.

According to our new identity papers Mutti was Mefrouw Bep Ackerman, and I was her daughter Jopie. I was now officially a little Christian girl from the Netherlands, but I felt strangely naked walking through the streets without the yellow Star of David stitched onto my coat. I'd detested every moment of wearing that yellow star, but I self-consciously held a magazine up against my chest to cover the space. We made our way silently across the streets of Rivierenbuurt, and into east Amsterdam.

Our first new 'home' was a small apartment owned by the Dekker family who had two little boys. The family was much poorer than I was accustomed to, and I was astonished to discover that the two rabbits living on the balcony were being fattened up for the Christmas dinner table. In the evening the rabbits were allowed into the apartment for the boys to play with, and we even went out to cut some grass for them to eat. Mutti and I settled into one bedroom and pretended to be relatives visiting from the countryside.

I couldn't relax, and kept nervously chattering away to Mutti. 'It feels so strange to be here, I can't believe that we could walk home in half an hour. I wonder where Pappy and Heinz are.'

Mutti looked sad but didn't say anything. She just patted my leg sympathetically.

Neither of us looked stereotypically Jewish so we often went out during the daytime, although this would have been very dangerous if anyone had scrutinised our false identity papers.

Our sense of anonymity didn't last long; one day we returned home to find Mrs Dekker standing on the doorstep looking frantic. One of her sons had gone to school and said, 'We've got an aunty and cousin visiting from the country, only I don't know who they are and I don't really think they're my family.' While we were out, the apartment had been raided by the Gestapo.

'I'm sorry you can't stay,' she told us, 'but we do know another lady across town who can take you in. You can go there.'

Without warning, we were on the move again, this time to Amsterdam Oud-Zuid. My nerves were rattling with the knowledge of how close we had come to being captured, and now it seemed we had miles to walk across the city. Finally we stopped and knocked on the front door of another house neither of us had ever been to before. The well-groomed Dutch lady who answered greeted us cheerfully as long-lost relatives. 'Come in! It's wonderful to see you again!'

Miss Klompe quickly ushered us over the threshold and clicked the door shut. Our false greeting of familiarity might not have fooled anyone for very long, but it was an essential part of the façade that we were old friends.

In Amsterdam, as elsewhere, resisting or collaborating with the Nazis was acted out in various shades of grey. In the first years of the war the Resistance was organised by small groups of individuals, who may not have even known of the existence of other groups. As time passed, hiding Jews became much more dangerous and the Resistance became more organised, but in the early days there were people like the Dekkers and Miss Klompe who simply hated the Nazis and were determined to resist them by hiding Jews.

There were people who would help Jewish families hide out of the goodness of their hearts, or because their church pastors told them their conscience required it, but there were also people who would only hide Jews for money. And just as there were people who would turn a blind eye if they saw you and suspected you were Jewish, there were also people who would report you to claim a few Dutch Guilders.

When nursery workers were smuggling orphaned Jewish children out of the Hollandsche Schouwburg building during the mass deportations of 1942, they would wait for the number nine tram to pass and then run alongside with a baby under each arm, before jumping on at the next stop. It was the only way to avoid being seen by the Nazi soldiers who stood guard on the other side of the road, watching the front door at all times to make sure that no Jews escaped. One nurse remembered that when she jumped on board with a Jewish baby 'all the people in the tram would start laughing because naturally they'd seen us, but they never said anything. That's typically Amsterdam for you.'

In truth though, it wasn't 'typically Amsterdam'. You

never knew who was really on your side, who would double-cross you – or even who was one of the feared 'Jew hunters'. This anonymous group of otherwise ordinary citizens roamed the streets to make a living out of turning Jews over to the Nazis, and almost certain death. In Nazi Amsterdam almost everyone was a stranger, and you never knew the motives of the people who watched you through their lace curtains, or lived in the house next door.

'You will have to be very careful,' Miss Klompe warned us over a cup of tea. 'You can't use either the bathroom or kitchen while I'm out.'

When Miss Klompe suggested Mutti might help with the cooking I gave my mother a sideways glance. This was her least favourite activity, and I expected to see a flicker of reluctance. Instead all I saw on her face was a grateful readiness, borne out of relief that we had found a safe place to stay.

We finished our tea and made our way up three flights of stairs to the attic where Miss Klompe had partitioned off a small bedroom for me, and a living room with a floral sofa for Mutti to sleep on.

While I took in our new surroundings, Mutti asked, 'How safe are we?'

The Germans often made raids, Miss Klompe admitted with chilling truthfulness, 'like rat catchers, trying to exterminate the "vermin" of hidden Jews' but, she stressed, the Resistance was equally determined to protect innocent people. Perhaps she meant to make us feel better, but when I heard that my stomach contracted with another lurch of fear.

Miss Klompe wasn't officially a member of the Resistance

(she just wanted to help, and opposed the Occupation and the new rules) but that night she introduced us to someone who was: Mr Broeksma, a teaching colleague from her home province of Friesland. Mr Broeksma was clever, reliable and resourceful and we felt completely safe putting our lives in his hands as he considered the best way to make us as secure as possible.

His first task, he told us, would be to build a secret hiding place that we could use if the Nazis raided the house. The best way to do this was to wall off the toilet at one end of a long bathroom, and install a hidden trapdoor covered by tiles.

Together with a trustworthy builder, Mr Broeksma began collecting materials and smuggling them over piece by piece at night. The two men didn't finish work until the third Sunday we'd gone into hiding. It was late in the evening and we were all tired, but the tiling still needed to be completed.

'You look exhausted, do you want to stop now?' Miss Klompe asked him.

After a moment's hesitation he said, 'No, let's get on and finish the job. Then it's done.' Eventually we all shook hands, Mutti and I full of gratitude. Mutti tried out the hiding place, disappearing seamlessly behind the freshly tiled wall. We fell into bed, too tired even to be anxious, and I was asleep within minutes. Not for long.

'Are there any filthy Jews hiding in here?'

The voices were loud and coarse. I was fast asleep and dreaming when the sounds of the vans in the street and crashing on the front door started to pull me back into consciousness. Suddenly Mutti grabbed me, and I was wide awake.

'Eva, cover the bed with the counterpane.'

I smoothed down the bed and we ran to the bathroom, but our urgent need to hide was complicated by another factor: Miss Klompe had her own secret – a married lover who happened to be a Jewish doctor. He was in the bathroom too – just about to climb into the hiding place in front of us. As the Nazis pounded on the front door, this gentleman tried to push us out and close the tiled door so that only he would be protected. Mutti implored him, and pointed out that if we were caught standing there he would surely be discovered as well. Reluctantly he allowed us to climb in beside him, and we shut the door just as the soldiers began to run up the stairs.

My heart was beating so loudly that I was sure the soldiers would hear it as they flung open the bathroom door and I heard them clomping about, gasping for breath and shouting instructions at each other – only inches from where Mutti was sitting, curled up on the toilet lid, and where I was crouching beside Miss Klompe's lover. Then the boots got further away as they searched the rest of the house, and finally we heard them stomping back down the stairs. The front door slammed and I could feel Mutti crying with relief beside me in the dark. We knew that only two hours and Mr Broeksma's goodwill in finishing the job had saved us.

Our time in hiding was to be a mixture of two emotions – utter terror and mind-numbing boredom. It is only when you are incarcerated, or incapacitated, that you realise a day is a very long stretch of time, and it can go on and on. Mutti and I usually woke early, got dressed and ate a small breakfast. We would hear Miss Klompe leave for work and close the front door and then the house would descend into silence. To make the morning pass more quickly Mutti would try to help me with my lessons, but I was as stubborn as ever and she would sometimes become frustrated enough to give me a sharp slap to the top of my head. I knew that somewhere in Amsterdam, Heinz would be occupying himself in hiding by reading voraciously, playing chess and making full use of his artistic talents. Mr Broeksma brought me books to read but I couldn't concentrate on them. Instead I filled the time by talking to Mutti about something that had happened, like a raid, or our plans for the future.

I found it hard to be cooped up with my mother day and night, and she found it equally difficult to spend every waking moment with a moody, exasperating, thirteen-year-old girl.

Food was strictly rationed and we were using false ration cards, so in the evening we ate a small dinner that always left me hungry. At some point we would have a brief chat with Miss Klompe, but she was usually occupied with marking schoolbooks or entertaining her boyfriend. It may seem strange, but in those days we didn't really know Miss Klompe very well. We were very grateful for her help, and we were lucky – later I discovered that many Jews had bad relationships with the people who were hiding them. Sometimes the children who were sent out to country farms were exploited, and women and girls were even sexually assaulted or forced to sleep with the man of the house to keep their hiding place. We didn't experience anything like that, but it was still a strain to live in someone else's house under those circumstances and know that you were at their mercy.

Every evening we would gather around the radio that Mr Broeksma had smuggled in and hidden in a cupboard. At 9.00p.m. we would tune into the BBC broadcast in Dutch from London, and listen to the progress of the war. It was from these broadcasts, and from Mr Broeksma himself, that we learned that almost all the Jews in Amsterdam had been rounded up and sent off to the East.

We were cheered to hear any bit of news that indicated the tide was turning against the Nazis, and I remember gripping Mutti's fingers with delight when we found out that Rommel had been beaten in Africa. But there was horrible worrying news, too. It was via that radio that we first heard about a Nazi death camp called Auschwitz in Poland. I remember I got goose bumps up my neck and felt sick when I heard that the Nazis were gassing Jews in this camp. We all sat slumped in disbelief, not meeting each other's eyes – surely it couldn't be true?

Later we turned in for the night and, in the dark, I kicked my feet up in bed, restlessly moving against the sheets – desperate for some release for all my pent-up fear and anxiety.

Maybe you can imagine living with this kind of routine for a few days, or even a few weeks, but we were in hiding for almost two years.

The only bright moments were when we managed to make rare visits to my father, and Heinz.

Leaving the house was a huge risk: we had to make our way through the city to the station and then catch a train to a small town outside Amsterdam called Soestdijk where Pappy and Heinz were hiding in a house belonging to a woman called Gerada Katee-Walda. I had to summon all my courage to appear calm and nonchalant when soldiers passed us on the pavement, or stood next to us in the train carriage, but the tension of the journey was quickly dispelled when we were all reunited.

As I suspected, Heinz was more suited to a life of solitary confinement than I was. He was painting more and more, and I could hardly believe the detailed and impressive oil paintings that he showed me. In one a young man, like himself, was leaning his head on desk in despair. In another a sailing boat was crossing the ocean in front of a shuttered window.

'How did you learn to paint like this?' I asked him. 'How did you even know how to mix the paints?' Heinz just grinned and shrugged.

Even Pappy was occupied with intellectual pursuits, filling thin-lined exercise books with page after page of business ideas that he could pursue after the war, as well as sketches and poems.

Sometimes these trips lasted for a day and occasionally we managed to stretch them out overnight. I knew that together we could get through anything, and I drew on the memory of each visit long after we returned to Miss Klompe's, until that finally gave way to a sense of building anticipation for the next visit.

I enjoyed going to Soestdijk so much that I even had my photo taken linking arms with Mrs Katee-Walda. She seemed like such a friendly and pleasant woman, and I was happy to think that Heinz and Pappy had found such a benevolent protector. Sadly, however, she was not at all the person we thought she was.

10
Betrayal

I was captured by the Nazis on my fifteenth birthday. It was 11 May 1944 and we were now living with a family we had known before, called Reitsma, in an old house on Jacob Obrecht Street, near the Vondelpark. Sheltering Jews had become increasingly dangerous, with the Nazis offering bigger financial rewards for turning people in. After one of our visits to Pappy and Heinz we returned to discover that Miss Klompe had been raided once again by the Gestapo. 'I'm sorry,' she said, 'but hiding you is becoming too much of a strain.' We had to move on.

I woke up early on 11 May looking forward to what my birthday had in store. I liked the Reitsmas; Mr Reitsma was a Frieslander and his wife was a Jewish artist. Their son, Floris, was also living in the house. When I went downstairs that Tuesday morning I discovered that they had prepared a special birthday breakfast for me. There was a vase of fresh hyacinths and tulips on the table, and Floris handed me a present wrapped in paper that Mrs Reitsma had painted herself. 'Keep this, it's a surprise,' he said. 'Open it after breakfast.'

It was half-past eight and we were just about to tuck in when there was a sharp ring on the doorbell. Everyone frowned in surprise, it was very early for visitors. Mr Reitsma went to open the door – and in the background

I heard the harsh German tones of the Gestapo. Suddenly it was mayhem. Soldiers pounded up the stairs, Floris leapt up, climbed out the window and ran across the rooftops, the dining room door flung open and Nazis pointed the barrels of their guns right into our astonished, petrified faces. I never got to open my present.

'It's them,' they shouted. *'Filthy Jews!'*

They grabbed us and pushed us downstairs and out on to the street. As we were marched along my mother started pleading desperately with the Dutch Nazi who held her arm, telling him that I wasn't really Jewish, I was the result of an affair she'd had with her dentist back in Vienna. He didn't believe a word and we soon arrived at the large brick building that had been a secondary school before the Gestapo took it over for their headquarters.

We were shoved into a detention room with other frightened looking people, who didn't look up to meet our eyes. We sat for hours on the hard wooden chairs that lined the walls, while I let the events of the morning run over and over in my mind. How had this happened? Who had betrayed us? What would happen now?

I could hear muffled screams and crying coming from the other rooms. One by one, people's names were called and they were taken away. No one spoke or offered any words of comfort. Eventually I heard Mutti's name being called out. My heart seemed to stop, but I felt her hand grip my arm in one silent squeeze that communicated strength and love.

Half an hour later they came for me.

A policeman led me into a sparsely furnished room with a picture of Hitler hanging on the wall. At one end there were two Gestapo officers sitting behind a desk watching me politely and intently. They weren't crass or boorish; when they spoke it was in quiet, well-educated German. 'Tell us everything we want to know and you can see your mother,' one said. Then the other spoke, and what he said made me gasp. 'You will be able to see your father and brother as well.'

I hadn't realised that Heinz and Pappy had been captured too, and I began to tremble violently. Suddenly the Gestapo began to fire questions at me. Where had we been living before and who had helped us? Who had given us our ration cards?

I fumbled my way through some answers without giving too much away, and I even managed to hide Miss Klompe's real identity.

They dismissed me and I went back to the waiting room to sit beside Mutti. Then I heard the sound of voices coming from the interrogation room, followed by screams. It was Pappy and Heinz. Soon the screams fell into silence again, and we waited and waited. The policeman reappeared and led me back into the room. This time the senior officer said to me, 'We will torture your brother to death unless you cooperate.'

I stood rooted to the spot in fear and disbelief. 'Do you want me to show you what we will do to him?' he asked. Then he took his truncheon and started beating me with hard blows across my back and shoulders. At first I tried not to call out, but they beat me relentlessly, so hard that I started to scream – deep screams that I couldn't control.

Eventually they picked me up and threw me into a room with other prisoners whose faces were also bloodied and bruised. I sat there all day, the day that was still my birthday, without food or water, listening to the noises of people being tortured in the interrogation room next door.

The policeman came again for me and led me down a corridor into another room. This time the door opened and Mutti was standing there with Pappy, Heinz and the Reitsmas. I started crying and fell into their arms.

Pappy explained what had happened; much of it I knew, but the most recent developments still shocked me. While we had found a new hiding place with the Reitsmas, Pappy and Heinz had also been forced to move, in even more difficult circumstances. At first, relations with Mrs Katee-Walda were cordial but as time wore on she became increasingly demanding. Pappy was already paying her a significant amount of money, but she said she wanted more. Soon she dropped her friendly façade and became unpleasant and insulting, giving them smaller and smaller portions of food. Things came to a head when we were visiting one weekend and she insisted that my mother take off her fur coat and hand it over. 'You don't go out much,' she told Mutti, 'so you wont be needing it. I can use it to get the shopping for Erich and Heinz.'

It was clear that Mrs Katee-Walda was blackmailing us – if Pappy couldn't meet her financial demands she would hand them in. He implored Mutti to help find somewhere else for him to stay with Heinz, so she went to visit a Christian friend and told her our predicament. Mutti's friend wasn't sure she could help, but she did know a family who were rumoured to be with the Resistance and we asked them to look into finding a new hiding place. They agreed, and we were delighted when they told us soon after that a family in Amsterdam would be able to shelter Pappy and Heinz.

Pappy and Heinz were thrilled to be leaving Mrs Katee-Walda but worried that she would hand them over if she discovered their plan, which would lose her a large part of her income. They crept out of her house early one morning and boarded a train to Amsterdam. Both Pappy and Heinz looked quite Jewish, and Heinz had dyed his hair blond in disguise, which did not suit him. They were both very anxious that they would be stopped and arrested and so they couldn't have been more relieved when a Dutch nurse from the Resistance met them at the station and told them she'd be escorting them to their new lodgings. They made it safely across town and met the friendly family who were taking them in and had even prepared a lovely meal – in stark contrast to the meagre portions available with Mrs Katee-Walda.

A few days later Mutti and I visited them. None of us suspected that the nice Dutch nurse and the welcoming family were all Nazi agents, waiting until Pappy and Heinz were comfortably settled before turning them in. The Gestapo saw us that day and followed us back to the Reitsmas. They waited a day and then arrested us all, simultaneously.

Now we were in Gestapo headquarters, heading for prison – and worse.

My parents tried to do anything they could to help us, and to help the Reitsmas. Our papers had been marked with the dreaded 'S' for *Strafe*, which meant punishment in German. Mutti made a deal with the Gestapo that she would tell them where all her jewellery was hidden on the condition that they removed the 'S' from our papers and released Mr and Mrs Reitsma. The Gestapo officer agreed and he returned to the house with Mutti where they found and unscrewed Mutti's talcum-powder box, which hid her diamond rings and diamond watch. Remarkably, he kept his word, releasing the Reitsmas and allowing them to live undisturbed through the remainder of the war. They survived the winter famine of 1944 by eating the food supplies we'd left in the trunk in the warehouse all that time ago, and it's some comfort to know that a good family benefitted.

At the time, I could only feel dismayed that we weren't all allowed to go free. 'Why can't they release all of us?' I sobbed to Pappy, back in the detention room at Gestapo headquarters. 'It's because they think we are the enemy,' he told me quietly.

Soon we were herded into a black prison van and driven to jail. Dutch prison officers pulled us out at the other end and separated men from women. I craned my neck and saw Pappy, he lifted his head up and mouthed, 'Chin up.'

I was led with Mutti into the women's section of the prison – a large dormitory with about forty other pitiful-looking women crammed into bunk beds, and a dirty toilet at one end. That night I climbed into the bunk with Mutti and we lay restlessly, slipping in and out of consciousness, as new prisoners were brought in, babies cried and one woman had chronic asthma attacks. I couldn't understand how any of this had happened to me. I was a young girl, just fifteen, and I'd already been hounded from country to country by the Nazis, forced from my home into hiding, and now I was in prison. My mind whirled with anger and bitterness, but all I really felt was empty.

In the morning we were handed a tiny piece of bread and some water and I ate ravenously, realising it was the first food we had seen since the birthday breakfast the day before, which I had barely touched. One woman, who I'd noticed trying to comfort the other prisoners, came and sat next to me on the bunk while I ate. Her name was Ninni Czopp and she was born in Amsterdam to a Russian family. She told me she'd been waiting to go to university when the Nazis invaded, but she'd managed to go into hiding with her younger sister, her brother and his wife and their baby Rusha. Her mother had been caught early on. 'At least we're in a Dutch prison,' she comforted me. The Dutch were known for being more humane.

At the end of our second day we were told that we were being moved to another location – a transit camp deep in the Dutch countryside called Westerbork. 'It will be better there,' Ninni said, pointing out the cramped and horrible conditions of the prison, 'and as long as we're in Holland we'll be safe.'

The soldiers crammed us into an ordinary train compart-ment, like the kind we had used once as commuters, and stood over us with their guns as we steamed through the Dutch countryside, which was blooming into a beautiful summer. It was a long time since I had seen fields and flowers and sheep and cows, and how I envied the farmers I saw en route, enjoying the freedom to plant their gardens, cycle down country lanes and work the crops. I clung to every detail of the journey, until we arrived at our destination.

Westerbork was originally built by the Dutch as a tem-porary housing camp for Jewish refugees arriving in the 1930s.

Once the Nazis occupied the country it became a detention camp for Jews – and then the deportation centre for Jews being sent to concentration camps and death camps.

We arrived at sunset and I looked out across the camp's flat expanse.

'It's not so bad,' Pappy told us, trying to keep our spirits up. 'We are still in Holland and at least we can be together. Perhaps there will be other people we know, like the others from the Lyceum, or some of the girls from Merwedeplein, Janny or Sanne and Anne.'

The wooden barracks and living conditions were primitive and people appeared tense and worried, but not hopeless. A muddy main street, nicknamed the 'Boulevard of Misery', ran down the middle of the camp and that was where most of the inmates met and socialised, exchanging news and gossip.

As new arrivals we were taken for registration at the reception desk and asked to fill in a number of forms and cards. The administrators and supervisors were Jewish inmates themselves, overseen by Nazi soldiers. A Central Distribution Bureau would have taken charge of our ration books but the Gestapo had already removed these. We were then passed on to a classification desk, for more detailed information. After that we were taken to the accommodation office, and then to the quarantine barracks.

Mutti and I were taken to one of the women's barracks, which had bunk beds and reasonable toilet facilities. Although we had been separated from Heinz and Pappy we soon found each other, and we were permitted to mingle outside in the fresh air. Heinz found a small patch of shade for us to sit and talk. That night we all ate together in a large communal dining area, and we had the traditional Dutch dish of stamp-pot, which is mashed potatoes with carrots covered in gravy. At dinner the other inmates filled us in on life in Westerbork.

Like all camps, Westerbork had quickly developed a unique and peculiar culture. At its height it had a large hospital with more than 1,000 beds, specialist consultants and an outpatients department, as well as a camp canteen and warehouse where people could, for a time, buy things unavailable elsewhere in the Netherlands including fish, cucumbers, pudding mixes and bunches of flowers. There were also large workshops and a tailoring department with a special machine that mended the ladders in women's stockings (freshly darned for arrival in Auschwitz). Until the time of our arrival the camp had hosted a famous cabaret show staged by inmates, featuring two well-known singers called Johnny and Jones.

The most dreaded day of the week was the day the transport left, carrying thousands of unfortunate Jews eastwards to their deaths. As each transport approached, the tension mounted; who would be on the list? The empty train rolled in overnight and inmates woke in the morning to see the long line of cattle trucks waiting for them in the siding.

As Dutch historian Jacob Presser described in his study of the destruction of Dutch Jews, these days were filled with anguish and despair but for those who were not on the list and had won perhaps an extra week's reprieve, there was also sharp relief. Inmates wrote about the incongruity of seeing Jews being shoved on board the train and the doors slammed shut, as across the camp the cabaret struck up one of its lively performances and the sound of music and dancing filled the air. Everyone at Westerbork was desperate to stay, knowing the only option for departure was the train that carried them to what Presser described as 'an unknown country from whose bourn no traveller returns'.

From 1942 Westerbork was run by camp commandant Albert Konrad Gemmeker and his mistress and secretary Elisabeth Hassel, who employed one of the inmates as her own personal dressmaker, and whose capricious cruelty towards any unlucky Jewish woman who caught her lover's eye was particularly feared.

Gemmeker was a typical Nazi; he combined unfeeling brutality with bursts of 'civilised' humanity, dispensed on a whim. One woman wrote that he never called anyone a 'Jew', only a 'camp inmate', while another person remembered that they had heard of commandants who kicked people onto the trains, but Gemmeker 'saw them off with a smile'. He once overruled an exemption from transport given to a sick child, ordering her onto the train with the chilling words, 'No, she will die anyway.'

Like other camp commandants, he treated the people unfortunate enough to come under his power as his personal playthings – and in the end more than 100,000 Dutch Jews and Gypsies would be dispatched to the horrors of the extermination camps under his 'polite' supervision.

At its height, from July 1942 until autumn 1943, trains left Westerbork every four days, carrying an average of 1,000 people in cramped dark cattle trucks. In the spring and early summer of 1943 some large transports carried up to 3,000 people at a time to the death camp at Sobibor.

(The Nazi leaders at Sobibor, in Eastern Poland, went as far as building a special station with an attractively decorated fake waiting room to make people believe they were arriving at a normal town.)

There were numerous ways of trying to stay off the transport list – some of them depended on what work you could do but most involved any personal connections that you could use to ensure the survival of your family. Pappy had already recognised some Jewish people he knew from before the war, including a man called George Hirsch who worked in the central administration office. Pappy told us, 'If I can, I'll make contact with people here to try and get us suitable work and manoeuvre our way into protected positions.'

With more time, he might have been successful, but luck was not on our side.

We had only been in Westerbork for two days when we received the dreaded news: our names were on the list for the next transport. By the summer of 1944 transports were becoming less frequent (almost all Dutch Jews had already been rounded up, deported and murdered). Tragically for us, though, our arrival coincided with a planned transport of Gypsies, and there were spare places to be filled on the train.

Early on Friday morning a woman prison guard came and woke us. She read out the list of people who were being deported that day.

'. . . Fritzi Geiringer, Eva Geiringer . . .'

I stared at her. I was so shocked I could hardly stand up, and I could see that Mutti's hands were shaking. There was a terrible tension in the barrack, broken with relief by those who were staying behind – but there was no relief for us.

Mutti took a deep breath and tried to pull herself together. 'Now, Evi, let's get our things. Don't forget to take the steel supports for your shoes, and your underwear.' She was trying to speak normally, but I could hear the fear in her voice, and she wouldn't meet my eye.

The other women in the barracks gave us extra food, blankets and shoes for the journey and then we walked outside where we could see a long stream of hundreds of people, men, women, old people and children hanging onto their mothers' skirts, all jostling against each other as they were steered up to the railway sidings. Suddenly Pappy and Heinz appeared next to us, and we clung together to make sure that we weren't separated on the train.

'Just hang on to me, Evi,' Pappy said. 'It will be all right.'

'Where are we going, Pappy?' I asked, with a trembling high-pitched voice that sounded to my ears as if I were a little girl again.

'I don't know, maybe we are going to a labour camp in Germany. The war is going very badly now for the Nazis and they need all the fit people they can find to work in their factories.'

We shuffled forward with the crowd, as Pappy gave us lectures on how to survive in a concentration camp. He told us to get as much rest as possible, and 'always wash your hands to avoid the possibility of germs or sickness'. Heinz and I exchanged a tiny grin at that.

'But Pappy makes it sound as if we are going to be separated when we get there,' I whispered to Heinz. 'I couldn't bear that!'

Heinz looked like he was going to cry. 'I think it's possible,' he told me. 'It's happened to other families.'

As I got close to the train I could see that many of the people in the first cattle trucks were Gypsies. The transport we were herded onto departed on 19 May 1944 and carried 699 people in eighteen wagons. Of the 453 Jews on board, forty-one were children. Children also made up half of the 246 Roma.

We were pulled and pushed on board one of the trucks, which was already crammed with people, and we made our way into one of the corners where Pappy could hold me, while Mutti put her arms around Heinz. Our suitcases had been pushed on board after us, and people from our barracks were standing in the siding shouting words of encouragement.

We stood there for more than an hour. Later I found out that there were more than 100 people in that truck, but at the time all I knew was that we were crushed together – with no room to sit or move. I looked up and saw two tiny barred windows near the ceiling and two iron pails in the corner. Finally there was a commotion on the platform as guards began slamming the doors shut. Ours was pulled across in a heavy motion and, as we descended into darkness, I heard the bolt fasten shut. With a long slow shudder the train began to move, and it felt as if we had begun a journey into hell.

II

Auschwitz-Birkenau

The train carried us slowly across Europe for three days and nights. We were pressed together in the darkness like condemned animals, with one small stinking pail for a toilet and another for water. Once a day the train would jolt to a stop and screaming guards would fling the door open, blinding us with daylight, and throw in some pieces of bread, before we lurched into the disorienting twilight world once more. People cried, prayed and wilted with hopelessness in the intense summer heat. One pregnant woman broke down completely in panic-induced hysteria.

Pappy tried hard to keep us calm but after a few hours Heinz said, 'I can't breathe!' The heat was stifling and I could hear his wheezy breathing and asthmatic cough.

'Don't panic,' Pappy told him. 'Let's push you through, so that you can get some fresh air.'

There was a tiny, high up slit in the side of the car, and Pappy managed to push Heinz though the throng of people, so that he could stand next to it for a while, and try to calm down.

Mutti looked on, silently, in deep shock at what was happening.

Sometimes we stopped for long stretches: a row of cattle trucks packed with hundreds of nauseous, sweating people, boiling in the sun in a railway siding, somewhere on what was supposed to be the most civilised continent on earth. But the journey was inescapable; eventually the engine would hiss and set off again – taking us closer, with a slow determination, to our final destination.

'Do you think we are still in Germany?' Heinz asked, as the journey wore on and on. We had been on the train for so long that we knew we couldn't be. After a moment Pappy simply said, 'I don't know, Heinz.'

Later Heinz said to me, 'Evi, remember those paintings I did at Mrs Katee-Walda's house?' Of course, I did. He went on. 'They are under the floorboards, next to the attic window. If I don't come back that's where I hid them.'

'Don't say that!'

'I'm just telling you. I hope that we can go and get them together.'

As we got closer to our destination the train stopped more frequently, and SS guards would throw the doors open and start screaming at us to hand over our jewellery and watches. It was all carefully planned to strip us of our valuables before we arrived and although many people held on to their things at first, after a few stops everyone had given up their wedding rings and watches and bracelets.

When the doors opened for the last time we saw that the train had brought us to the place we dreaded the most – the flat, fetid swamp lands of south-west Poland. We had arrived at Auschwitz, a death centre the size of a small city with thousands of workers busily dedicated to perfecting mass murder, and the extermination of the Jewish race.

In the course of my lifetime I have seen amazing technical advances. When I was born it was unusual to have a motor car, but by the time I was forty years old man had landed on the moon. We have cured diseases, built nuclear weapons, mapped our DNA, surfed the web and developed genetically modified food and medicine. In the West at least, most of us have become wealthier than a generation like my grandparents' could ever have imagined. Yet in terms of our humanity, it seems that thousands of years of experience have led to little progress.

Anne Frank wrote at the end of her diary, just before she was captured, that she still believed people were good at heart, but I wonder what she would have thought if she had survived the concentration camps at Auschwitz and Bergen-Belsen. My experiences revealed that people have a unique capacity for cruelty, brutality and sheer indifference to human suffering. It is easy to say that good and evil exist within each of us but I have seen the unedifying reality of that at close hand, and it has led me to a lifetime of wondering about the human soul.

Like all things truly German, the Nazi concentration camp system was organised with supreme, and rigid, efficiency. All camps came under the central control of the SS, but different camps had different designations. Some, like Westerbork, were transit camps intended to dispatch Jews to the East, while others, like Dachau and Buchenwald, were officially 'work camps' where Jews were subjected to hard labour. Tens of thousands of people died in these camps, but they were not designated as 'death camps'. After the 'Final Solution' was decreed at the Wannsee Conference in January 1942, four camps were built in Poland, at Treblinka, Chelmo, Sobibor and Belzec, with the single purpose of killing the Jews – and the people who were transported there were virtually all murdered upon arrival. These were the 'extermination camps', and they were actually very small in size – there was no need to build barracks or administration buildings as the huge numbers of victims were led through the woods and gassed immediately.

In total the Nazis operated more than 300 concentration camps across Europe. The largest of these was Auschwitz-Birkenau, a vast extermination and labour complex consisting of thirty-eight separate camps. Auschwitz-Birkenau encompassed an industrial plant that manufactured the Zyklon B gas used to kill millions of people, which was operated by IG Farben, as well as a coal mine and a farm.

The Nazis were very proud of Auschwitz, it was the jewel in their concentration camp crown. Top leaders, including Himmler, personally oversaw the camp's expansion and development. Once the first experiment of gassing had been carried out on Soviet prisoners of war at Auschwitz in 1941, a specially designed series of gas chambers and crematoria was built for the inmates of the newly built Birkenau camp. Those death machines puffed away day and night until late 1944, covering an area for miles around in grey sooty ash. Sometimes they broke down under the strain of sending more than one million people to their deaths. When we stepped off the train that day at Auschwitz, terrified, dazed and confused, we were being herded straight into the engine room of the Holocaust.

'This is it,' someone moaned, 'We are all going to be killed!'

'Don't say that!' Pappy snapped at them. Then he gripped me and Heinz and said, 'We are all strong and fit, and the

Germans need people to work. We will work hard for a few months and then the war will be over.'

Just as we were about to get down from the cattle truck, Mutti handed me a long coat and a felt hat. 'I don't want it,' I told her. It was boiling hot and I couldn't wait to get outside and breathe some fresh air.

'Put it on,' she told me severely. 'We don't know what we'll be allowed to take with us, they might not let us take our suitcases.'

On the platform I could hear the SS guards shouting harsh German commands, and dogs barking and straining at the leash. Embarrassed, I slipped on the coat and hat, feeling ridiculous.

'You look like a very smart young lady,' Pappy told me.

'If there are any people who are too ill or too tired to walk, get on the truck and we will drive you to the camp,' an SS guard shouted.

Many people were exhausted from the journey and with huge relief they hobbled over to the trucks and jumped on board. 'We'll see you up there,' they shouted back to their relatives left on the platform. The trucks set off, led by a car decorated with a false symbol of the Red Cross to add legitimacy to the façade. No one realised that it was a ploy to weed out those too weak to work, and that they were being driven directly to the gas chamber.

'Get down and put your belongings next to the train. Stand in rows of five,' the guard shouted at us.

The scenes on the platform were wildly emotional and I was overwhelmed by the sounds of people wailing and crying, shouting desperate goodbyes.

There were hundreds of people; old people, mothers

with babies in their arms and small children, all in a state of total commotion and a kind of primitive desperation. But with the ease of practice, the SS guards began to rifle through us like clothes on a rack, until we were sorted into lines of men and women – and then into rows of five.

I turned and saw that Heinz's face was white with fear, and I hugged and squeezed him. Mutti drew Heinz close and ran her fingers through his hair, kissing him. Then my parents gave each other a frantic embrace – and we were parted. 'God will protect you, Evertje,' Pappy said, hugging me tightly, before he was moved away.

We moved up the ramp slowly until we could see the SS guards at the top, directing people into two columns going left and right. A woman in front of us began screaming when she realised that she would be forced to hand over her baby to the other column. An old woman held out her arms to take him but the young mother cried and cried, until Mutti told her that the old woman would know she was the baby's mother when it was time to collect him. I don't know if any of us believed this, but the young mother handed her baby over and slumped into silent defeat.

Then I was at the front of the ramp and it was my turn. There were several SS officers waiting, and one was clearly in charge. He was slim and neatly dressed with a cool demeanour. For a moment he looked me up and down – and indicated left with an indifferent gesture. Mutti was also sent left, and I felt her behind me, holding my arm.

I didn't know then that we had just undergone our first selection by the notorious camp doctor, Josef Mengele – or that the coat and felt hat had saved my life. There was no need for Mengele to take part in the platform selections, but he particularly enjoyed being intimately involved in the mechanics of torture and murder. Later I would encounter him again, and 'Dr Death', as he was called, would play a decisive role at several points in our story.

All I knew at the time was that I was by far the youngest girl in our line. I realised that Mutti's determination to dress me up had made me look older. All children under the age of fifteen were automatically sent to the right – the line that led straight to the gas chamber – and I was one of only seven out of the 168 children on our transport to survive.

One of the main reasons why Auschwitz had been chosen as the site for a large camp was good railway connections, and sprawling tracks and roads spread out in different directions. The road from the station forked in two – one way to the men's camp at Auschwitz, and the other to the women's camp at Birkenau.

It was a beautiful hot spring day, but all around us the earth was dry and barren, with not a tree or flower in sight. Mutti and I joined the women's line, for what turned out to be a long trudge up to the camp. After our brief embraces and few words of comfort, Pappy and Heinz disappeared into the throng of the men's line.

We set off up the dusty road, hundreds of hot, tired and thirsty women, knowing that in the surrounding farms and houses there were ordinary people going about their lives. Auschwitz had originally been a Polish town called Oświęcim with 12,000 people of whom 5,000 were Jews. Most of those people had been moved out of their homes after the Germans invaded, renamed the town and built and expanded the camp across a huge area.

By 1944 the sight of long lines of arriving prisoners, or emaciated men and women in striped uniforms being marched out to work, was familiar to the local people. Poland had a strong tradition of anti-Semitism and many of the local population were actively involved in building the camp, working as labourers on the crematoria, erecting barbed wire or digging ditches. Many returned after the war to reap the gruesome rewards of what has been called a 'golden harvest', digging up the remains of the victims and sifting through the ash and bones to find any gold teeth or valuable materials that had been overlooked when their bodies and possessions had first been looted by the Nazis.

By the time we arrived at the gates of Birkenau my feet were aching and my throat was as dry as sandpaper. I longed for even the tiniest drink of water. Before me was the entrance that is now familiar to most people who have seen images of Auschwitz-Birkenau: a long brick building with a guard turret, and an arch large enough for a train to pass through. We had arrived at the main Auschwitz train station, but the SS had recently built a railway spur, taking the tracks right into the heart of the camp itself and nearly up to the crematoria. We did not know it, but this was part of a frenzied expansion plan to cope with the expected influx of hundreds of thousands of Hungarian Jews who were almost all murdered upon arrival.

I looked around and saw a tall electrified barbed wire fence stretching far off into the distance, guard posts manned by SS soldiers with snapping dogs, and long rows of dark and decrepit barracks. There was an unfamiliar acrid smell in the air.

We soon discovered what the smell was. Once we had been marched into an airless barrack that served as the reception area, a group of eight women *Kapos* arrived to oversee our induction. Kapos were prisoners themselves who the SS used to administer the camps. Mostly they were Polish Christians who had been incarcerated in Auschwitz since the start of the war. Some still retained a spark of humanity, but many were criminals who held onto the closely guarded privileges of their positions by exercising cruelty and barbarity.

'Welcome to Birkenau,' they sneered, pushing their way amongst us and lashing out with punches. 'Your luck has just run out. Can you smell the camp crematorium? That's where your dear relatives have been gassed in what they thought were shower rooms. They're burning now. You'll never see them again!'

I tried to turn inside myself, not listening – not believing. I was dimly aware that Mutti was asking for a drink and swaying in an almost dead faint, and I heard a kinder Kapo whispering that we mustn't drink the water because it carried typhus and dysentery.

Eventually we were told to strip naked and leave all our last belongings behind. As a teenager I felt acutely embarrassed about having to undress in front of hundreds of people, but I saw that Mutti and Ninni, my friend from the prison in Amsterdam, were taking off their clothes in a very matter of fact way. 'Don't forget your steel supports,' Mutti hissed, handing me the hated metal arches that she made me wear in my shoes to correct my flat feet.

Two Kapos at the far end of a room were roughly shaving off all our hair. 'Open your legs,' one commanded, drawing the razor sharply down across my skin. Then she picked up a pair of blunt scissors and began chopping off the hair on my head. 'Leave a little,' Mutti asked them. 'She's very young.' Surprisingly the Kapo complied, and I was left with a shorn inch of blonde fringe on an otherwise bald head.

Still naked, we were taken to another desk for processing where I noticed that everyone seemed to be inventing useful occupations, claiming they were cooks or cobblers. When it was my turn I said I was a secretary. From time to time male SS guards would wander in, laugh at our nakedness and leer over a few women. I jumped from shock when one walked behind me and pinched my bottom.

Mutti put her arms around my shoulders as another Kapo picked up the needle and the bottle of ink to tattoo my camp number on my left arm. 'Don't hurt her too much, she's just a child,' Mutti said, and the Kapo made my number fainter than the others.

Then an SS guard marched in and started screaming at the Kapos – someone had got the registration numbers wrong. This was the kind of administrative problem that caused endless delays and upheavals in camp life, and we were lined up and re-tattooed, with the Kapo scoring through the old number just as if she were crossing out on a blackboard.

Still holding my steel supports in the palms of my hands, I was moved along into a large room with pipes and shower nozzles. The door closed and everyone began to tremble. My heart pounded as I wondered – is this really a shower? What if we are going to be gassed? Mutti held me tightly. After an agonising few seconds the water dribbled through, and we scooped it up to rub over our dirty, dusty bodies.

Naked and soaking wet we emerged outside where there were piles of rags and broken-down shoes. 'Where are your steel supports?' Mutti whispered. I shrugged. 'Oh Evi,' she scolded. 'How will you ever correct your feet?'

As the final indignity, we were handed random ill-fitting clothes, and mismatched shoes, and we tried to swap them until we all had something that we could wear. At that point Mutti and I realised that my steel supports would have been useless anyway.

I was sure that we must be almost done, and all I could think of was finding something to drink. Eventually we stumbled on and joined the camp proper. I ran to the nearest tap and began to gulp down mouthfuls of water, not caring if it was infected with deadly diseases. Around me, Birkenau was bustling with tens of thousands of people, all trying to hang on and eke out an existence in the harshest conditions imaginable – but I was too intent on slaking my thirst to take it in.

In the future I would have to develop a finely tuned awareness of my surroundings and maintain the steeliest determination, if I were to survive. I was now prisoner A/5272 – part of a process intended to strip me of my pride and identity. When I was marched away from Auschwitz railway station, I left the girlish Eva Geiringer and her dreams, behind. We had spent our last moments together as a family, and I would never see my brother again.

12

Camp Life

Auschwitz-Birkenau was its own world, and almost nothing about it could be compared to life before. Occasionally I would stop and remember that not so long ago I had been a girl playing marbles on Merwedeplein, and I would wonder where Janny Koord and Susanne Lederman and Anne Frank were, and what they were doing. Were they and their families suffering like us?

Auschwitz was a world of filth, starvation, depravity – and small gestures of solidarity. Pappy had once warned me never to sit on a toilet seat because of the germs, but now I had to squat over a filthy sewer with thirty other women. I had never planned for anything more complicated than a game of marbles, but now I learned to fight for my food ration – and, if necessary, starve myself by bartering my bread for other things I needed more. I soon saw that civilisation is a thin veneer easily stripped away and I real-ised life's true necessities, like having your own cup for food and drink so that you could make sure you always got your share. When I got my own cup I tethered it to my ragged clothes and never let it out of my sight.

Not everyone could adapt. People who could not adjust to camp life acquired a vacant gaze, gave up hope and died. In camp language these people were called 'muselmann' because their lifeless stoop made them look like Muslims bent over in prayer. A large part of my survival was down to pure luck – no amount of willpower could have saved me if I'd been selected for the gas chambers. Yet I vowed never to join the ranks of the 'muselmann'. I never gave up hope, or the determination that I would outlast the Nazis and go on to live the full life that I, and all victims of the Holocaust, deserved.

Birkenau covered a vast area, more than 432 acres, and was teeming with many different groups of people but I was only ever exposed to small parts at a time. In four years the camp had housed Jews of all nationalities from as far away as Norway and Greece, as well as Gypsies, political prisoners, criminals and, at one stage, a 'family camp' with a kindergarten that was eventually 'liquidated', with all the children being sent to the gas chambers.

There was even a Birkenau orchestra led by a Viennese violinist called Alma Rose. The orchestra was forced to play during executions and entertain the SS guards at camp concerts. Alma Rose was the daughter of the leader of the Vienna Philharmonic Orchestra and the niece of Gustav Mahler – and she was known to exact the same professional standards she'd been used to before the war.

In one memorable incident she told some SS women guards to be quiet when they were chatting in the middle of a piece and, with German respect for 'authority', they recognised her role as the orchestra leader and fell silent. Like most things at Birkenau, however, the orchestra ended in tragedy when Alma Rose was murdered. Many suspected another prisoner, who was jealous of her position.

I did not know about the kindergarten, or Alma Rose, but I did understand very quickly that there were many divisions within the camp, which could lead to solidarity or strife. The main one was whether or not you were Jewish.

Over time, non-Jewish prisoners accrued small concessions and benefits. They could receive food parcels, and in Auschwitz I camp, some could even avail themselves of a rudimentary swimming pool (really a water tank with a wooden plank diving board) and a brothel. Non-Jewish prisoners also had access to better medical care and better sanitation and could sometimes rise up the camp hierarchy into positions of authority over other prisoners.

Jewish prisoners received no concessions – the Nazi goal was extermination, by any means possible. For Jews the world was turned on its head, with all the normal experiences of life perverted. An ill non-Jewish prisoner might get a brief consultation with a doctor and some basic medicine; an ill Jewish prisoner receiving 'medical attention' might be injected in the heart with a lethal dose of poison. Pregnant women were either subjected to late-term abortions or had their babies killed at birth.

Of course, there were divisions between the Jewish prisoners, too. We were kept in fenced-off areas of the camp according to nationality, and some groups fared better than others. Polish Jews, who were already accustomed to very harsh conditions in the ghettoes, usually outlasted Dutch and French Jews, who had been living much more comfortable lives.

Survival also depended to some extent on what work you were assigned to, and there were many different 'occupations'. Birkenau had a team of *Sonderkommandos* – the prisoners who worked in the gas chambers, sorting last possessions, pulling out gold teeth and clearing away the bodies. This was a truly horrible task but these prisoners usually got extra food and better living conditions (although they were frequently gassed themselves after a few weeks). There were also German-speaking Jewish women employed in the Gestapo office.

Most of us were ordered to take part in different types of manual labour, whether that was working in the laundry, joining an external labour unit making German ammunitions or working in the warehouses, sorting out the endless piles of clothes and belongings taken from people arriving on the transports.

At first, Mutti and I were held in quarantine with the other women from our transport. We were consigned to one of the dark, dismal barracks and kept apart from the rest of the camp for three weeks. At night we slept in the middle shelf of one of many three-tier bunks that lined each wall, squashed together on a wooden board with eight other women. During the day we sat outside in a bare courtyard with the sun and rain beating down remorselessly on our shaved heads. A Kapo lived in her own area at one end of the barrack to guard us, and she cooked her own food there. We had one bucket to use for the toilet overnight, and it was full to the brim by morning. Each barrack housed hundreds of women.

Day broke on our first morning in Birkenau at about 4.00 a.m., and we were called outside for the morning roll call, which was known as 'appel'. This was one of the most hated parts of the day at Birkenau. Every morning and evening all the women lined up in front of their barracks and stood motionless, often for hours on end, while the Kapos and SS guards counted and re-counted the prisoners.

The slightest mistake could prolong the agony of standing there in our thin clothes – sometimes in suffocating heat, sometimes in a damp chill.

My first few days in Birkenau proved to be the ultimate test in survival. Both Mutti and I almost fainted standing in the first 'appel' for two hours. Neither of us had eaten for days on the train and we had missed our rations on the evening of our arrival. As soon as were back in the barrack I wolfed down some food – a four-inch-thick slice of black bread, not realising that this was my ration for the entire day.

After a few days I began to feel unwell and it seemed that I was paying the price for my foolish disregard of the warning about drinking the water. At first I was gripped by crippling stomach pains, and I had to run outside and relieve myself in the yard. This was strictly forbidden – we were only allowed to visit the toilet block, en masse, three times a day, regardless of how ill we were.

The Kapo who managed our barrack was determined to punish me. She narrowed her eyes. 'You little shit-bee! You people can't even control your own mess, no wonder you have diseases.'

Then she made me kneel outside in the courtyard holding a heavy wooden stool above my head, while the other women prisoners circled around and watched. Within moments my arms were aching, but I knew I couldn't let it drop. 'Come on, you can do it,' one of the women urged me. Then my arms would fall, and another stab of pain would grip my stomach. 'Don't give in, Eva,' someone else would whisper. Mutti stood right in front of me looking into my eyes, giving me strength through the agonising ordeal. Two whole hours passed with me holding the stool over my head before the Kapo decided I'd been punished enough. I don't know how I'd managed it for so long, but when finally it was over I fell to the ground in relief.

I'd hoped that my illness would soon work its way through my system, but instead my temperature climbed and I became weaker, and then delirious. The other women in the barrack started to grumble that I should go to the hospital block. They were sure that I had contracted typhus.

I begged Mutti not to make me go, and cried hysterically. The hospital block was a cruel joke: it had the appearance of a normal medical facility, yet we knew it was anything but. By the time we arrived at the camp the 'hospital' had spread over a compound of many barracks. It had an official air, with nurses and doctors wearing white coats and consulting patient notes. Their purpose, however, was to kill Jewish patients, not heal them. Often, terribly sick people lay moaning on their bunks, surrounded by their own filth, while SS camp doctors made 'rounds' looking at charts – but never at the patients themselves. Why would they bother? They didn't care how much their patients were suffering, and had no intention of helping them to recover.

'Please don't let them send me,' I begged Mutti, but eventually I became so ill she felt she had no choice but to request permission for a consultation. She was sure that without some intervention I would die.

I was so delirious that I was only vaguely aware of Mutti helping me across to the hospital. Once inside we took our seats on hard wooden chairs beside the entrance, and I drifted in and out of a dream world.

Eventually I was ushered back to see a hospital helper

Here are my maternal grandparents with my mother, pictured in 1909.

Here are my paternal grandparents with my father and his sister, pictured in 1909.

Our lovely house in Vienna which was my home until 1935.

My parents pictured in 1920. My mother was just fifteen when they met.

My favourite portrait of Pappy, taken in 1921.

Gino, my mother's dashing
Italian boyfriend.

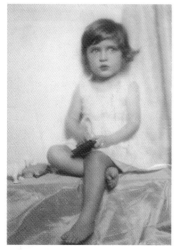

Me at two years old.

I love this photo of
myself and Heinz
with Mutti.

Here are all the staff at my father's shoe factory in Vienna, Geiringer & Brown. My
father is in the second row, the seventh person from the left, wearing a white shirt.

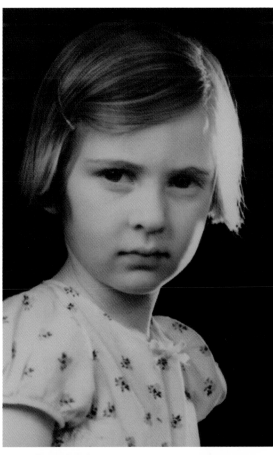

Looking very stubborn (typical of me), aged four years old.

Here I am with Martin Hahn, my first love. Martin and his parents escaped to Shanghai in 1939.

Heinz as a toddler.

Quite a formal portrait
of Heinz and I!

This was taken in Belgium,
with my friend Jacky, who was
the son of our landlady. We were
going to a fancy dress party.

This is the last photo of Heinz
ever taken, just before we went
into hiding. He loved reading,
writing and painting. The photo
of me on the front cover was
taken at the same time.

A couple of the paintings Heinz painted
while we were in hiding. It's hard to
believe he was just 16 at the time.

This was taken with the Leica camera that Otto later gave to me.

Anne was popular and had lots of friends – she was always smiling and laughing.

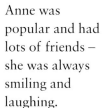

Anne's diaries were found by Miep Gies, one of the people who helped to hide the Frank family.

Anne and a friend playing outside the Merwedeplein, Amsterdam. We lived on the left side, the Franks lived on the right.

Here is Anne with her sister Margot, taken in 1933.

The railway line into Auschwitz-Birkenau.

We were sent to the camp in cattle trucks, and when we arrived the elderly, young and those too weak to work were separated from the rest of us.

Our heads were shaved on arrival, but Mutti persuaded
the guard to leave a little of my fringe.

I was put to work sorting through people's belongings in 'Canada' – an area of huge
warehouses filled with shoes, spectacles, and even false legs.

The Rosenbaums,
with whom we stayed for
a while after our return
from Auschwitz.

My cousins Tom
and his little brother
Jimmy. Tom was the
first person I shared
my experiences with.

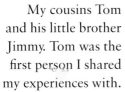

Otto Frank, Miep and Jan Gies and their baby Paul. This picture was the first
commissioned job I took with Otto's Leica camera.

who confirmed that I had typhus and gave me some pills. This in itself was little short of miraculous. We knew that Jewish people didn't receive medication. I don't know what made my case different. Perhaps it was just that Mutti was there, loudly pleading for someone to help me, and it was easier to get rid of her by giving me something.

No one knew if I would survive the night, but when I woke the next morning the fever was gone. I was weak, but I was going to make it.

My illness had consumed most of our period in quarantine, and soon it was time to join the main camp and be assigned to a work unit. As usual we lined up and looked ahead, not daring to meet the eyes of the SS soldiers who marched up and down inspecting us. I could feel that one was paying close attention to me and I heard him say, 'This one can go to Canada.'

I knew that 'Canada' was the most prized of all work units. It was so called because it was the 'land of plenty', a vast area behind the camp where enormous piles of prisoners' possessions were waiting to be sorted and classified. People working in Canada often managed to find extra food, or cigarettes and small items they could barter back in the barracks for more rations. Working there would mean a real improvement in our situation.

My eyes suddenly snapped to the SS guard. 'Can I take my mother, too?' I asked. Everyone was stunned; speaking to the SS was generally a very bad idea. But the SS man was so surprised that he took a step back, and then looked at Mutti, prodding her like a cow. 'Yes, why not,' he said, with a shrug.

Small improvements in the worst of conditions often led

to spurts of what seemed like happiness, and I marched off to Canada on our first day there, feeling cheerful. We were outdoors and away from the main camp and those thousands of emaciated faces that reminded us of the truth of our situation.

Canada itself seemed like a grim wonderland, full of surprising things. I approached one huge metal pile, glinting in the sunlight, and discovered to my amazement that it was composed of thousands of pairs of spectacles. Another warehouse was piled up to the ceiling with eiderdowns, while another housed nothing but false legs and arms. There were thousands and thousands of shoes, and suitcases and trunks of every shape and size. One area had children's suitcases, most of them with the name and date of birth of their owner carefully painted by their parents on the front. Another room held hundreds of empty prams, like a perpetual waiting room for a nursery that no babies ever returned from.

The purpose of Canada was to plunder every conceivable piece of Jewish property, and send it back to Germany, where it was then distributed to soldiers and their families, and ordinary people. German men were shaving with Jewish razors while good German mothers pushed Jewish prams, and grandparents put on Jewish glasses to read newspaper reports about the war effort. In July 1944 2,500 wrist watches were sent to the residents of Berlin, who'd lost their homes and property in the Allied air raids. A Polish former inmate called Wanda Szaynok remembered watching a transport of empty baby carriages, five abreast, making its way to Auschwitz station. There were so many prams it took an hour to go past.

In a crazed effort not to 'waste' anything, the Nazis even piled up the hair they had shaved off prisoners, and made it into carpets and socks. All clippings over 2cm in length were used to make wigs, and many proud Aryans of the Third Reich ended up walking around wearing the hair of dead Jews.

It was theft and plunder on a truly mammoth scale, and the amount of money that the Nazis made from stealing Jewish property of all kinds should not be underestimated as one of the reasons why they waged their vicious war against us.

In the crematoria a team of workers pulled out gold teeth from the victims. The teeth were then soaked in acid to remove tissue and muscle, and melted down into gold ingots for shipping to Germany. This gold was supposed to be reused by the SS dental service (one year's supply from 1942 would have been sufficient for the whole of the SS for the full five years of the war) but inevitably much of it made its way into the hands of camp guards and Swiss bank accounts, including the International Bank of Settlements in Basle.

The Nazis regarded 'stealing' by guards as a major problem. All officially plundered property was supposed to be accounted for in Berlin, but many soldiers in the camp engaged in full-scale corruption, and founded their own personal fortunes on stealing from Canada. At one stage, before our arrival, the Nazis had launched an investigation into corruption at the camp and had arrested many guards, as well as temporarily removing the founding commandant Rudolf Höss. (He was in fact promoted to overseeing all concentration camps from Berlin, but he loved Auschwitz so much he had returned by the time of our arrival.)

I was put to work on that first morning in Canada picking open clothes and coats, looking for hidden 'treasures' – and I was innocently amazed by what I found. People had hidden money and jewellery as well as food, watches, documents and any other items, like cutlery, that they thought might come in useful.

While the SS frequently worked themselves up into an orgy of greed, desperate to get their hands on everything and anything they could steal from their victims, my most common discovery brought home the devastating reality of what was really happening at Auschwitz. Sometimes the 'treasures' I found were nothing more than carefully trimmed and folded family photos – a tiny picture of a smiling baby, or an old photo of someone's parents, stitched into the seams of a jacket.

I stood and stared at one photo of a mother and father holding their little child and realised, with absolute horror, that this was the only thing that had mattered to the person who had hidden it – and that none of these people would ever see each other again. They were all dead.

Canada was nothing more than a gruesome graveyard of things – and behind the tall trees that separated this strange world from the rest of the camp were the Birkenau gas chambers and crematoria which were, at that moment, working beyond full capacity to murder more than 400,000 Hungarian Jews.

There was little to suggest that Mutti and I would not share the same fate, but one meeting while we were in Canada would play a hugely important role in our survival.

I developed an ugly sore on the back of my neck and, although I ignored it at first, it grew bigger and more painful. Finally Mutti told me I would have to go to the hospital and get treatment.

As before I was reluctant to go, but eventually I agreed and we put our names on the medical list and waited for our turn. When the day came, Mutti accompanied me to the hospital barrack where we stood in line hoping to get help.

Soon after our arrival a nurse appeared. I wasn't paying much attention, but I noticed that she was wearing white, and that she looked sturdy with a full head of dark hair. Then I heard Mutti scream, 'Minni!'

'Fritzi!' the nurse replied in astonishment. It was Minni, Mutti's cousin from Prague. We had spent many holidays together; she and my mother had grown up as close as sisters.

Minni was married to a well-known doctor, a skin specialist who had been treating the Nazis in Auschwitz for several months. Although they were both Jewish prisoners, Minni and her husband had managed to find a protected position – and Minni used her role as a nurse to look after as many people as she could.

Minni and my mother had an urgent, whispered conversation about how they had both ended up in Auschwitz, and Mutti managed to tell Minni about my father and Heinz.

'I will do my best to look after you,' Minni whispered to us. 'Come and find me if you need me.'

As it turned out, Minni really was our angel, for, during our time in the camp, she saved both our lives.

13
The Bleakest Winter

L ife in Auschwitz-Birkenau was full of horror and fear
and at first, only Mutti's support sustained me.

Imagine, if you can, the nights. We slept, packed literally
like sardines, with eight other women. When one person
turned over, we all turned. Bed bugs would drop onto us
from the bunk above, and you had to be alert enough to
pick them off or they would prick your skin and cause
infection. One morning I found that the bugs had fallen
and formed a thick crust around my mug. I was almost
sick when my fingers squished into them, causing a huge
spurt of blood. During another night I woke from a horrible
dream to find an enormous rat chewing my feet, and I
screamed with disgust and terror.

The ordeal I hated most was being the last person to
use the toilet bucket. It was always full, and the last person
would have to carry it twenty barracks away to empty it.
No matter how I planned it, invariably this job fell to me.

One thing kept me going and made the nights more
bearable – having Mutti by my side and sleeping in her
arms in our bunk.

Imagine, also, the hunger. Our official food rations
consisted of some watery lukewarm soup at breakfast, or
a few mouthfuls of a grainy coffee substitute, followed by
an evening meal of one slice of black bread. Our calorie

intake fell well below that of non-Jewish prisoners; the intention was to slowly starve us to death. As the food was shared you could sometimes miss out on your ration altogether, and the more substantial parts of the meal, like the vegetables in the soup, were usually kept for prisoners who had secured a favoured position with the Kapos. If you kept some of your ration to eat later, another starving inmate would usually steal it from you.

Again, Mutti came to our rescue. She quickly found the pile of food scraps discarded from the kitchens and she would wash and tear up a green carrot top, for example, and pretend it was some kind of vitamin-packed salad. People would barter for anything nutritious and we found a busy market in our barrack for potato peelings and vegetable tops. Mutti and I also established a brisk trade bartering handkerchiefs we found on the ground where the new arrivals had dropped them. Minni helped out as well, sending us bits of cheese and sometimes even sausage, from the hospital. These were small but important ways to stay alive.

Try to imagine the filth. On one memorable occasion a Kapo punished us for some misdemeanour by throwing the toilet bucket all over us, and my clothes and skin were coated in faeces for days until I was finally allowed to shower it off. A small mercy, I suppose, was that none of the women in Birkenau had their periods after the first week they arrived. We speculated that the Germans added bromide to the soup, which left us with a strange floating sensation.

Not having your period was a blessing in another sense. It seems hard to believe that the German SS guards would take a sexual interest in the starving, dirty, ragged women they were ruling over – but some of them did. These men had plenty of other distractions, and they were living a life of luxury compared to the other option – serving in action on the Eastern Front. The SS guards had a good canteen, a cinema and theatre, plenty of plundered food and drink and frequent day trips to take their minds off the nasty activities that might be troubling their conscience. In truth though, very few guards who were questioned after the war admitted to feeling troubled. Some had brought their families with them, and their children played innocently just outside the camp. Others enjoyed spa breaks at the Solaheutte retreat in the nearby mountains. There they entertained women SS guards, and were photographed laughing, having tea parties and relaxing in deck chairs on the veranda. A few even went to church.

I suppose they did not think of us as human beings. Perhaps they really did believe we were 'vermin' who needed to be eradicated. But I can't imagine a mindset, even one subjected to full Nazi conditioning, that allowed them to be so carefree in the midst of mass-murder. The wife of camp commandant Rudolf Höss cautioned her children always to wash the strawberries they grew in the garden of their villa; the fruit was covered in a grey soot from the crematoria next door. The stark contradiction of an innocent childhood pleasure like picking strawberries existing side by side with the Holocaust is one that still makes it impossible for me to understand the Nazi mind.

Suffice to say that the SS guards enjoyed the full pleasures of life at Auschwitz, and for some that also included sex – and even love. One woman prisoner wrote a fascinating account of how an SS guard fell in love with her, and believed that their time in Birkenau was one of true romance. He was astonished to discover, when the camp was liberated, that she wanted nothing to do with him. Thankfully I never had to contend with that, but I did have to be alert at all times in case one of the SS guards took it upon himself to rape me. If they were going to choose a woman prisoner, the women in Canada were usually in better condition and, as we were allowed to have showers, there was also more opportunity.

I'd been warned by the other women to always take care in the showers, which were outside and surrounded by a low wooden fence. I noticed that one young guard was starting to pay particular attention to me. I saw him watching me in the showers and I noticed him in other parts of the camp too – keeping an eye on where I was and what I was doing.

One day the Kapo ordered me to take a message to someone in the warehouse. When I turned I saw this guard behind me, walking quickly after me with his rifle. I sprinted into the warehouse and dived under the nearest pile of clothes, where I lay breathlessly for at least half an hour, feeling the sorters reducing the pile on top of me piece by piece, and praying the soldier would be gone by the time I was forced to emerge.

The threat was very real, but Mutti did her best to protect me, standing in front of me in the showers or lying in front of me in the bunk. There was little the women of Birkenau could really do for each other – but Mutti did everything she could to help me.

If Mutti was my constant companion, Pappy was my ray of hope.

For three weeks in June 1944 I was kept very busy working in Canada. The camp was buzzing with the kind of frenzied activity never witnessed in the full four years of its existence. In March of that year Germany had struck a deal with Hungary and taken control of the country: finally the Nazis could get their hands on the last, large Jewish population in Europe that had remained just out of reach. The arrival, and immediate gassing, of half a million Hungarian Jews, sent the Auschwitz-Birkenau killing machine into overdrive. Rudolf Höss returned from Berlin to personally oversee the operation. He immediately ordered the building of a railway spur right into the middle of the camp, and refurbished the crematoria so that they could operate at full capacity. He even gave the walls of the gas chambers a fresh coat of paint. Höss knew from his previous experience that the main logistical problem was not killing people but disposing of their bodies, so he arranged for several vast new pits to be dug behind the crematoria, where corpses could be burned in the open air.

The first transport of Hungarian Jews arrived on 15 May, just a few days before us. They were soon followed by trainload after trainload of people, the vast majority of whom were sent straight to their deaths. Of course, not all could be murdered immediately, even with the gas chambers working beyond maximum capacity – so large groups would be sent to sit in the trees and grass behind the gas chambers until it was their turn. It is harrowing to see photos of these people, sitting with their parents and playing with their children, almost as if they are on a picnic – still unaware of the fate that awaited them.

Many of these people brought a lot of belongings with

them, and the piles of their possessions grew bigger and bigger, extending out past the thirty warehouses until they covered much of the surrounding ground. Working in Canada had never been busier, and one lunch break I squatted down outside in the sunshine to have a rest and eat my rations. A group of male prisoners were walking past on the other side of the electrified wire fence, and I recognised one.

'Pappy!' I shouted, and ran over to him.

He looked thinner in his prison uniform and beret – but it was definitely my father.

'Evi!'

Pappy came to the fence, and we stood looking at each other, as close as possible. I could have reached out and touched him, but the electric fence made that too dangerous.

He asked where Mutti was and I told him she was working in Canada too. 'What about Heinz?' I asked him. He replied that Heinz was fine, working in the farm and getting fresh air and exercise.

'Listen, Eva,' he whispered. 'I'm working in the lumber office and I've got a responsible job. I think I can try and come here at the same time tomorrow – can you arrange for Mutti to be here, too?'

Mutti was of course thrilled and relieved to hear that Pappy and Heinz were well, and we both managed to be near the fence the next day. As promised, Pappy appeared, and I watched my parents exchange a few short words.

'Fritzi,' he said, 'what about your hair!'

My mother ran her hand over her bald head and smiled self-consciously.

'Don't worry, Erich, it will grow back.'

My father looked inconsolable, however, as if the sight of her had brought home the reality of our true situation. 'Oh Fritzi,' he said, 'what will become of us?'

Soon Pappy had to move on, but he promised to come again, and asked me if I could bring some cigarettes for him from Canada that he could barter for extra favours on his side of the fence. Sometimes the guards would see me throwing a pack over to him, but I never got into too much trouble.

Then one day, Pappy stopped coming. I continued to wait for him every lunchtime but he never reappeared. I was frantic with worry. I told myself that he had been transferred to another job, one that he couldn't leave so easily, but I couldn't push away the nightmarish thought that he had stopped coming because he was dead.

In any case, activity in Canada was winding down, which meant that Mutti and I would ourselves be moved to new positions. More Jews, the vast majority of them Hungarian, had been murdered in two shorts months at Birkenau than in the previous two years. An average of 3,300 people had been transported every day, rising to 4,300 on some days – and three quarters of those people were sent straight to the gas chambers. The flames from the crematoria had burned brightly, night after night and all night long, but now everyone was dead – and we had sorted out the belongings that they had been forced to leave behind.

We were transferred to other work units, first carrying heavy rocks from one side of the camp to the other and breaking them down into small pieces – and then to a barracks where I had to plait tough pieces of rubbery material into ropes used to throw hand grenades.

Working in the barracks proved to be the toughest, and bleakest, time in my life for one simple reason – I was there alone. In autumn, Mutti had been 'selected'.

I had noticed that my mother was getting thinner and that the heavy labour was taking its toll on her but I hadn't realised how precarious her situation was becoming.

One day we were called into the showers, which was always a frightening ordeal as we were terrified that we would be gassed. This time we washed as normal – but then the doors opened at the other end and Mengele was waiting for us outside. Wet and naked, we paraded in front of him in a cold inspection, while he decided each of our fates. He viewed us with narrow-eyed clinical precision – this one to live, this one 'selected'.

I started shaking with relief when I was quickly sorted into the group of survivors. But this time something was different – Mutti was not behind me. I turned around and could hardly believe my eyes to see that Mutti was being herded into the side of the 'selected' women.

I let out a terrible scream and Mutti immediately tried to come over and comfort me – but the Kapo beat her back with a leather belt.

'Try and tell Minni,' she whispered, as she was pushed out of the door – and as I saw her being shoved out, still naked, I believed it was the last time I would ever see my mother.

The months that followed were black, without hope. I did manage to tell Minni, taking a huge risk by evading the guards and the searchlights to make it to the hospital block in the middle of the night. She promised to do what she could, but she could not guarantee anything.

Without Mutti, believing that Pappy had probably also been killed, with no idea whether Heinz was alive or dead, I felt myself immediately spiral into a decline. In the barracks I was alone for the first time, crying myself to sleep. At daybreak I trudged across the barren ground to work, noticing the winter setting in with a sense of despair. What did life matter? What did it matter if a person was good or bad? What consolation could anyone find in 'God'?

In the work barracks I talked very little, occupied with my own depression and the endless plaiting of rope, plaiting and plaiting for fourteen hours at a time – tearing the hard material with my teeth and sore fingers, and praying that my work would not be weeded out as substandard. I knew that people who fell behind were quickly picked out and gassed. Soon my feet developed frostbite, and holes in the skin filled with an infected yellow pus that reduced me to a painful hobble. I was losing the will to live.

Then one day the Kapo called to me and told me to step outside. I ignored her, as any deviation from the routine was usually bad news. 'Go outside,' she shouted, 'there is someone to see you.' I shuffled out, hoping that this did not mean that I had caught the eye of another SS officer – but when I looked up, to my astonishment, I saw my father.

'Pappy!' I cried, and threw myself, sobbing into his arms.

He looked much thinner and older than the last time I saw him, but his arms held me tightly. 'Don't give up,' he urged me. 'We can make it, the war won't last long now. Just hold on.'

Then he asked, 'Where is Mutti?'

I wish that I had been able to restrain myself, but at that

moment I was bursting with the relief of being able to share my anguish.

'She was selected,' I told him. 'Oh, Pappy, she has been gassed.'

I felt his arms stiffen and he stepped back, looking at me with such horror and pain. I could see that he was trying not to cry, but his eyes betrayed his feelings.

He promised me that he would try and come again, and that he would also see if he could get the kitchen to give me some extra food. I nodded, weeping, desperate with relief and gratitude that he was alive, that Heinz was still alive, that I was not completely alone.

He wiped his eyes and kissed me goodbye. We couldn't even speak a word to one another.

Despite his anguish over the news of Mutti's fate, my father was as good as his word, as I discovered that night in the kitchen barracks. I don't know how my father was able to secure such favours; he was not under the protection of the SS, but he did have a good job in the lumber office – not to mention a great deal of personal charm.

'Oh, what a man your father is!' the Polish girl in the kitchen barracks clucked that night, laughing and rolling her eyes. Then she handed me a bowl of warm vegetables – an almost unimaginable luxury.

He always had a way with the ladies, even starving and in prison stripes.

My father did manage to make one more visit. He told me to keep going, that the Allies were advancing across Europe and he was certain that the war would soon be won.

I can still see his face as it was that day, earnest and

yearning, and full of love for me – and I bitterly regret that he could not have come to see me one more time so that I could tell him the news that I was about to receive: Mutti was alive. She was staying in the hospital block – Minni had saved her life.

14
Liberation

Mutti and I spent the final weeks of the war huddled together in her hospital bunk, hardly aware of the snow falling outside or the arrival of Christmas. We had lost any sense of time and we drifted in and out of half-starved daydreams about the future, talking endlessly about all the food we would eat when we were free. I longed for roast chicken while she told me how wonderful it would be to sink our teeth into pancakes filled with jam and cream.

Since I had last seen her at the 'selection' Mutti had come within moments of being killed several times. At first she was rounded up for the gas chambers and taken to the death barracks where women were locked up, waiting for their last day on earth. My mother told me there were terrible scenes inside those barracks; women prayed and cried, some lost their minds and clawed at the locked doors in madness. True to her word, however, Minni made a personal intervention to Josef Mengele, who indicated that he would see what he could do. Minni did not know if he would save my mother or not, but when the door to the barracks were opened and the women were led away, Mutti discovered that she was not on the list – she would live.

Then, just as she thought she was safe, Mutti was selected again to fill a last-minute quota. Another guard had put her back on the list to make up the numbers. As she approached the final administration desk where guards were ticking off prisoner numbers Mutti spoke up and said she believed her number was not actually supposed to be on the list. The guards checked, and were furious to discover that she was right. Finally, at the last second, Mutti was saved again.

As she looked on, the other women in her group were led away, screaming, towards the gas chambers – and then later the flames of the crematoria shot up into the sky, carrying their final remains. At one point, Mutti told me, she had resigned herself to death. Her only prayer was that Heinz and I should live, get married and have our own children one day.

In the meantime I had undergone my own torturous journey to be with her, narrowly avoiding being selected myself. Now we pinned all our hopes on living out the remainder of the war under Minni's watchful care.

When I found Mutti again she was reduced to a pile of rags, lying on one of the hospital bunks under a thin blanket. She was still a young woman, just about to turn forty, but she looked ancient and I could see that she was close to starving to death. Our enforced separation had brought about a crucial change in our relationship – I now understood that it was time for me to look after my mother.

By the winter of 1944 things were changing at Auschwitz-Birkenau. The war had turned decisively against the Germans. While British, US and Canadian forces were advancing across France and Belgium, the Soviets were moving in across the Eastern Front, coming closer to Auschwitz every day.

Reichsfuhrer Heinrich Himmler, who had overseen the extermination of the Jews on behalf of the SS, saw the writing on the wall and understood that those responsible would not be treated kindly when the nature of their crimes came to light. In October he had ordered the end of the liquidation of the Jews, and in November he decided that the gas chambers and crematoria at Auschwitz should be blown up. The intention was to hide all trace of what had happened there.

One night there was a massive explosion and a huge fireball burned in the darkness as some of the crematoria were destroyed.

Discipline and order were also breaking down, although this often replaced familiar dangers with new ones and did not make us feel any safer. At the same time that Himmler was ordering an end to the gas chambers, hundreds of Sonderkommandos (the prisoners who worked in the gas chambers) led an October uprising against the SS. They fought hand to hand with the Nazis, killing several guards and escaping to nearby villages. The Sonderkommandos had realised that they were key witnesses to the atrocities that had taken place, and that they were about to be moved out of the camp and murdered. Their uprising was ultimately doomed and they were all caught and executed, but the rebellion did lead to at least one gas chamber full of people being set free before they could be killed.

I wasn't aware of the Sonderkommado uprising but I did notice that we had more time to ourselves, as the guards seemed to have other things on their minds, and that the hated roll calls stopped altogether.

We were still subject to the random whims of the SS,

however, and being killed in an outright attack replaced the fear of organised gassing. We were well aware that we too were living witnesses – and that the SS were terrified of what the Soviets would do to them. They might be tempted to murder us all rather than leave any of us to tell the tale.

By the beginning of January these fears seemed very real. SS guards began tearing down the electric fences, guard towers and some of the barracks. Some of the documents and all their meticulously kept paperwork relating to the Final Solution were set on fire, and the corpses that were buried behind the gas chambers were dug up and burned in open pits.

The Soviet army was making strong headway. On 12 January they overwhelmed German defences at Baranow and headed towards Krakow. On 16 January, the Soviet planes swooped low out of the sky and bombed Birkenau's food depot.

The Soviet advance and air raids created near panic among the Germans. One morning several SS guards appeared in the doorway to the hospital and shouted, 'Everybody who can walk – outside!' Mutti was so weak she had hardly been able to climb out of the bunk for weeks but, at Minni's urging, we gathered together our blankets and hobbled to the doorway.

The camp beyond was eerie but breathtaking. The sky was blue and a heavy blanket of snow had fallen. We stood, teeth chattering and bodies frozen, for several hours. Nothing happened except the crack of gunfire in the distance from the advancing USSR forces. When an air-raid siren started wailing, the guards reappeared and started shouting at us to get back indoors. At dusk they returned and made us march out into the snow again, but another air-raid siren seemed to make them even more nervous, and we were allowed back into our bunks.

That day had a terrible effect on some of the women in the hospital. The sub-zero temperatures had fatally weakened them, and many died in the night. In the morning I saw Minni, sad and drawn, as she carried out their bodies. She came over to Mutti, laid a hand on her head, and said, 'Hold on.'

This new procedure of being marched out into the freezing cold continued for several days but I noticed that many of the women were staying in their bunks. Eventually I said to Mutti, 'Let's just stay here and hope that no one notices.'

It was a fateful decision. We slept through the night and I woke up on the morning of 19 January 1945 to the most curious sensation – total quiet. I opened my eyes and looked around the barrack, but it seemed almost empty, and there was none of the ordinary morning activity. I crept out of the bunk and stepped outside to explore further. There was no one to be seen. A few months ago Birkenau had been home to tens of thousands of prisoners but now there were no SS guards, no dogs, no soldiers in the watchtowers, no doctors in the hospital – and no Minni.

Overnight the Germans had turned off the telephone switchboard, left piles of documents burning and marched thousands of women from Birkenau (and men from Auschwitz I) out of the camp in long, bedraggled columns back towards the heart of the Third Reich. Unlike other work camps that were simply abandoned, Hitler had ordered that no man or woman at Auschwitz who was fit for work should be left behind. There appeared to be only a small band of prisoners in very frail health, like us, remaining.

We were only skin and bone but we immediately began to organise ourselves for survival until the Soviets found us. It was a truly liberating feeling to know that the Germans had gone – how I had wished for that day – but we knew that there were steep hurdles ahead. I worried that no one would find us after all, and that we would starve to death waiting. Worse, I was petrified that the Germans would return and retake the camp, condemning us to death when we were so close to freedom.

Before I could even consider such scenarios, I had to find the strength and willpower to carry out the day-to-day tasks necessary to keep us alive.

Some of these tasks were gruesome. On that first morning without the Germans, Olga, a Polish prisoner, told me that I would have to help her carry out the bodies of the people who had died in the night. I recoiled from the very thought – I had never touched a dead body, and although death was all around us at Birkenau, I had found a way to shield myself from its reality. But I was one of the few remaining women who was strong enough to complete the task, and I understood why she was asking me to do it.

Carrying out the stiff bodies of the women I had come to know so well was the worst thing I have ever had to do. I could feel as I held them that they had wasted away to nothing and I looked into their staring, open eyes and gaping mouths and knew that they had held on for so long – with so much hope – almost until the end. I saw more people die in those few days than in the rest of my time at Birkenau.

Other duties were less horrible, but still exhausting. On our first morning we found a storeroom full of food and we stuffed ourselves with the loaves of black bread lining the shelves. The next day I climbed through a hole in the electric fence and found barracks full of warm clothes, eiderdowns and more food than I could have imagined in my wildest dreams. There was cheese and jam, flour and potatoes. We sat down on the floor and just ate and ate, cramming our mouths with as much food as we could.

I took two eiderdown quilts and found myself some riding boots – my first proper shoes in years. I thought they looked wonderful and it was only later that I realised they were not even a pair. I found some clothes for Mutti, too, and she put on a dark blue woollen dress that was much too short for her, grey woollen stockings and lace-up ankle boots. With her shaved head she looked quite awful.

We each wrapped a quilt around ourself. We must have looked like two strange, bald, padded creatures as we wandered across the barren landscape looking for more food that had been left behind.

Collecting water was also a major problem. A few hours after the Germans had abandoned the camp on 19 January, Russian planes had bombed the IG Farben industrial complex that had used slave labour from Auschwitz and Monowitz to process chemicals, including Zyklon B. The bombing raid had cut off water and electricity supplies to the camp and surrounding area, leaving us with no lights or drinking water. At first we melted snow, but then I went with some of the stronger women to hack down into the ice covering the frozen pond at the entrance – then I had to stagger back to the barracks with heavy buckets.

It was wonderful to have survived the first few days, but there were still many problems. Living in the barrack made us feel vulnerable; the bunks were just as hard and cold as they had ever been, and there was a real possibility that the Germans would return.

On 25 January an unexpected detachment of SD troops (the SS intelligence organisation) did indeed return to the Auschwitz I camp, under express orders to kill all remaining prisoners. Just as they had pulled all their sick and frail victims out of their bunks and made them line up in the snow to be shot, another Soviet air raid swooped down. 'Return to barracks!' shouted one of the officers, and the soldiers vanished as suddenly as they'd arrived.

The next day the SS returned to Birkenau, arriving in armoured cars during the early hours of the morning. They set fire to Crematoria V and then drove off to blow up nearby bridges. Overhead, German and Russian planes engaged in dogfights in the sky.

When dawn broke the next morning we were already deep in discussion about what to do and where to go. The conversation went round and round for what felt like hours. Suddenly, the door to the barrack flung open and a woman shouted, 'There's a bear at the gate – a bear!'

This seemed unlikely, but in Birkenau anything was possible. Nervously, we made our way down to the entrance and peered at the peculiar sight. Indeed, there was a 'bear'. A large man covered in bearskins, staring back at us with the same startled expression. Perhaps I should have been more cautious, but all I felt at that moment was unrestrained joy. I ran into his arms and hugged him. It was 27 January 1945, and Soviet forces had arrived to liberate us.

Since the end of the war there has been much revisionist history about the role, and acts, of the Allied forces. Some of it challenges the idea that one side was 'evil', and the other 'good', and perhaps rightly so. Documents showed that the British and Americans were well aware of the extermination of the Jews in Auschwitz as far back as 1943 – and dismissed a petition to bomb the gas chambers in the summer of 1944. A British Foreign Office official wrote that bombing Auschwitz might lead to a 'flood of refugees' who would head towards Palestine, then still a British protectorate, and demand an independent homeland. Maybe the bombing of Auschwitz would have made little difference, most of its victims were already dead by then. Maybe even more people would have been killed in the attack – who knows. What is certain is that winning the war and maintaining a strong anti-immigration policy were more important priorities for the Allies than helping the Jews.

Much has also been written about the role of the Russian soldiers, and their campaign of rape against German women. I wish I could say that I can find it in my heart to feel sorry for those women but, given what happened to my family at the hands of the Nazi regime they supported, I cannot. You will have to understand that I cannot be objective about this subject – my own suffering and loss will always be too deep and too raw. Intellectually, however, I do believe that human rights apply to everyone, and that atrocities committed against anyone are wrong.

My experience of the Soviet soldiers was that they were

my liberators, and my friends. Those first soldiers were from the 60th Army of the 1st Ukrainian Front, under the command of General Pawel Kuroczkin. Over the next few days, small and then larger groups of soldiers set up base in the camp. They cooked hearty food for us, talked to us and let us warm ourselves around their fires.

Mutti still believed that it was safer for us to leave the barracks, and we set up a temporary home in an abandoned guardhouse with Olga and Yvette, a French woman. The guardhouse was small and cosy, and we slept in proper beds for the first time since our arrival at Auschwitz.

There we waited, tensely, for the war to be over or for some sign that the Germans were gone for good. We were still worryingly close to the front line and Soviet troops moved in and out as the fighting dictated. 231 were killed in fighting during the liberation of the camp and in battles with retreating Germans.

Tension, uncertainty and danger were palpable. One day, Mutti was out collecting water when she was accosted by SS soldiers who screeched to a halt in a lorry. I watched, horrified, from the window of the guardhouse as she was ordered to march off down the road with some other women from the camp. Yvette and Olga tried to comfort me as I became distraught: how could I lose Mutti now? It wasn't until late that night that she returned. Mutti explained that she had seen the Germans shooting the other women and understood that the only way to survive was to lie down in the snow and pretend to be dead. She duly wavered on unsteady legs, coughed and pretended to faint, only getting up several hours later. She made her way back down a road littered with bloody corpses.

These were precarious and desperate days. The fact that we were so close to freedom made death seem even crueller. It's hard to accept that many women died not at the hands of the Nazis, but from eating the good hot food provided by our liberators. After starving for so long their bodies simply could not cope with the sudden change in diet.

I found myself committing extraordinary acts to survive. One day we were out getting food when we came upon a dead horse from the Soviet army that had just been shot. 'Come on,' Olga whispered, ushering me over to its corpse that was lying, steaming, in the snow. She took a knife and began to cut into its belly, 'Look at this!' she urged. I peered over, not really wanting to see. Inside there was a semi-formed foal. I retched at the sight, and looked away, but Olga said 'That will be good for the stew!' Eating an unborn foal seemed appalling to me, and I shuddered, closing my eyes at the thought. But I was a starving person, too, and the urge to eat meat was strong and primeval. I didn't eat the foal, but that night I took my place around the fire and we ate the horsemeat.

As we regained our strength, day by day, we began to look ahead with tentative thoughts about the future. Mutti and I talked constantly about what had happened to Pappy and Heinz, and we desperately wanted to go to the men's camp at Auschwitz I to see if we could find them. Olga left us to go back to her home in Poland, but Yvette was still living in the guardhouse and she also wanted to go to the men's camp. Apart from looking for Pappy and Heinz, we knew that there was a larger contingent of Soviet troops there, and we hoped that it might offer us more safety.

I decided it was safer and easier to make the first trip

without Mutti. Yvette and I set off for Auschwitz I, a long and exhausting trudge in the snow. Eventually we saw the three-storey brick compound and lines of Soviet trucks on the roadside. As soon as we got to the entrance Yvette peeled off to talk to the soldiers, but I continued.

I walked beneath the metal sign, crafted by a prisoner on Nazi instructions, that famously lied *Arbeit Macht Frei* – 'Work makes you free'. I remember thinking that it looked like such a small and insubstantial representation for the most evil ideology the world had ever known.

I'd never been inside the camp at Auschwitz I and its built-up streets of bleak-looking buildings were very different to the much larger, open expanse of Birkenau. I was determined to find Pappy and Heinz, though, and I approached the first occupied barrack of men that I reached. They were delighted to see me, and they peppered me with questions about their own missing wives and daughters. I had no useful information to give them and they had little good news for me in return. I wandered on, asking any and every person I passed, entering every single barrack. Eventually I found someone who knew Pappy and Heinz. He told me that they had left days earlier, on the forced march led by the German troops. My heart sank – I had so hoped and believed that we would find them. Still, they were alive, they had somehow managed to evade being gassed. All four of us were alive, against the odds, and that gave me hope. I believed that they were strong, and that they could make it.

I did recognise one man. He was thin and gaunt with hollow eyes, wrapped in a blanket. He raised himself from the bunk as I approached.

I said, 'I think I know you. I'm Eva, the little girl who used to play with Anne in Merwedeplein.'

It was Otto Frank. He remembered me, and nodded. 'Do you know where Anne and Margot are?' he asked in a tone as desperate as my own had been when I was asking for Pappy and Heinz. I had to explain that I'd never seen anyone I knew from Amsterdam in the camp.

By then it was late afternoon and time to start the walk back to the guardhouse, but when I found Yvette she refused to come with me. Now that she had made it to the main camp and met up with the men again, there was no way that she wanted to walk all the way back to Birkenau. I begged her to come with me – it was a long way, and you could still hear the sound of fighting close by, but she said no.

Trying to summon some courage, I set off, my feet carrying me down the dark road as I imagined bullets whistling overhead. When I finally arrived, and Mutti anxiously opened the door, I collapsed in exhaustion and relief. We both agreed that it would be better to move to Auschwitz I, and the next day we gathered our belongings, while I told her about meeting Otto Frank again.

In fact, as we took our first steps forward into our new life, I didn't realise that I would see very few of the people I had known before – and that even those I did meet again would be tormented and changed beyond recognition by what we had all been through.

Mutti and I would soon be leaving Auschwitz, but most of my friends were not that lucky.

Susanne Lederman, the girl I'd admired so much, was transported from Westerbork to Auschwitz on 16 November 1943, and was gassed on arrival on 19 November.

Herman de Levie, the boy who gave me flowers and wanted to be my first boyfriend, was transported to Theresienstadt on 4 September 1944, and died on 15 December.

My best friend, Janny Koord, was transported to Auschwitz with her brother Rudi and their parents on 7 September 1943. Janny was gassed on arrival on 10 September, while her brother was sent to work in the coal mines where he died on 31 December.

Anne and Margot Frank were deported with their parents Edith and Otto on Sunday 3 September 1944 – on the very last transport to leave Westerbork for Auschwitz. In October 1944 Anne and Margot were sent to another camp, Bergen-Belsen, in Germany. Edith stayed behind in Birkenau and died ten days before liberation, in January 1945. In the appalling conditions at Bergen-Belsen both girls became very ill, and in March 1945 – shortly before liberation – they too perished.

More than one million Jews were murdered at Auschwitz-Birkenau, and there were only 6,000 of us still alive at the time of liberation. Even though the Germans had hastily sent as many plundered items as possible back to Berlin, and then burned down the warehouses at Canada, the Russian troops found more than one million items of clothing at the site, as well as 43,255 pairs of shoes and more than 15,000 pounds of women's hair. When hair samples, including those reused by German companies, were later tested they showed signs of prussic acid, one of the ingredients of Zyklon B gas.

Mutti and I had survived through luck, willpower and the protection of Minni. We had outlasted what I believe was the most evil ideology of ethnic cleansing, and killing, in history. The Nazis had chased our family across Europe, driven by a crazed obsession and a determination not to stop until every last Jew was dead. I was alive, but I would have to relearn how to live, and find my place in a world that often didn't want to know about the horrors that I had seen.

In January 1945, however, little of this entered my mind. I was overwhelmed with the joy of being alive, the relief of not being hungry and the pleasure of wearing warm clothes. My thoughts, such as they were, were focussed on returning home to Amsterdam – and being reunited with Pappy and Heinz.

15
The Road Back

'I wonder what Pappy and Heinz are doing right now?' I asked Mutti.

'Maybe they are having some stew, and talking about us,' she replied.

We liked to imagine them, somewhere out there – we didn't know where – thinking about us and our future.

In January 1945 we found ourselves in limbo: our imprisonment was over, but the war was not yet won. Top Nazi generals understood that devastating Allied bombing raids on supplies and infrastructure made defeat and surrender unavoidable, while war-weary German civilians trudged on in ever-worsening conditions. Capitulation seemed the only solution, but Hitler refused to countenance the idea. He swore never to surrender, and demanded that the fighting continue long into the spring of 1945, sacrificing the lives of hundreds of thousands of soldiers and reducing Europe to rubble.

Mutti and I were still living with danger and uncertainty. After we left the guardhouse at Birkenau, we found an empty room in one of the barracks in the men's camp at Auschwitz, and settled in. There was some normality in sleeping in real beds, even if they were bunk beds, and we could shut the door and have a little privacy and some time to ourselves. We ate the hot potato and cabbage soup served up by the soldiers, and even made new friendships with other prisoners. Even so we had no idea what the future would hold. We watched the activity in the camp, and the comings and goings of the Soviet soldiers, with great trepidation. Our lives were literally in their hands.

Three weeks into our stay, we lay awake for a whole night listening to the boom of artillery and crack of gunfire. Somewhere, close by, a major battle was underway.

'Do you think the Germans are advancing again?' I nervously asked Mutti.

'I don't know, Evi,' she replied, 'but I'm sure the Russians will look after us.'

The next morning, an agitated Ukrainian soldier appeared in the doorway to tell us that the Germans were fighting back, close to the camp, and that it would be safer to move all the camp survivors further behind Soviet lines. Nothing was more terrifying than the thought of being recaptured, and surely murdered, by the Nazis, so we gladly agreed to leave.

On a cold February morning we picked up our two eiderdowns and a small cloth bag Mutti had sewn to hold our possessions, and started walking towards the station. Soviet army trucks drove past, carrying other inmates of Auschwitz-Birkenau towards the railtracks. Behind us, one of the world's biggest crime scenes disappeared into the cold Polish fog.

Now we were beginning another journey – and I hoped that this one would eventually lead us home to our family.

At Auschwitz station we saw the train waiting for us with a long line of cattle trucks, just like the one we had arrived on. This time, however, the trucks were left open and there were frequent stops for food and the toilet. Mutti and I bedded down on the floor on our eiderdowns, and warmed ourselves around a small stove that had been lit in the middle of the cattle truck.

We didn't know our ultimate destination, but we found out that we were heading to Katowice where we would wait for the Soviets to decide what to do with us next. Although we were immensely grateful to the Russians for saving us from the Nazis, our lives were still governed by unknown forces and it seemed that we had little say over our destiny.

Today you could drive from Auschwitz to Katowice in a couple of hours, but our progress on a Russian freight train was painfully slow. Poland had been devastated by the fighting, losing a fifth of the country's roads and 10,000 miles of railway. Added to that, our train was frequently stopped in sidings while Russian troop trains rushed past on the way to the front.

The countryside we passed through seemed barren and empty; more than four years of German occupation had hollowed out whole communities. Three million Poles had been killed and there was an almost total absence of Polish Jews.

When we stopped in small stations to stretch our legs we saw the wreckage of bombed, burned out villages. Much of Europe looked this way. Whole cities had been reduced to piles of rubble, their populations were living beneath destroyed homes, often in holes in the ground. Time and time again we would stop in a broken-down village, only to find hunched shapes emerging from craters – old women wanting to sell eggs and potatoes in exchange for anything we had to offer. It looked like a land of old women and children.

As we rocked slowly across the Polish landscape I fell into an almost dream-like state of sleeping and eating, feeling nothing but the strengthening physical reality of being alive. Sometimes Mutti and I struck up conversations with other people around the fire, but more often than not everyone was lost in their own thoughts and memories. When we stopped and got down for a break beside the tracks we often had more animated conversations with the Soviet soldiers. Those soldiers that were Jewish would shake our hands enthusiastically, and we shared a deep kinship with them. Others, haunted by the war, would pull out photos of their families and ask if we had seen their loved ones anywhere. Regardless of religion, or background, they all appeared to be fervent supporters of Stalin, and their long suffering at the hands of the Nazis had left them with an overwhelming desire to seek vengeance on the German people.

We also talked to people from other carriages at these rest stops, and younger men and women began to pair up along the way. Often, I drifted back into sleep listening to people having sex in the dark.

Three weeks after we left Auschwitz, on 5 March we arrived at our first destination.

Departing Nazi troops had crushed thousands of years of culture and heritage into the dust, razing cities like Warsaw to the ground, but we discovered that despite an air of depressing neglect Katowice was relatively intact. By now the first hint of spring was in the air; it was still cold but the trees were coming into bud. We were allocated to billets on the edge of the town, with straw mattresses to sleep on, and I had my first bath in more than two years.

'Mutti, it feels wonderful!' I called out, feeling myself slip into the warm water. 'I feel like a person again!'

By now I was even well enough to turn my nose up at some of the coarse yellow maize bread the Soviets handed out. 'Eat it!' Mutti ordered, but I wrinkled my nose. 'No, I don't like it!'

During the day we wandered through Katowice, enjoying walking the city streets and looking in shop windows, even if they were largely empty of any goods. As the days passed we waited anxiously to find out what would happen to us next. We'd heard that the Germans were fighting back strongly in Poland, and there was talk that they might even be able to recapture Katowice. Rumour was that the Soviets might move us on, to an unknown destination.

By 31 March we were heading east. At the first rest stop I climbed down from the train to stretch my legs, and saw a familiar but forlorn figure down the tracks, standing alone. It was Otto Frank. Mutti and I had met a mutual friend, Rootje De Winter on the train, and she told us that Otto was on the same transport as us. She also told us that Edith Frank had died in Auschwitz, and that Rootje had had to break the devastating news to Otto. 'That's awful,' Mutti said. 'That poor man – I'd like to talk to him and tell him how sorry we are.'

Now she had her opportunity. I helped her down from the wagon and slowly we walked over to Otto. I reintroduced them. 'Mr Frank, this is my mother.'

Mutti said, 'Yes, I came to your flat once to ask if Anne

would like to join Eva in the private school lessons. I'm so sorry to hear your terrible news.'

Otto nodded but seemed too weary and sad to hold a conversation. With that, we climbed back on board and travelled on.

We were now crossing hilly countryside dotted with small wooden houses. In villages where the fighting had been intense, people were making do with homes made from straw, but in other places we even saw pigs and chickens, which we clung onto as symbols of life amidst the desolation.

I'd hoped that our dramas were over, but there was more in store. On the third day of our journey we stopped outside the town of Lemberg (now called Lviv) and Mutti climbed down to relieve herself. After a few minutes the train started to move off again, but Mutti was still crouching down beside the track.

'Mutti, Mutti!' I shouted, holding out my hand to her as she ran down the track. She was still weak, and she couldn't grasp my hand to let me pull her on board. Other people in our car held out their hands too, but she just couldn't reach. 'Stop!' I shouted as we pulled off. 'Wait for my mother!'

The soldiers were oblivious to the fact that Mutti was now standing by the side of the track, helplessly, watching us disappear.

'She will find us, it will be all right.' The others tried to console me.

'How can she find us when even we don't know where we're going?' I replied, in despair that once again we had been separated. I could only hope that somehow she would find her way back to me.

We rode on for another three days until we arrived in the Ukrainian city of Czernowitz where we were billeted in a deserted building that had once been a school. I was sick with anxiety; I could barely believe that I had lost Mutti again. She was all alone and there was nothing I could do to help her. I simply had to wait, and try not to give up hope.

One night the lights in the hall were snapped on and soldiers woke us from bleary-eyed sleep by clanking past with enormous buckets of potatoes. 'More coming! More coming!' they explained. There were more soldiers arriving on their way to fight at the front, and they needed to be fed. I was tired, but of course I got up, ready to help.

Then I heard that many of the women from the camp were refusing. 'Why should we peel potatoes?' they complained. 'We've already done so much hard labour. We are victims.'

At that moment I decided that I would not be a victim, no matter what had happened to me. I would never let myself have that mentality – it was almost like accepting the role of utter helplessness that the Nazis had wanted to instill in us. I wasn't helpless. I was a survivor.

That night I peeled more potatoes than I ever would again in the rest of my life, all fuelled by the vodka liberally handed out by the soldiers, who also entertained us with bouts of wild Russian dancing.

I collapsed into an exhausted tipsy slumber, only to dream of potatoes. 'Leave me alone!' I moaned, when I felt someone poking me awake what seemed like only moments later. Then I felt hands shaking me. 'No. Let me sleep!' I pulled my eiderdown tighter around my shoulders and rolled over. The hands shook harder. 'What?' I finally gave in, exasperated, and opened my eyes. It was Mutti.

Since she'd missed the train outside Lemberg, Mutti had been on quite a journey of her own, crossing lands that were formerly part of Austria, and staying with a returning Jewish family in Kolomea. A group of Soviet soldiers had managed, using some complicated sign language, to communicate to her that they thought the Auschwitz train was heading for Czernowitz, and took her part of the way. She had finally caught a ride on a train with some British prisoners of war who had agreed to carry her first letter in three years back to Grandpa Rudolf and Grandma Helen.

'Evi!' Mutti said, with tears of relief in her eyes. She was delighted to see me, but instead of welcoming her with open arms I was overwhelmed with intense anger.

'Where have you been?' I shouted. 'How could you miss the train! I've been so worried about you . . .' On and on I went, raving like a mad woman, until finally I ran out of breath.

Mutti was so patient with me. She only hugged me, and explained what had happened. 'Even when I knew that you were in Czernowitz I was terrified I wouldn't know where I was because I couldn't read any of the railway signs!' Thankfully the sign at Czernowtiz station had been in German, not Russian, or we might never have found each other.

Then I hugged her back, feeling how thin she still was. I clasped her in my arms.

'Evi,' she said, 'I promise that we won't ever be apart again.'

Czernowitz held one other memorable delight for me – a cinema. The usher let us in only grudgingly. We still looked shocking, even by the standards of war-ravaged people who surrounded us. Inside, the grainy yellow light of the projector trapped particles of dust between the dark auditorium and the screen, holding time static. In front of us the Emperor Franz Josef talked and danced, and went about the old business of Empire as if the world would never change. The gardens of Schönbrunn Palace dazzled with all the magnificence that I remembered from my childhood. The characters spoke in a rich, unpolluted German that struck the deepest chord in my memory; it was my mother tongue and my own language long before the Nazis tainted it for me.

Then the lights came up and we were sitting in a row of lumpy velvet seats that made my legs itch beneath my ill-fitting second-hand clothes. I rubbed my corn-stubble hair, aware that it marked me as a concentration camp survivor just as much as the yellow star had told people I was Jewish. Mutti and other women from Auschwitz sat beside me, and as I listened to the music of Johann Strauss play out over the credits, I wondered – how did we ever get from there to here?

Still asking everyone we met for news of what had happened to Pappy and Heinz, and thinking and talking about them constantly, Mutti and I prepared to set off on yet another stage of our journey. This time we were heading across the devastated lands of eastern Ukraine and down to the Black Sea port of Odessa.

Ukraine had suffered brutally in the war, with the same tracts of land often being fought over several times, and towns burned down by both the Soviet and German armies in retreat. This flat farmland had been the bread basket of the Soviet Union, with Ukrainian farms producing legendary grain and vegetables and sausages. Now we saw nothing but the detritus of war, burned-out tanks and military vehicles, roads turned into useless rutted tracks, shell craters and trenches. The Soviet Union lost twenty-seven million people in World War Two, and seven million of them were from Ukraine – nearly one in five of the population.

This desolate situation only eased slightly when we pulled into the station at Odessa and felt the warmth of a tropical sun on our backs. In Odessa the climate was warm, and the city nestled beneath dense green hills that ran down into the clear waters of the Black Sea. Although war had taken its toll on basic infrastructure and there was no running water, the colourful blooming foliage and liveliness of the people brought us back to life. I discovered that Odessa was a city of man-made beauty, too. We were staying at an abandoned summer palace that had belonged to the Tsars, and I marvelled at the beautiful murals painted on the ceiling, and the delicate parquet floors.

I marvelled even more at the toothpaste and toothbrush given to me by one of the Australian soldiers who were camped out with us in the grounds of the palace, waiting to return home. Imagine – I hadn't brushed my teeth since before we arrived in Auschwitz and the feeling was exquisite.

For six weeks I swam in the waters of the Black Sea in a makeshift bathing suit, lay on the beach, greedily soaking up the sun and explored the city of Odessa by tram with

Mutti. On 11 May it was my sixteenth birthday and we had a small celebration. One of the other girls in our group gave me a lovely handmade necklace of seashells.

Red Cross parcels regularly arrived for the prisoners of war – but, as Jews, we never received anything from the Red Cross. The Australian soldiers were friendly and generous though, and gave us chocolate and treats. My mother struck up quite a friendship with a soldier called Bill who wanted to whisk her back to his station in the outback. She assured him that she was happily married and waiting to be reunited with her husband, but he said, in words that chilled an otherwise sunny day, 'Remember Fritzi, you may be a widow.'

That was a possibility that neither of us was prepared to think about.

On 7 May 1945 we heard the news everyone had been waiting for – the Germans had unconditionally surrendered. Hitler had committed suicide a week earlier. The war was over, and the grounds of the palace broke out in unrestrained jubilation, dancing, singing, laughing and drunken declarations of love. That day we all celebrated together: soldiers, prisoners of war, Soviets and refugees. Then, a few days later, we woke and found that once again we were alone – the Australians had left in the night. Friendships in war could be deep, but were usually transient.

Mutti and I were also preoccupied with the future. With the war over we could finally hope to return to Amsterdam, but even this final stage of our journey was complicated. When Mutti went to register to return to Holland, a Jewish Dutchman said, 'But you are not Dutch, you are Austrian.

We have enough Jews of our own without taking you back to Holland.' As we were to discover, the end of the war was not an end to prejudice – far from it.

Mutti insisted that we did not want to go back to Austria. Finally we were added to the passenger list for a New Zealand troop ship called the *HMS Monowai* that was docked in Odessa and would take us as far as Marseille.

On 20 May we boarded the ship before a line-up of naval officers dressed in their white uniforms and entered into what seemed another world. There were crisp bed sheets, linen tablecloths, bone china teacups and all the food we could eat. The sight of the neatly laid out dining room reduced Mutti to floods of tears. On the second day aboard, the Captain announced over the tannoy that people did not need to hoard food in their cabins – there was plenty, and anyone could eat whenever they wanted. After all we had endured, it was overwhelming to be treated as decent human beings again.

We sailed though the Bosphorus strait, past Istanbul and into the Mediterranean – a raggedy group of concentration camp survivors, still looking haggard in our tattered outfits. The women stayed in cabins on the top decks, but occasionally we saw the men, who were sleeping in hammocks below. Once or twice I saw Otto Frank but he looked withdrawn, his thoughts obviously far away.

After a week we arrived in France, to great fanfare and celebration. As we got off the ship I waved to the cheering people on the quayside, but when we were followed down the gangplank by a group of German prisoners who were also being sent home, the French turned their backs and fell silent.

Much to my annoyance, Mutti stayed behind to help with the registration process, but once again I stuffed myself at the welcome banquet. When she eventually turned up I was a little drunk and shouted at her, 'Where have you been, you busybody? You've missed all the food!'

The next day we boarded a train that carried us up through France, and I noticed that many of the towns we passed through had an effigy of Hitler hanging from a gallows. When we stopped at a station the faces of ordinary people would appear, pushing bread and wine through the window – which I thought was wonderful until I realised that this was for the benefit of the returning French soldiers, not for us.

Europe was a continent in chaos, with the biggest movement of displaced people the world had ever seen. As many as twenty million people were on the move, trying to make their way home. The result was confusion, and often a complete breakdown in law and order. It seems like an astonishing number until you remember that it included millions of forced labourers, as well as huge numbers of people fleeing the devastation of the Eastern Front, ethnic Germans on the run from the advancing Soviet army in Poland and the Czech Republic and Hungary – and up to four million Germans who were displaced refugees in their own country. And that doesn't even take into account the Allied forces and the huge numbers of surrendered German soldiers.

We managed to travel as far as southern Holland and then waited for the Allies to build pontoon bridges over the rivers so that we could drive the final miles by road. Through the bus window I could see the flat tulip fields that I had once loved, as well as the windmills and the farms of the country I'd come to think of as home.

Finally we entered the outskirts of Amsterdam, and pulled to a stop outside the vast nineteenth-century monolith of Central Station. I climbed down the steps of the bus and stood on free Dutch soil for the first time in years, tingling with excitement but also lost in the enormity of the moment. We were home, whatever that meant, but there was no friend to welcome us, no smiling faces or brass bands as there had been in France. Most importantly, there was no Pappy or Heinz.

A group of city officials were sitting at trestle tables waiting to take down our details, but they had no interest in where we had been, where we should go now or what our future would hold. Every moment of our lives had been watched over and controlled from the moment we had been captured by the Nazis, but now there didn't seem to be a soul alive to direct our fate.

I was truly liberated, and terrified.

'The rest of my life starts now,' I thought, 'but I have no idea what to do with it.'

'Where should we go?' I asked Mutti.

The city looked drab and depressed, even at the height of summer, and people hurried past with their heads down.

Mutti shrugged, frowning. 'Let's try the Rosenbaums,' she said, remembering our good friends from before the war.

We picked up our one small bag and made our way slowly through town. The buildings and canals all looked the same but something essential in Amsterdam's character was different.

Life had been hard for the Dutch in the latter years of the war, and most people had no interest in hearing about the problems of the few returning Jewish refugees. At that stage the horrors of the concentration camps, and the Holocaust, weren't widely known. Some people's attitude could be summed up as, 'We took you in and looked after you in the 1930s, what are you doing back here now? What more do you want from us?'

In 1944 the Nazis had announced that Dutch men between the ages of sixteen and forty would be deported to Germany for forced labour. This caused massive resentment, and a surge in the number of ordinary people who supported the Resistance. In total a third of all Dutchmen, nearly 500,000 people, ended up working in Germany either as forced or voluntary labour.

Then in the winter of 1944, Amsterdam fell into the grip of 'The Hunger Winter'.

The southern Netherlands had been liberated by the Allies in the autumn of 1944, but Amsterdam and the rest of the country remained under German control. In September 1944 the Dutch government-in-exile, based in London, called for a railway strike to bring German troop transport to a standstill and facilitate Allied airborne landings near Arnhem. More than 30,000 railway workers took part in the strike but the Germans continued to run their own troop trains and the Allied landings were a failure. The real consequence of the strike was that the Germans decided to punish the Dutch by cutting off food supplies. The ban only lasted for six weeks but even when it was lifted, food supplies couldn't return to normal as the railway network remained crippled. The transport of coal from the liberated south of the country also stopped, and gas and electricity were shut off. By winter the situation had become desperate: people chopped down trees on the street for firewood, and went on 'hunger expeditions' into the countryside where all they could find to eat were flower bulbs. More than 20,000 people died of starvation.

Travelling through Amsterdam on that first morning back we could see a pinched, hard look on the faces we passed, so when Mutti and I reached the Rosenbaums' house we knocked on the front door with some hesitation. We wondered if they would still be there, and whether they would be pleased to see us.

Luckily, we needn't have worried. Martin Rosenbaum opened the door and exclaimed, with a beaming smile, 'Fritzi Geiringer!'

There was another reason why Martin looked so happy that day. In all of the misery of the war the Rosenbaums had produced some wonderful news. After years of failing to conceive, Martin's wife Rosi had just given birth to their first baby – a little boy called Jan who was only three days old. Before the war the Rosenbaums had been heavy smokers, so perhaps the years of austerity had done some good. Rosi was still in the hospital but we happily agreed to stay for a while to help with the baby when she came out.

Mutti discovered that, unlike many returning Jews, we would be able to move back into our old flat at 46 Merwedeplein. Thanks to Pappy's foresight it was still registered in the name of the Christian woman who owned it, as was our furniture. At first, though, we were too scared and intimidated by all our experiences to go back there alone, and we were very grateful to the Rosenbaums for their kind offer of somewhere to live. (In fact, I adored their gorgeous baby boy, who grew up to be a lovely man and is a very good friend today.)

Mutti could see immediately that even the Rosenbaums had little food or fuel, and she wondered if any of our hidden supplies had survived. After we'd settled in we went in search of the Reitsmas, the family who had been sheltering us when we were captured. Like the Rosenbaums they were still living in Amsterdam, and they were delighted to see us. Mrs Reitsma had been asked to design postage stamps to commemorate the liberation, and their son Floris was enrolled at the University of Amsterdam. They told us that there was nothing left from our food store – they had eaten it themselves to survive the war.

Not that it tasted very good. 'Even the chocolate tasted of mothballs,' Mrs Reitsma told Mutti, 'but we didn't mind.'

'I'm just happy that someone could make good use of it,' Mutti replied.

16

Amsterdam Again

A few days after we arrived back in Amsterdam I answered a knock at the Rosenbaums' front door and found Otto Frank standing on the doorstep. He looked calm, but just as thin as when I'd last seen him on board the ship from Odessa. I let him in and ushered him through to where Mutti was sitting. She smiled, but he clearly didn't recognise her.

'We've met before, haven't we?' she asked, 'We met on the train.'

He frowned for a moment, as if he were trying to dredge up something from the depths of his memory. Then he shook his head.

'I'm sorry, I don't remember,' he said. 'I got your name from the list of survivors. I'm trying to find out what has happened to Margot and Anne.'

Otto sat down with Mutti and they talked for a long time, trying to build up each other's confidence that we would all be reunited with our families.

After a few weeks we realised that it was time to go home, even without Pappy and Heinz, and Mutti collected the keys to our apartment. As I walked into the square at Merwedeplein and climbed the steps to the flat, I was struck by the feeling of stepping back in time.

Mutti put her key in the lock and opened the door: before us the living room sat silently, full of all our furniture, but lifeless. The chairs were turned in the same position, as if we had just got up, and the same curtains hung at the windows, waiting for someone to come home and draw them shut.

I reached out and touched the mark on the bedroom wall where Pappy had pencilled my height. Outside there were the same noises of children playing.

That night I heard a car pull up outside and the doors slam, and I was sure that it was Pappy and Heinz coming home to us. But the voices trailed off into the darkness, and I was left with a strange dizzy feeling that everything had been turned upside down.

Eventually I fell asleep, longing to see my father and brother again, and for the first time since leaving Auschwitz I dreamed about the horrors of the camps. In my dream a bottomless black hole appeared in front of me and grew and grew until it swallowed up the whole world – and I woke Mutti with my feverish screaming.

In the weeks that followed, life took on some of the shape of a normal existence, although fundamentally everything had changed.

Mutti and I did everything we could think of to try and find out what had happened to Pappy and Heinz, but the situation was chaotic. Everyone was looking for their families. Mutti even put a notice in the newspaper asking for more information about them, but we heard nothing.

As the head of our household, Mutti also had to pay for our upkeep and the rent for the flat at Merwedeplein. During the first few months after our return she taught herself how to use some of the leather left over from my father's business to make belts. I would often come back to find a flat full of cut out parts ready to be sewn together. In the beginning orders were good, and Mutti even thought about exporting, but eventually it became harder to sell enough to make a living and she started to look elsewhere. My mother had already demonstrated that she was amazingly adaptable and resilient, and she did so again. She agreed with Martin Rosenbaum to begin work as a secretary at his tie factory.

Just as she'd once had to learn to cook, mend and make belts, she now had to learn typing – and it proved to be an equally difficult skill to master.

'Oh Evi,' she'd sigh, as she walked in the door in the evening. 'How will I ever get the hang of this?'

Her bag would be full of bundles of paper, covered in hundreds of typing errors.

'I can't let them know how bad I am,' she'd tell me, vowing to practise and improve.

I now suspect her co-workers may have had some idea of her initially rather low level of productivity.

I also took up a new money-making activity, painting flower designs on small wooden brooches. At one stage I even had an order to make 600.

To supplement Mutti's wages we took in two women lodgers who were also Jewish refugees. One was Truda Heinemann, a member of the publishing dynasty.

Living in our flat with two unknown women felt odd but then again, I had no interest in resuming normal life. Even so, Mutti was determined not to let me sit around and mope. When we were still living at the Rosenbaums she wrote to the headmaster of the Amsterdam Lyceum and explained my circumstances. Although I had missed a large chunk of my education, Mutti asked that I be allowed to return and finish school – it was imperative to my future. The headmaster, Dr Gunning, agreed. Mutti told me that I would begin classes again at the end of August.

At the same time as we were trying to pick up the thread of day-to-day life we were also involved in ever more frantic efforts to find out what had happened to Pappy and Heinz. More and more people were returning from various parts of Europe, and there were notices plastered all over the city asking for information about missing loved ones. Mutti anxiously scanned the lists from the Red Cross, but there was no mention of them.

Otto Frank visited us often over that first summer. On 25 July he found out that both Margot and Anne had perished. He found two sisters who had been with them in the camp who confirmed the worst: they had died in Bergen-Belsen of typhus. He was utterly devastated by the news – at that moment it felt like the end of his life, too.

We all cried bitterly, and after Otto had left that evening I curled up on Mutti's lap and we held each other for a long time.

'At least we have each other, Evi,' Mutti said, stroking my arm, 'That poor man has no one.'

Otto continued to visit us, for mutual support. It was during one of those afternoons in our apartment that I first heard about Anne's diary. Otto arrived carrying a small bundle, wrapped up in brown paper and string. He was almost shaking with emotion as he told us that Miep Gies, one of the people who helped to hide the Frank family, had found the diary in the attic after they were arrested, and kept it waiting for Anne to return. When it was confirmed that Margot and Anne had died she gave the diary to Otto. He'd started reading it straight away, but could only read a few pages at a time.

Then, with great feeling, Otto unwrapped the parcel and began to read some extracts to us. He read slowly, but he was trembling, and couldn't get far without breaking down in tears. He was astonished by the daughter he discovered in the pages, an Anne he did not recognise, with deep thoughts about the world.

Mutti and I were equally surprised. In that moment, none of us could have imagined in our wildest dreams that the diary would be published – let alone that it would become an historic piece of literature that would change the world.

On 8 August 1945 we too received the dreaded letter from the Red Cross. All across Europe these letters were falling through people's letterboxes, delivering their few, cold and official lines to be read with a mixture of horror and dread that turned into disbelief and overwhelming grief.

I remember almost nothing about the day the letter came. It is still so painful I have always blocked it out, and it remains virtually blank.

Our letter confirmed in stark, almost clinical language, that both Pappy and Heinz were dead. They had left Auschwitz on the forced death march and arrived at Mauthausen concentration camp in Austria on 25 January 1945.

Pappy had been assigned to a work unit, but died at 6.20 on the morning of 7 March. The letter said that Heinz had died of exhaustion sometime between April and 10 May 1945.

Mutti sat at the kitchen table for hours afterwards, just holding that letter. I remember that I walked around and around the flat in a daze, not believing.

Over the years we received more letters from the Red Cross, listing conflicting information and even different dates of birth for Heinz. Mutti pursued the Red Cross until the 1950s, trying to find out the truth, but we never got a clear answer, nor met anyone who had been in Mauthausen who could tell us. I have to accept now that we will never know what really happened to them.

It is such a familiar thing; the sound of the metal letterbox opening, the grate of the paper being pushed through, the soft thump of the envelope hitting the mat. Then the feel of a single sheet of crisp white paper in your hand, the official stamp at the top, and the plain few paragraphs setting out your fate. Even today it is impossible for me to describe the feeling that runs through your body like a flush of sudden cold poison, when you realise that the most ordinary occurrence, receiving a letter, means the end of your world.

Just before Christmas 1945 Mutti wrote to her mother, releasing her feelings in a way that she never did with me, and already drawing some solace from her friendship with Otto Frank.

Herr Frank says that when we are sad it is very egotistical. We feel sorry for ourselves because we are missing something so vital to us, but we can't help those that are missing because they can't feel pain any more . . .

I can't agree with him about that because my biggest

pain is that their lives are so senseless, interrupted and unfinished . . .

With 'Heinzerl' I always think that perhaps he would have become blind because our biggest worry was always his eyes – but he has been spared this experience. So we must not complain. It's a fact that we don't know what sadness life brings . . .

. . . If I spoil Evi it is less that I want her to forget what she's suffered, but more that I don't want her to feel what she's missing. I don't want her to think, 'Pappy would have allowed me to do this.' Or, 'I could have discussed that with Heinz.'

I would like to replace those two dear ones to her and that's why I want to earn enough money so that she can learn and do as much as she wants to – as if her father were still alive . . .

I hope it won't spoil her sweet character, and I hope that I don't do things wrong . . .

There was one particular thing we could do together – and it would bring us closer to Pappy and Heinz. I remembered that, on the train to Auschwitz, Heinz had told me that he had hidden his paintings beneath the floorboards of his former hiding place. I persuaded Mutti to come with me to Gerada Katee-Walda's house to find out if they were still there.

It felt so strange to make the journey from Amsterdam, knowing that it was the same route we had taken to see Pappy and Heinz only a year and half earlier. I almost had to pinch myself to believe that they wouldn't be there at the other end, waiting for us.

Mutti and I were both nervous about seeing Gerada Katee-Walda again, but when we knocked on the front door we discovered that she was gone, and a young couple was living in the house. When I explained our situation they looked wary and the man held out his hand to stop us, saying, 'Look, we really don't want to get involved.'

'Oh, please let us in,' I said. 'Just let us look . . .'

But the man was adamant, and Mutti started to pull my sleeve and lead me away.

After we'd walked a few steps she turned back and blurted out, 'I know it sounds suspicious, but the paintings are all we have left of my son and it means a lot to my daughter to be able to look for them.'

I could see that the woman in particular had been affected by Mutti's words, and reluctantly the man moved aside and let us into the house.

We walked up the stairs and into the room where Pappy and Heinz had hidden. I sat down on the floor underneath the attic window and ran my fingers over the wooden board that Heinz had told me about. I imagined him touching the same board, and I thought, 'Oh Heinz, why can't you be here now to get your paintings back?'

I'm not sure that I was expecting to find anything, but when we lifted the boards up and peered underneath we could see some flat canvases. I put my hand down and felt one painting, then another, and then another. Mutti lifted them out with shaking hands and we saw all of Heinz's wonderful imagination and talent before our eyes.

'Look at the sailing boat,' Mutti said. It was sailing across a sunny bay as though the person who had painted it had no cares in the world.

We found twenty of Heinz's paintings and ten of Pappy's, still intact.

One painting in particular made my eyes fill with tears, and I had to steady myself. Heinz had painted himself studying at a desk; the calendar on the wall was marked the 11th, my birthday. It made my heart ache to realise that he had been thinking of me, just as I was thinking of him. I desperately longed to see him and hear his excited stories and laughter, just one more time.

17
A New Life

Despite her best intentions, I was so anguished and upset that I did blame Mutti for bringing me up the wrong way – and I often lashed out at her.

5 January 1946

Fleur is gone. Why did she have to do that? Does she not know that I can't do without her.

As long as I have been reading, it was not too bad. But I can't read any more. This is not the right book for me. I wonder if Fleur knew that? I would always read the book first before I gave it to my child.

I am so miserable, I don't know why. I want to kill myself.

I have no respect for myself, I despise myself. Fleur does not understand me.

Pappy would understand me. I don't know what it is, but I can feel that Pappy and Heinz are still alive. They will come back to help me.

I don't understand why Fleur does not bring me up properly. She knows that's what I want. If a person is old enough they can do what they want. I see more and more how bad Fleur is for me. She is much too good. If I were a boy, who knows what I would do with my life?

*I am very, very unhappy, in despair. I am disgusted with
everything, and with myself the most. I love Vaz
Dias and the Czopps. Why does Fleur not help me to
love more? Jealous? Bah!*

You can see from this letter that I wrote to myself what
my state of mind was like by January 1946. Fleur is my
mother. We gave her that name in Brussels because we
thought Mutti sounded too Germanic. I can't remember
the book that I was objecting to, or where my mother had
gone (probably to the shop – certainly nowhere very
dramatic). I was a desperately confused and unhappy
teenage girl, and I strongly believed my father and Heinz
were still alive.

Sometimes people did turn up unexpectedly after they
had been missing for years, or even reported dead, so my
conviction was not beyond credibility. Then there was the
confusion with the Red Cross letter in which they had given
the wrong year of birth for Heinz. That only added to my
feeling that it was all a horrible mistake.

For years afterwards I jumped whenever I heard a car
stopping outside, believing that they might be in it. It
seemed unthinkable that I, a young girl, had survived, but
my father – the tough active man I'd always looked up to,
had not. I blamed myself, with a terrible feeling of guilt,
for telling him that I thought Mutti had been gassed the
last time I saw him at Auschwitz. I convinced myself that
he had given up the will to live.

I expect many teenage girls would identify with the senti-
ments I express towards my mother. Mutti was the closest
person in the world to me, and the person I sometimes

resented the most. Underlying my hostility towards her was a feeling that somehow the wrong two people had been left behind. I was my father's daughter and Heinz was his mother's son. Yet here we were, Mutti and Eva.

(In case you're wondering, Vaz Dias was a boy I'd gone out with a few times. I certainly don't remember being in love, in fact I'm sure that I wasn't – but obviously at that moment I felt strongly about him!)

This letter sat buried amongst my other papers and photos in my flat in north London for many years. When I took it out and re-read it, what surprised me most was that I'd said I wanted to kill myself. I vividly remember my feelings of self-disgust, worthlessness and despair, but if you'd asked me if I remembered feeling suicidal I'd have said no.

In my work today I often meet people in bleak circumstances who tell me they are either contemplating, or have attempted, suicide. I usually try to convey to them through my own story that there is always hope, and that life's circumstances will always change – sometimes for the better, sometimes for the worse. Nothing ever stays the same. Now I can see that I did indeed contemplate suicide, and I can truthfully say that those feelings do pass.

Recovering from traumatic events and loss is such a slow and gradual process that at the time you can hardly recognise your snail's pace back to normality. Of course, there are days when I am still very sad, upset and reflective, but I can tell anyone who is in the depths of depression or despair that in time it is possible to get over things, and move on with your life.

When I read this letter it seemed impossible to believe that my deep misery wasn't evident to everyone but it

appears from another piece of correspondence that even
Mutti had no idea about how bad I really felt. Just after
her birthday in February that year (only two weeks after
my letter of despair) she wrote to tell my grandparents
that I had made her a wooden serving platter, painted it
with flowers and written 'Mes Fleurs' across the top. 'You
write that I should have a lot of pleasure with Evi. She's
really such a good hearted, brave and loving child. What
pains she took to make me happy for my birthday . . .'

On my fiftieth birthday in 1979 Mutti typed out a four-
page tribute to me, looking back over our lives, and in one
passage she mentioned how well I adapted back to life in
Amsterdam.

*You went back to school and, as you had studied during
the two years we had been in hiding, you could adjust
quite well in the Lyceum. But you did not feel very
happy being more mature than the other pupils due to
all that you had experienced.*

*It was fortunate however that you met a former
girlfriend, Letty. She had returned from Theresienstadt
with her mother, while her father and brother* [Herman,
my first 'boyfriend'] *had died. She had the same
problems as you. As time passed you found other girl
and boy friends, you were invited to parties, you went
sailing, you led a normal life.*

*I think I did my best to be your mother, father and
brother in one.*

I'm deeply touched to read that last sentence where my
mother mentions what must have been a huge ordeal for

her. Yes, she had to be everything for me. She had to take over where previously my father had made every decision, and somehow, she had to try and maintain a positive frame of mind in the face of her own despair and shepherd and cajole her troubled daughter into leading a life worth living.

But I can't believe that she really thought I was happy and well adjusted. I did go sailing, and out to parties, but only because she made me. Left to my own devices I would not even have crawled out of bed. Later she adds, 'You had a busy life, but I think that you liked it.' Nothing could have been further from the truth.

Grudgingly I attended the Amsterdam Lyceum, feeling so much older than the other students. Before the war I had often seemed quite young for my age, but now I was weighed down with terrible experiences I believed no one else would understand.

A few of my old friends and acquaintances did return to Amsterdam, and I enjoyed the distraction of the days I spent with Ninni Czopp, whom we had met in Westerbork and who had been by our side when we arrived at Birkenau. Ninni was now living with her sister out in the town of Hilversum, and they were looking after her brother's little girl, Rusha. Ninni's brother and his wife had been deported and perished in a camp.

Mutti and I took a great interest in the child, and another little boy, Robbie, who was the son of the woman who had hidden them before they were captured. We even wrote to England to ask our family to send over some children's clothes.

We discovered that our cousin Minni, who saved our lives in Birkenau, had also survived although her husband had not. After liberation Minni returned alone to Prague for a short time, and then visited us en route to starting a new life in Palestine with her two sons, who were living there already. We remained close to Minni for the rest of her life, which was marred by a further tragedy when her youngest son Stephen was killed by a land mine in Israel's War of Independence in 1948.

The truth was that life was hard for everyone who survived.

Ellen, the girl who had so captivated Heinz before we went into hiding, came back to Merwedeplein and we were delighted to see her. The strain of the war proved too much for her, however, and she slowly went mad. Sometimes she would turn up and ask me vacantly, 'Where's Heinz? I don't understand where Heinz is.' Eventually her family was forced to admit her to a mental hospital where she remained for the rest of her life. I visited her once, but she had no idea who I was.

Even those who had not been deported, such as the Rosenbaums, suffered mental anguish. Martin Rosenbaum had managed to stay in hiding and survived the Occupation physically unscathed. As the years progressed, however, he became more and more anxious. He was so terrified of the threat of capture and persecution that he became an over-protective father who was scared to let Jan cross the road by himself. Eventually he too was admitted to hospital, which was a very sad end for one of our dearest and most loyal friends.

All of my new friends were Jewish. We never expressed any outright sense of solidarity, but we instinctively wanted to stick together. Even so I always felt false, smiling and talking to them, when it felt like a wall of glass separated me from the rest of the world.

There was just one person I poured my heart out to: my little cousin, Tom, who was still only ten years old.

It was extremely difficult for us to travel to the UK in the immediate aftermath of the war, partly because Europe was still in a state of chaos and partly because we were classified as Austrians, and therefore technically 'the enemy'. Grandma Helen tried to get permission to visit us in Amsterdam, but this required many letters and two references from people in the Netherlands.

Mutti applied to visit the UK, but at first we were turned down via an extraordinary letter, handwritten on a piece of torn off notepaper from the Home Office. It stated that despite a request from the Secretary of State to treat our case sympathetically, our visa application was denied. I can only assume that, in addition to England's other problems in 1945, there was a shortage of stationery.

Nevertheless we persevered and as soon as we could, Mutti arranged for us to cross the channel and make our way up to northern England to be reunited with my grandparents, aunt and uncle and cousin.

Tom was only three when he left Vienna, but he grew up in Darwen, Lancashire, hearing stories about my parents and what Evi was getting up to with her big brother Heinz. Then, for two terrible years, the letters stopped and we disappeared from view. Everyone feared the worst, until the day that the letter from my mother was delivered, carried all the way home by that British solider she'd met on the train.

'We were scared to death,' Tom says now, 'but when we

got the letter from Fritzi we all collapsed in tears and hugs, followed by even more tears of relief that she and Eva were safe.'

Seeing my grandparents again was unbelievable. They had existed for so long almost as figments of my imagination. I could tell that the war had changed them, too. They were no longer comfortable middle-class Austrians, living in a city they knew well, with my grandfather visiting his friends at the tavern every Sunday, and my grandmother being scolded by their maid, Hilda. Instead they had arrived in a new country as poor refugees without a word of English, and had set up home in a small three-bedroomed semi-detached house in an industrial northern town.

My grandmother had adapted well. She soon learned English, and read the *Daily Express* every day from cover to cover. She also looked after the house, cooked for the entire family and even set up her own dressmaking business to make some extra money. It was quite amazing, considering that back in Vienna she had never lifted a finger and had relied on Hilda to do everything.

I think my grandfather found the adjustment much harder. He never learned more than a few words of English and he always listened to the BBC radio broadcasts in German. In time he was able to put his old musical skills to good work, playing the piano by ear in various Darwen pubs and making new friends who bought him a pint of his beloved beer. He loved those evenings, being the centre of attention, and I'm happy to know that he was able to feel proud of himself, and once again become someone that other people in the community could look up to.

We stayed in Darwen for quite a while, and I shared a small bedroom with my ten-year-old cousin, Tom. My visit is perhaps seared even more strongly on his mind than mine. He vividly recollects the night that I kept him awake until dawn telling him about the war, and about Auschwitz.

I told him about the hunger, and the cold and the fear of being killed. I told him about the dirt and the disease – and the brutality of the SS. I talked and talked all night. I showed him the tattoo on my arm and told him how I got it, and I even told him about the rags we had to plait together and how I was terrified about not making my quota.

What a frightening burden to put on a little boy. I would never have talked like that to anyone else, but perhaps I opened up to him because he was a child. I think I felt that he was too young to understand what I was telling him.

That episode shows that I was still physically and emotionally fragile, and I can see now that I was in a deep depression. Until the middle of 1946 I was kept on a strict diet of soft food, like pasta and rice, to allow my starved digestive system to recover. My gums bled and my body was weak and anaemic. At night I was still plagued with nightmares about the camps; during the day I frequently wept and shouted at my mother in fits of rage.

Perhaps Mutti had to keep some of those emotions at arms' length so that, especially once we were back in Amsterdam, she could continue to hold what was left of our family together. If she had given in to her own grief and loss I'm sure we would have collapsed into a dark hole that we might never have emerged from.

We obviously deeply misunderstood each other. At the time I wondered how she could seem so cheerful. Sometimes I would come home and find her working away making a belt, whistling and singing – a fact I complained about in letters to my family in England.

'I'm not happy with Fleur. She's obsessed with working, but not with housework – with making belts. Now she cuts and whistles and sings and it makes me completely crazy – you know she was never very musical.'

In addition to that harsh judgment, I added that my mother was also lacking in love. 'The worst thing is that Fleur is not cuddly or affectionate enough,' I told them. *'She says that you, Grandma Helen, weren't like that either – and that I don't need it. But that is very, very wrong. I need it very much. I need a lot of love. I'm a very needy and loving young person.'*

Mutti must have seen my letter to my grandmother because she then writes to them, too.

What do you say about how she talks about me? It's not really that bad, but she would like to sit on my lap the whole time and cuddle, and I can't do that. I have to go to work. Obviously she needs a lot of love and attention . . . The other day I was sitting working on the belts, when Eva played something on the gramophone and I thought – as always – of the past. I suddenly felt that my previous life was just a dream – that I've always lived only with Eva and that I only dreamed that I had a husband and son. And then I cried desperately because my memories are not real any more. I just can't believe that I had that other life.

I had no idea that this was how Mutti *really* felt. It makes me so sad to realise now, far too late, that we were both so miserable and brokenhearted, and that neither of us could share our feelings and comfort each other.

In his quiet, understated and thoughtful way Otto Frank was playing a bigger role in both our lives. He had more than enough to think about – after a long struggle to find a publisher, the first edition of *The Diary of Anne Frank* was printed in Holland in 1946. Soon afterwards, Otto's life became consumed with arranging foreign publications and translations – and, once the American edition was published, overseeing an international sensation.

So I'll always be grateful that he cared enough to think about my future when he was still reeling from the knowledge that his own daughters would never come home. As someone who had also lost a child, my mother could sit with him and ask his advice. Often that advice involved how she could support me and help me with my problems.

As ever, Otto did his best to help, in very practical ways. He arranged for me to visit Paris with his younger brother Herbert, and then to accompany him to London for a World Progressive Judaism conference.

London was a revelation to me. We had all looked to it as a beacon of freedom and possibility, but when I arrived I discovered a war-ravaged city with bombed buildings, harsh food rations and little of the sophistication of cities like Vienna. Even so, I loved London's vast energetic anonymity, the cheerful unconquered spirit of its people and the almost audible hum of a city always pushing forward into the future. There were none of the stagnant splendours of old Imperial Europe.

For five days I stayed in a magnificent tall white town-house near Regent's Park and was whisked around by a relative of the Jewish scion Lady Montagu, taking tea in Park Lane and visiting expensive private clubs.

I enjoyed my trip very much, but one of my most vivid memories is waking one morning to discover that my bleeding gums had dripped onto the crisp white sheet beneath me, turning it pink. By now I was already suffering from the crippling shyness and lack of confidence that would continue to afflict me for many years. Rather than explain what had happened, I decided to rub the sheet with an orange from the fruit basket to try and remove the stain – but unsurprisingly, this resulted in an even bigger mess. Eventually I turned the sheet around so that the mark was near my feet, and I hoped that no one would notice.

After our London trip, Otto encouraged my mother to take me to Switzerland, and meet him afterwards. Looking back it's clear that they were becoming very attached to each other. Even my grandmother, who visited us in Amsterdam for a few months, was well aware of it. She told Mutti that, with a seventeen-year age gap, 'Otto is more my age than yours'. At the time, however, I was completely blind to all this, and I had no idea about their burgeoning relationship.

On Otto's advice my mother and I duly departed for the Alps. I was thrilled to be in the mountains again but hated the evening activities. Mutti would force me to go out dancing. She was determined not to let me slip into the life of a solitary misfit, but I detested clomping around hot dance floors in the clutches of various Swiss soldiers who were always wearing heavy woollen military uniforms and sweating profusely.

Nevertheless, these holidays offered me some light-hearted relief from my world – but back in Amsterdam the same heavy feeling of depression returned.

The question was, what was I going to do with my future?

As my mother mentioned early on in her letter to me on my fiftieth birthday, I was 'not a brilliant pupil', with no interest in reading or spelling. Although I worked hard to graduate from the Lyceum and got excellent grades, the thought of spending three or four more years in a university lecture hall studying obscure academic subjects was more than my traumatised psyche could contemplate.

My time in Auschwitz and then in the Ukraine, had left me restless. Amsterdam now seemed like a small drab town where everyone knew everyone's business and the pace of life was ponderously slow. 'I don't want to stay here,' I wrote to my grandparents. 'This is the most disgusting country in the whole world.'

I'm deeply embarrassed to see that I wrote that. The Netherlands is now very close to my heart, and as you can see in earlier chapters, we were very happy there before the Occupation. But in those years after the war, everything seemed bleak. Like many people, I had survived experiences that made it impossible for me to return to life as I had known it before. I needed to go out into the world and make a new kind of life – but I had no idea what that entailed.

Mutti wrote in her letter, 'What profession should you

choose? I realised that you had artistic qualities but you were also very technically-minded. So I thought that becoming a photographer would be a good choice, and you agreed.'

It was a good idea, and the original suggestion was Otto's. He had been an avid amateur photographer before the war and had a vast collection of family photos taken with his Leica. Now that he knew that Edith, Margot and Anne had been murdered he had no interest in his hobby, or any use for his camera.

I was always the 'practical' one in our family, while Heinz was the 'artistic' one but Otto could see that I was talented in my own way. Not only did he suggest a career for me but he also helped me arrange an apprenticeship in a studio by the Herengracht – and he gave me his precious Leica to work with. That camera is quite a piece of history, and I treasure it.

During my last year at school I combined afternoon work in the studio with classes at the Lyceum. The studio mostly made slides of art works and architecture. My work was largely confined to the darkroom, but I found that I loved the combination of artistic vision needed to find and frame a shot, mixed with the scientific knowledge of light and aperture, and the technical expertise to develop a photo.

More importantly, I was fully occupied. I hated the empty hours between school and sleep; I could never get engrossed in a book and socialising rarely took my mind off losing Pappy and Heinz. Occasionally I enjoyed myself, I remember going to a bar in what is now Amsterdam's Red Light district and seeing some American sailors teaching local girls how to swing dance and jive. That was quite something!

Another incident made me smile. Mutti invited an Israeli soldier from the Jewish brigade home for Friday night dinner, but he displeased her by roughly putting his feet up on the coffee table and asking what we were having to eat. That dashed Mutti's hopes for a future son-in-law, but there was another young man that she thought might fit the bill.

Henk was the son of a family friend from the synagogue, and his charming smile and fun-loving personality had won me over. Henk took me out on quite a few dates, and our relationship started to blossom into something more serious.

However much I enjoyed spending time with Henk, though, it wasn't long before I would look up and expect to see Pappy walking around the corner, or remember a conversation I'd once had with my brother. I couldn't bear to think, and so I was more than happy to fill my days with exhausting, time-consuming, activities.

When I graduated from the Lyceum I went to work in the studio full-time. I liked the people I worked with, especially my flirtatious boss, Jaap, who made me sit on his knee to demonstrate photographic techniques and took me for rides on his motorbike.

But it still wasn't enough. I was moody and difficult with Mutti, and in a photo of me sitting by the canal during my lunch break I look utterly miserable. Amsterdam seemed to be suffocating me with deadening memories: putting the past behind me and building a real future would require something more radical.

Otto and Mutti could see this too. Otto asked around and found another contact in a studio where I could work for a year. It was in a city I already knew slightly – one so vast and sprawling and anonymous that the old Eva Geiringer could get lost there, and I could try to move on. London.

18
The Trial

Outside of the day-to-day business of trying to rebuild our lives, the years we spent in Amsterdam after the war were marked by one major event: the trial of those people who had betrayed us to the Nazis.

There were so many informants in Amsterdam during the war that many families never found out exactly who had betrayed them. In some cases it may even have been more than one person.

There were the official 'Jew Hunters' from a unit called the Colonne Henneicke (an investigative division in the Bureau of Jewish Affairs named after the lead investigator, a ruthless curly-haired young man called Wim Henneicke whose previous occupation had been running unlicensed taxis). The 'Jew Hunters' were usually poorly educated young men, who had joined the Dutch Nazi party, the NSB. They often bragged that they lived 'high on the hog' receiving a premium of seven and a half Dutch Guilders (£50 in today's money) for every Jew that they arrested.

Then there were the civilians that the Colonne Henneicke recruited as their informants and paid handsomely for every Jew that they turned over. Some people betrayed members of their own family, like the woman who turned in her sister-in-law because of a dispute over a radio. One Jewish woman informed on eighty other families but was still arrested and sent to a concentration camp, where she perished. Of course, there were also the Nazi ideologues, committed to Hitler's cause, and legions of ordinary informers and snitches, each with their own motive that was sometimes little more than pure nastiness.

During the Nazi Occupation, Amsterdam was teeming with thousands of people willing to go out of their way to betray the Jews – and by the late 1940s they faced a reckoning with justice.

Unlike Otto, who was never certain who had betrayed his family, we knew the names of the people whose actions led to our arrest.

There was Gerada Katee-Walda, the woman who had blackmailed my father for more money. She demanded that my father increase his payments from 400 to 700 Dutch Guilders a month, an astronomical amount that is equivalent to 5,000 Euros today. She set in motion the whole chain of events that led to my father and Heinz having to move elsewhere, and ultimately to their demise. After our arrest the Gestapo paid a visit to Mrs Katee-Walda. In order to ensure her own safety, she provided them with the location of another family who were hiding four Jews. That family and the people they were hiding were rounded up and deported. They all perished.

Gerada Katee-Walda went on trial in 1947, and was sentenced to seven months in an internment camp. Later she changed her name and disappeared.

Then there was the group of people who had conspired to deliberately lead us into the hands of the Nazis. The 'nice' Dutch nurse who had met my father and Heinz from the train and led them to the house where they were arrested, was a woman called Miep Braams. Braams was the girlfriend of a Dutch resistance worker called Jannes Haan, and she was supposed to be helping him protect Jews and help the Resistance. As the war progressed Haan became suspicious that his girlfriend was really a double agent for the Nazis: an awful lot of the Jewish families he entrusted to her were vanishing without trace, or being rounded up. When she became aware of his suspicions Braams betrayed Haan to the Gestapo, and he was executed.

It was later estimated that Miep Braams was responsible for betraying as many as 200 Jewish families, including ours. She was acting as part of a larger group of informers under the control of a Dutch policeman, and brutal anti-Semite, called Pieter Schaap. Two of the women working with Schaap were Jewish, Ans van Dijk and Branca Simons.

Ans van Dijk became notorious in the Netherlands as the only woman to receive the death penalty for her role in the Occupation, and she was executed in January 1948. Van Dijk was a thirty-seven-year-old shop assistant who had escaped deportation in 1943 by agreeing to inform on other Jews – and she had accepted her task with enthusiasm, turning in more than 100 people.

Branca Simons, who was also Jewish, was the woman who had welcomed my father and Heinz to their new hiding place – and fed them such a lovely meal while she waited for the Gestapo to arrive. Working with Pieter Schaap, Simons set up a supposed safe house at 225 Kerkstraat where she would pretend to be married to another member of the group, petty criminal Wim Houthuijs. Together they welcomed scores of unsuspecting, desperate Jewish families into their 'home', which was, in reality, a terrible trap. Simons also received the death sentence for her activities, but it was later commuted to a prison sentence.

The case I remember most vividly was the trial of Miep Braams, because Mutti was called to testify.

The Dutch government had devised a system for bringing collaborators to justice, while it was still in exile. Under the Special Justice Act a series of tribunals would be set up across the Netherlands, including Special Courts for the most serious cases. In newly liberated Holland the Political Investigation Department, under the control of the Office of the Public Prosecutor, looked into hundreds of thousands of cases.

To give you some sense of the staggering number of people under investigation, a total of 450,000 dossiers were compiled. Nearly half of those were forwarded to the prosecutor and 50,000 people appeared before tribunals, while 16,000 were tried in Special Courts.

Miep Braams had already been tried for her role in working with the Nazis, but the case had collapsed due to difficulties with producing evidence. In May 1948 we heard that she was to be tried for a second time.

'I have to be there too,' I told Mutti. 'I want to go and see her for myself!'

'I know, Evi,' Mutti said, 'but they are not allowing children or young people into the court. Maybe they think it will be too upsetting, or disruptive.'

I couldn't believe it. 'Disruptive! She is the person who sent us to Auschwitz. If it wasn't for her, Pappy and Heinz would still be alive!'

Mutti tried to soothe me, but there was no way of getting around the rules of the court – she had to go alone.

The day arrived and, as Mutti told me later, Miep Braams sat in the dock looking cool and composed. Her hands were folded tidily in front of her; her bland expression never flickered when she heard Mutti describe what had happened, how she had betrayed our family – innocent strangers who just wanted to live our lives. While Mutti looked at her with the anguish of a mother and wife who had lost almost everything, Braams returned her stare without emotion. She showed no remorse.

'I just wanted to climb over into the dock and scratch her eyes out!' Mutti cried later, with a deep bitterness and grief that I rarely saw. 'She wasn't even sorry for what she'd done!'

Braams was not only cool but also cunning, and she had a trump card up her sleeve. During the war she had saved the life of one Jew, who just so happened to be very famous.

Paula Lindberg-Salomon was a well-known operatic contralto from Berlin who had escaped from Westerbork transit camp with her husband in 1943, and remained hidden in southern Holland for the remainder of the war. Lindberg testified about the immense gratitude she felt for Braams, who had helped her hide and survive.

The trial was long but in April 1949 the verdict came in. Braams was guilty, but was only sentenced to six years in prison.

We were outraged. 'How can someone only serve six years in prison for arranging the murder of 200 people?' I shouted at Mutti.

'I can't believe it either, Evi. After a few years she will

be out and leading her normal life again – but we have lost Pappy and Heinz for ever.'

And that is exactly what Miep Braams did.

As I discovered later, lenient sentences were often a feature of the trials of Nazi collaborators. Anything could sway sympathy in favour of the accused – the statement of a Jewish person whom they had helped in some way, or a plea from a wife or mother. Although 140 people received the death sentence, 100 of these were later commuted to life in prison because the Dutch government feared that too many executions would be bad for public morale. The average prison sentence served by a 'Jew Hunter' was ten years, but some were as low as twelve months.

I wish I could say that I believed these people, and Miep Braams in particular, faced true justice after death but my experiences in Auschwitz stripped me of any belief in the divine power of 'God' or an afterlife.

Justice must exist in this world, or it doesn't exist at all.

19
London

The weather in London was particularly cool and wet that spring, but I arrived with the small seed of hope that this was a new beginning. It seemed that the whole country felt the same way. It was May 1951, and England had decided to throw off the shackles of drab post-war austerity with the launch of the Festival of Britain.

More than eight and a half million people flocked to the South Bank in London to see the concrete-clad Royal Festival Hall. Next to it a 300-foot steel and aluminium cigar-shaped tower called the Skylon shot up into the clouds to proclaim a confident thrust towards modernism. Britain was ready to move forward and rebuild, and there were plans for new towns, new types of housing and investment in the National Health Service that had been founded three years earlier.

Furthermore, the war-battered population was ready for some fun, with millions more enjoying the fair at the Battersea Pleasure Gardens, riding on the miniature railway and strolling in the European-style wine garden. The future looked promising – perhaps even inviting.

Mutti saw me off tearfully at Amsterdam Central Station and promised to visit, but my own feelings of sadness were mixed with anticipation.

Me aged seventeen after the war, taken by a
friend who wanted to become a photographer.

My old boyfriend Henk. Our relationship became quite serious before I moved to London.

I took this photo of Mutti in 1948 and it remains one of my favourite images of her.

Minni saved our lives in Auschwitz. Here she is with her two sons in 1948.

Zvi with his mother Isle, father Meier and half-brother Shlomo, before they left for Palestine in 1936.

Zvi with Mrs Hirsch, the owner of the boarding house where we met in 1951.

We were married in Amsterdam 1952.

Zvi going to meet my family in Lancashire. We also took our first holiday together there.

Nini, Irene and Rusha, our best friends in Holland after the war.

Mutti, Grandma Helen and I with our first daughter Caroline in 1956.

My daughters Caroline and Jacky playing in 1959, with the same kind of wagon I used to play with Heinz in.

This was taken in Devon in 1966.

I always made my own Christmas cards to send to friends.
This one I took of our daughters Caroline and Jacky in 1960 with my Leica.

Mutti and Otto with Audrey Hepburn. They wanted her to play Anne in the first film of 'The Diary of a Young Girl'.

Mutti and Otto with my daughters in Cornwall 1965. We had many wonderful holidays together.

Otto with my youngest daughter Sylvia, on holiday in Switzerland.

Otto aged 76 on a beach in Italy. He was always full of energy when he was with the children.

Outside my beloved antiques shop which I opened in 1972.

I have also been lucky enough to meet some talented people. Demi Moore took an active part in the production of 'And Then They Came for Me, Remembering the World of Anne Frank' at her theatre in Haley, Idaho.

I love visiting schools and talking to the children. Here I am with the pupils of Battersea Junior School.

My name up in lights at the Egyptian Theatre in Boise, Idaho.
I was amazed when so many people arrived to hear me speak that
the police and fire service had to be called!

I learn as much from
schoolchildren as
they do from me.
They give me such
hope for the future.

With my daughter
Sylvia and
granddaughter Ella
at the opening of the
first exhibition of
Heinz and Pappy's
paintings, at the
Resistance Museum
in Amsterdam. Two
paintings by my
father of my mother
are behind me.

Zvi and I with Sylvia, Jacky and Caroline at our diamond wedding anniversary celebration in 2012. Since it was the year of the Olympics they gave us gold medals. I am very proud of my family.

In 2012 I was awarded an MBE by Prince Charles, for my work with the Anne Frank Trust and other Holocaust charities. It was a great honour.

'You must take care of yourself,' Mutti said, 'and write me lots of letters telling me everything that you're doing.'

'I will,' I promised.

'And I can come and visit you, and we can see Grandma Helen and the family in Darwen.'

With a kiss and hug I jumped on the train. In truth, I wanted to get away, and with the typical blitheness of young people, I assumed that Mutti would understand.

Henk and I had already said our goodbyes. I was very fond of him but I didn't know what to make of the relative ease with which I set off for this adventure without him. He had asked me to marry him and I had said that I would consider it. Somehow I felt curiously detached from my feelings about the whole thing.

Otto had found me a place to work for a year and a young man I knew from Amsterdam, called Sam, found a boarding house where I could stay. I got the train from Amsterdam to the Hook of Holland and then caught the boat to England. Then I caught another train to Liverpool Street station where Sam was waiting to take me to my new lodgings.

My initial impression on this second visit to the city was far from favourable: the area around the station looked like a bombed-out wasteland, and even the narrow streets and the buildings that were still standing looked poor and dirty.

Sam explained that I would be living in north-west London, not far from thousands of other German-speaking Jews who had settled in Golders Green and Hampstead including, most famously, Sigmund Freud.

With the tiny salary I expected to earn from my new

employer, I would sadly not be living amongst them. We caught the tube and got off at Willesden Green, walking towards Cricklewood past rows of houses and arcades of shops that looked to me like a curious version of the English dream. Everything was squashed together, with mullioned windows, tiny gardens and rose bushes. Frequently there would be gaps between the buildings, and groups of ragged laughing children would emerge from a wasteland of rubble, courtesy of the heavy bombing that the locals referred to as 'Mr Hitler's town planning'.

My landlady, Mrs Hirsch, opened the door of 91 Chichele Road when I knocked, and, as the only female resident, I was immediately enfolded into her hearty warm embrace. Cricklewood was a working-class Irish area, but Mrs Hirsch was a Czech Jew, and I was assured that I would be well looked after.

Even after the variety of conditions I had recently endured, life in an English boarding house came as a shock. Of course, it was infinitely better than the burned-out villages and falling-down homes I'd seen passing through Eastern Europe, but it was not nearly as luxurious as our old home back in Vienna, or even as comfortable as our small apartment in Merwedeplein.

The house was dark and narrow, with a clammy chill that you could only shake off by sitting so close to a gas fire that it almost singed your eyebrows. The bathroom held a strange coin-fed contraption, mounted on the wall, and meant to heat the water. I quickly came to view this beast as a dangerous monster, to be approached only with extreme caution. After I had hurriedly fed in as many small coins as I could lay my hands on, I would lean back so as not to be scalded by the fierce hissing spits of boiling water that spurted forth in all directions. After a few moments the water would go cold again.

At night we closed our bedroom doors and shivered beneath heavy flannel pyjamas and nightgowns, wrapped in sheets so freezing that it felt like slipping into a cold sea. The wind whistled through the gaps in the draughty windows. I would drift off to sleep listening to the singing hum of the overhead lines as a trolley approached the terminus at the end of the street, and turned around with a noisy clatter.

I liked this strange new country, but it puzzled me that on the Continent we had believed that England was the hub of modernisation.

'What is that?' I shrieked one evening, pointing at my dinner plate.

Mrs Hirsch took a step back and glared at me. 'What do you mean?'

'That is what you feed to a donkey!' I said, lifting a huge fat carrot off my plate and dangling it in front of her.

I'd never been very good at keeping my inconsiderate opinions to myself. In Austria I'd only eaten carrots that had been thinly sliced, or cut into batons. Even in Amsterdam the Dutch served them mashed up. But here was a nobbled monstrosity that I was supposed to chew on for supper. It even had a green stalk attached to the end – it looked hilarious.

'Very good for you,' Mrs Hirsch said, staring through narrowed eyes. 'Vitamins to build you up.'

I had often failed to appreciate how much Mrs Hirsch looked after me. Food was rationed in Britain until 1954, but Mrs Hirsch often favoured me by sneaking me a packed lunch with a jar of potato salad, or a sausage. In this instance she had clearly bought and saved this carrot just for me, rather than portioning it out to the other residents.

I was still obsessed with food after my near starvation in Auschwitz, and I struggled to adapt to British cuisine. I noticed that when my co-workers and neighbours wanted a treat they would buy a bag of greasy chips and a pickled onion – and then sigh as if this was the height of pleasure. By contrast, I greeted food parcels from Amsterdam as if they contained the wonders of the world, and fell upon them greedily.

One of the items in one of my first food parcels was good Dutch chocolate – a very rare delight in 1950s London – and it attracted the attention of the young lodger who was living across the hallway from me in the other attic bedroom. One evening he knocked on my door and introduced himself. His name was Zvi Schloss, and I knew that he was originally from Germany. That night we discussed mysteries like how to use the bathroom water heater – and when he saw my food parcel, his eyes lit up at the sight of the bar of chocolate.

Before long I felt very comfortable with Zvi; he was studying for a Masters degree with the LSE and he had a keen intelligence and a dry sense of humour. Neither of us was very tall, but I liked his short trim build, handsome face and dark hair receding at the temples. There was something about his appearance that reminded me of my father, and I warmed to any connection to him.

In London those family connections were now memories, rather than a daily reality that I encountered on every street corner. Travelling alone across the city I felt comforted, rather than afraid, to be a nameless young woman – only one person amongst thousands of strangers who each had their own story to tell.

Every morning I walked down to the underground station at Willesden Green and caught the tube into town. I knew that some people hated the closely packed compartments and the miles of claustrophobic tunnels, but I felt comforted by the rhythmic jerking of the tube train, the darkness and the odour of sweat, cologne, rain and cigarette smoke. The mass of huddled people were polite but would not dream of speaking to you or meeting your eye.

My new job was working for Woburn Studios, in Bloomsbury. The large studio was spread out across the ground floor and basement of one of the buildings on Tavistock Street, and we produced enormous prints that were made by projecting large images against the wall. The work was quite difficult and demanding, but I was engrossed in learning new things. I still worked in the darkroom, but now I could broaden my horizons a little, and even go out on some assignments (although this usually meant little more than holding the reflectors for the light).

One day my boss, Mr Peck, asked me to go out on a shoot with him at Heathrow Airport. Back then Heathrow had only been operating as a civilian airport for five years, and work had just begun on building the first proper terminals. The journey seemed to take a long time as we drove far out of London into the countryside, and we finally came to a stop on the tarmac, right next to a new passenger jet, the de Havilland Comet.

I climbed on board the plane, behind Mr Peck, and we

spent the day taking photos of models dressed up as glamorous air hostesses who were pretending to hand out delicious meals. Now when I fly around the world, cramped up with hundreds of other people in economy class, it makes me smile to remember how excited I was to be swept up into the glamorous world of air travel – and a little nostalgic about the more relaxed attitude towards security.

In those days I was painfully withdrawn and quiet, with only schoolgirl's English, but I made friends at work. We shared some of the pleasures of being young and poor in the city, like buying a single newspaper every day and sharing it amongst everyone. My life was not exactly a social whirl, but as well as my work friends, I met people at the boarding house where one of the lodgers, an Irishman, took me to the dog races. I also became fond of an older man who was a kosher butcher because I loved the way he smelled of sausages. I even started to go out with a couple of young men.

There was still the matter of my half-promise to marry Henk when I returned to Amsterdam, but I was also seeing more of Sam. He worked as a car mechanic but wanted to become a Rabbi and, if possible, he was even shyer than me, with a nervous stutter. We often went to public talks and events at the Quaker Meeting House on the Euston Road, and after the speaker had finished I would sense that Sam was working himself up to ask a question. His shoulders tensed and his face would turn red with effort – but he always made himself stand up and ask something, no matter how long it took him to actually articulate the words. I admired his efforts, but shrivelled inside at the thought of having to go through that myself.

Having helped me so much, and found my lodgings with Mrs Hirsch, Sam probably understandably believed that we had a growing attachment. But, much as I liked him – and Henk in Amsterdam – there was another young man playing a bigger role in my life. As we became more friendly, Zvi started to accompany me to various activities, too. We often went to the Festival of Britain together and we picnicked with the rest of the lodgers in an outing to the Battersea Pleasure Garden, where I noticed – with some jealousy and annoyance – that Zvi had taken quite a fancy to another woman, a blonde and busty German who was much more forward than me but already married.

One night we went to watch a play in the small hall at the bottom of the road, and then panicked when we couldn't find our way back in the thick pea-soup smog. Zvi almost choked on the rank air. On other days we would walk up to Hampstead Heath, with the City of London and St Paul's Cathedral a rather magnificent backdrop, and talk about all sorts of things – but never about what had happened in the war.

I was impressed when Zvi invited me to play tennis, although his terrible performance revealed that sport was not his forte. Despite all his efforts, I was still not really sure whether Zvi was attracted to me, or my chocolate confectionery, but I had other suitors to go out with and keep me free from any deep emotional entanglement – which, I thought, was just the way I liked it.

20

Zvi's Story

While I was a little girl growing up in Vienna, and then travelling across Europe seeking safety with my family, Zvi was also undergoing a traumatic childhood over the German border in Bavaria.

His father, Meier, was born in a Bavarian village and his family were Jewish farmers and business people. Then World War One took Meier far from home, and when he returned he was a defeated soldier and a weakened man who suffered from glandular rheumatism and a serious heart disease.

Instead of going back to his village, Zvi's father moved to the town of Ingolstadt, north of Munich, and set up a business dealing in the local hops used to make beer.

By the time Zvi was born in 1925 his father was an established business and family man. His first wife had died giving birth to Zvi's half-brother, Shlomo, and Zvi's mother, who came from a family of wealthy wine dealers in Württemberg, was his second wife.

From the beginning, Zvi was the adored baby of the family. When German children start school they are given a huge decorated paper cone filled with sweets. Zvi's parents commissioned an artist to paint a portrait of him with his cone, to hang in the middle of the living-room wall.

But before long, things started to go wrong for the family.

The economic turmoil in Germany in the 1920s meant that the business was struggling, and arguments were a constant backdrop to family life. Eventually Zvi's father started selling cloth for suits and clothes; later he tried to sell life insurance, and even cigars.

Zvi's grandparents moved in to their house to help economise. His grandfather was a well-respected local doctor who often saw patients for free if – as many people were – they were going through hard times. Soon he became an official doctor of the local Social-Democratic party.

It was Zvi's grandfather who gave him an interest in learning languages that has lasted throughout his life. In the evenings he would call Zvi and his brother Shlomo over to his writing desk and they would read the stories of Rudyard Kipling, with Shlomo learning the English words and Zvi chipping in with occasional comments.

But despite these bright spots, the Schloss family were struggling. They had few friends in Ingolstadt, and anti-Semitism was increasing.

'I did not have a single friend at my local school. The boys would shout "Jew! Jew!" at me,' Zvi told me, much later. 'There were about forty Jewish families in town at the time, but none had children in my class and so I felt completely isolated. Once, the boys chased me until I reached the top of a steep flight of stone steps. I slipped at the top and crashed all the way to the bottom, hurting my back and ribs very badly. On the streets of Ingolstadt we could feel people turning against us, no longer speaking, or even meeting our eyes.'

One year after the Nazis assumed power, in 1934, Zvi's father was rounded up and arrested 'for his own protection'.

He was transported to the nearby camp at Dachau, which then housed mainly Communists, opponents of Hitler and criminals, as well as some Jews. Dachau was described as a work camp but thousands of people were unjustly imprisoned there, and few emerged alive.

'Family life became even harder. We were allowed to write only occasional letters to my father, on pre-prepared cards with a small section for handwritten comments. He could reply to us this way, too. It was the only contact we had with him.'

You can imagine Zvi's thoughts and feelings when he looked out of the window one day and saw an open-topped car slowly making its way through screaming crowds, carrying none other than Adolf Hitler.

Ingolstadt was a Nazi stronghold and Hitler was visiting a friend of his who was the local party boss. 'It seemed like everyone in town had turned out to see Hitler, the Swastika hung from every building and people were almost hysterical with delight.'

Zvi told me about the load of feelings he had when he recalled this incident later, with the benefit of hindsight. 'People have sometimes said to me – if only you could have thrown a bomb straight into his car. But I was just a child, and in any case, none of us could have imagined what was to come.'

Zvi saw Hitler three times in Ingolstadt. 'I found him unremarkable. It was hard to believe that someone who looked so ordinary could be responsible for so much murder, for almost wiping out the Jewish people.'

One day Zvi opened the front door and found the person he had been longing to see: his father. Meier's return was

completely unexpected, and he had changed dramatically.
Now he looked thin and nervous, and he couldn't bear to
be in a room with the door shut. After two long years Zvi's
father had been released from Dachau, but on the condition that the family leave Germany within two months.
Immediately, Meier set about trying to get visas so they
could all flee to another country.

It seemed like an impossible task. By 1936 most countries
were refusing to take penniless Jewish refugees and they tried
everywhere to no avail. Finally, as the deadline approached
and they really began to panic, someone told them that the
British consulate in Munich kept a handful of visas to
Palestine in case of extreme emergencies. They applied – and
thankfully they qualified.

'I left Germany with my brother and my parents, first
catching a train to Munich and then travelling down across
Austria to the Italian port of Trieste,' Zvi remembered.

At Trieste they boarded an Italian ship and made their
way to Haifa, in what was then British-controlled Palestine.
Zvi was eleven years old.

'Before the Nazis came to power we were respectable
citizens and business people, but we got off that boat as
poor immigrants, with my father a physically and emotionally damaged man after his experiences in Dachau. This
new land we found ourselves in was completely alien to
us in its smells, sunlight, surroundings, language and
people, but it was to be the foundation for the rest of my
life. And we were free.'

Wearily, and rather warily, the Schloss family shrugged
off their heavy German habits and started a new life in
this messy and sometimes poverty-stricken country where,

to German eyes, everything appeared to be in a state of disarray.

Life was tough. Back in Germany Zvi's father had managed his own business, but now he was reduced to pulling a heavy handcart up and down the hills of the town, laden with barrels of a popular local drink. In his state of health it was the worst possible occupation, but it was better than seeing his family starve.

Zvi's father paid to enrol him in a small private school where he could begin to study Hebrew, and try to get used to his new country.

'I no longer had to run away from gangs of German boys pushing me over with shouts of "Jew", but in Haifa I had to dodge and weave my way through the hot streets, always aware of the tensions and animosity between the Jewish community that jostled up against Arabs from the Old Quarter. I remember the British authorities walking around in their khaki uniforms, knee-length shorts and pith helmets.'

Soon, however, family life changed irrevocably.

In 1938 Zvi's grandparents visited from Germany for his Bar Mitzvah, and even though the situation under Hitler was becoming intolerable, they decided to go back. 'It seems like an astonishing decision,' Zvi says now 'but they were elderly, with no other home, and they had lived their entire life as Germans. They hoped that their country would soon come to its senses, and get rid of the Nazis.'

As it turned out, their hopes couldn't have been more misplaced. Zvi's grandfather couldn't bear life in Nazi Bavaria, or the humiliation of being stripped of his professional prestige as a highly respected doctor, and he may have committed suicide. Then, when the war began, Zvi's grandmother was deported to a concentration camp in Latvia. She never returned.

There were big changes in Haifa, too. Zvi's father's health deteriorated under the strain of his heavy work and he died of heart failure. Zvi desperately wanted to continue studying, but he knew that he was going to have to leave school and find some work. 'It seemed to me that the best place to earn money was in a bank – so that was where I started, aged thirteen, as a general errand boy.'

Before he died, Zvi's father had found him a place with a bank called Feuchtwanger, which was owned by a German Jew. Zvi kept up his studies in the evenings for many years, until he'd had passed his examinations.

At the same time, he was becoming very involved in Zionism. The war in Europe was creating turmoil in Palestine. The Nazis and their partners were keen to capture the Middle East and get access to both oil and the Nile Delta. Italian planes regularly bombed Haifa, blowing up the storage tanks and the oil refinery and sending massive fireballs shooting into the sky.

'We were terrified that the Nazis would take over, but we were also deeply unhappy with British rule,' Zvi says.

The British White Paper of 1939 had proposed setting up an independent Palestine, governed by Arabs and Jews. Representation would be proportionate to their respective populations in that year. The paper placed restrictions on Jewish immigration and the rights of Jews to buy Arab land.

A limit of 75,000 Jewish immigrants was set for the following five years, consisting of a regular yearly quota of 10,000, and a supplementary quota of 25,000 to cover emergency refugees over the same period. After 1944, further immigration would depend on the permission of the Arab majority.

At the end of the war, the first reports of the Holocaust trickled in. Zvi recalls the reaction. 'We all felt totally devastated by the terrible catastrophe that had befallen the Jewish people. We had heard rumours of what was going on in Europe, but they were almost unbelievable. Surely things couldn't be that bad, we thought. We had been living in denial.

'Then we watched as boatloads of Jewish refugees washed up on the beaches, only to be rounded up, arrested and turned back by the British, who sent them to displaced persons camps in Cyprus. It was shocking, and completely unbelievable.'

In 1945 Zvi joined Haganah, the underground Jewish paramilitary organisation. His corps met for training in the evenings in the Haifa flour mill. 'I was ready to fight for an independent Jewish state, and for my people.'

In November that year the UN voted to accept a partition plan that proposed that the British withdraw from Palestine, and establish two separate Arab and Jewish states. Tensions between the communities reached fever pitch. Many on both sides disagreed with the proposed plan and the future boundaries.

On 30 December 1947 a group of Arab militia broke into the refinery and killed thirty-nine Jewish workers.

'Although I had been trained to shoot, and even to throw grenades, I walked the streets in fear,' Zvi says, 'Once, in the old quarter in Haifa, I heard a car idling behind me. I turned just in time to see an Arab man pulling out a pistol and aiming it at my head. Quickly I ducked, and narrowly avoided having a bullet shot through my brain.'

On 15 May 1948, when the State of Israel was founded, Zvi immediately joined the Israeli Defense Force, the successor of Haganah, where he served for two years, first as a paymaster and then as a censor in the army intelligence unit.

He was always far better equipped with brains than brawn – and army life was not really for him.

'I remember once having a terrible bout of dysentery and stopping in a Druze village to clean my bottom in a cattle trough while the local girls looked on. What a lovely experience for me, and for them!'

In off-duty hours Zvi sat in his dusty army tent reading and studying, and when his army service was finished he went back to his position in the bank.

'I realised that if I wanted to advance my career I would have to leave Israel for a while and get more experience abroad,' he says. The bank helped him to find a job in London, and he arrived in England in 1950, wearing an ancient German winter coat that made him look like a character from a nineteenth-century novel.

I well remember that coat – it was hideous, but Zvi seemed to love it. Even in the early days of our relationship I looked forward to the day when I could dispose of it! At the time Zvi didn't realise he was going to need a new coat. European winters were only a temporary inconvenience because he was completely dedicated to returning to Israel and his job in finance. If I hadn't appeared in his boarding house one day, full of mystifying opinions and carrying a decent supply of good Dutch chocolate, he certainly would have.

Instead we met, and both our lives changed for ever – and for the better.

21
The Wedding

The morning I got married was a beautiful summer's day in Amsterdam. There was only one blot on my horizon – my mother-in-law to be. Frau Schloss had disapproved of me from the moment she heard of my existence. She was grief stricken that I would be taking away her beloved son, her darling Zvi.

Zvi had asked me to marry him one day, months earlier, when we were walking on Hampstead Heath.

'Eva, I love you and I think you're a wonderful girl,' he suddenly blurted out, rather nervously, 'would you like to marry me?'

If this was a romantic novel I would have accepted on the spot, but two things held me back. I liked Zvi tremendously but I was still very confused about my feelings – and I wasn't sure whom, if anyone, I wanted to marry. It was only a few years since I had lost Pappy and Heinz, and although I had managed to move to London and pick up day-to-day life, I couldn't feel any deep love for anyone.

I told Zvi that I was very happy he had asked me, but that I needed to think about it and spent the next few weeks trying to reach an understanding of what I really wanted. There was one person in particular that I needed to consult.

'Who do you think I should marry?' I asked Mutti during one of her visits to London.

She frowned in concentration. Zvi was the intellectual choice, but there was also Henk, back in Amsterdam, and our 'semi-engagement'.

'I think you should marry Zvi,' Mutti said eventually. 'Not only is he a nice man but he is clever and interesting. It's very important for you to have a husband that will keep you interested. Henk is a darling boy too, but I think Zvi is the right choice.'

I had to agree that Zvi was clever and mysterious (with that exotic past in Palestine) but there was one other thing standing in my way – Mutti herself. I had never told her this, but after all that we had been through I had no intention of moving to another country permanently and leaving her behind. So my answer was no.

'Thank you very much,' I said to Zvi, because we were very polite in those days, 'but I can't marry you. My mother is a widow and I want to be near her in Amsterdam.'

Without giving it too much further thought, and without too much heartache, I went back to working in Woburn Studios and continued with my normal life at Mrs Hirsch's boarding house. Zvi appeared to accept my decision quite calmly, although he tells me now that he was always sure he would win me over, that I just wouldn't be able to resist him. At the time I believed that nothing would change my mind – but, of course, I was wrong.

'Well, Eva, now I have some news to tell you.'

This time I was talking to Otto Frank, and he looked nervous. Otto had come to London on business and I'd been looking forward to seeing him. He had been seeing my mother every day in Amsterdam and she had already told him that I had turned down Zvi's proposal. Now Otto was determined to tell me something.

'You may have noticed that your mother and I have been getting closer . . . We've fallen in love and, once you've settled down, we've decided to get married ourselves.'

I was completely taken aback to hear this. Their deep feelings for each other had been obvious to everyone in Amsterdam for some time, but I had never seen them as having anything more than a supportive friendship. Many other ladies had their eye on Otto, but he was deeply attached to my mother – and it turned out their relationship was based on far more than companionship and mutual understanding: it really was a romance.

While I was settling in to London life, Otto was writing long letters to my mother from his travels in the States to promote *The Diary of Anne Frank*. In these densely typed pages he told her everything – including what he had eaten and how much it cost (he thought a meal for 99 cents was quite expensive). Then he promised to tell her even more details when he saw her in person, and made plans to move in with her when he returned. Back in Amsterdam, my mother would set off for work every day on the tram and, rather sweetly, Otto would ride alongside on his bike. At each stop my mother came out onto the platform and they blew kisses at each other.

I was stunned, but happy that my mother would not have to spend the rest of her life alone. My own feelings were more complicated, but I was truly fond of Otto and I knew that it would be selfish to express the spurt of pain I felt for my own father upon hearing this news.

One thing was clear, I was now free to lead my own life, and accept Zvi's proposal if I wanted to.

I gave it some thought and decided that I would tell Zvi that I could accept his offer of marriage after all, 'but first you will have to ask my mother's permission. She's visiting next week and you can talk to her then.'

Mutti arrived and the following day, the three of us strolled up to Hampstead Heath, which was evidently a popular spot for discussions in our family.

Zvi seemed very tense as he nervously told her that he wanted to marry me. Mutti agreed – with one request. She asked him not to take me back to Israel. After all that we'd been through she couldn't bear to be so far away from her only child, or face the possibility that we might not see each other for years.

Zvi looked genuinely shocked by her request. I knew that he felt an enormous pride and loyalty towards Israel, and was committed to helping build up his new nation. Although he loved studying in London, like me he'd never considered the city to be his permanent home. And of course, his mother, like mine, would have no desire to live thousands of miles away from her only child. Getting married would involve a far greater sacrifice than he'd envisioned. I could see all the ramifications of Mutti's request playing out across his face as he thought it through but, taking a large gulp, he agreed.

'I wonder what the time is?' Mutti said suddenly. We had been so involved in this deep conversation that we'd forgotten Mutti had to catch a train. None of us was wearing a watch, so Zvi ran over to a crowd of people and asked for the time. I watched him with dismay.

'Oh no, look at the way he runs!' I said to Mutti. 'He is so flat-footed, he runs like Charlie Chaplin.'

I'm sure Mutti said something consoling, but the truth was I still felt deeply ambivalent about getting married and unsure about the proposal I'd accepted.

We saw Mutti onto the train and, after it left, I said to Zvi, 'I'm still not sure if I want to marry you. I thought you were athletic, but you're not. I wanted us to go skiing and climbing together.'

These issues seem rather trivial, especially now that I understand all of the ups and downs that a long marriage entails. What I was really trying to say, of course, was that I had a strong idea of how I'd imagined my future husband to be – and I didn't know if Zvi could be that man. It was like taking a huge leap into the dark.

We talked for two more hours, and Zvi made an impassioned response, telling me that I needed to take more risks in my life and promising that he could, and would, change everything about himself to be exactly what I wanted. Of course, I was still too innocent to realise that people can rarely, if ever, do this.

He talked me round, and with a feeling of excitement, and some trepidation on my part, we set the wedding date for a few months' time. We would marry in Amsterdam. Meanwhile I finished my year at Woburn Studios as planned and took Zvi up to visit my family in Darwen.

Little did I know that, despite her encouragement, Mutti later wrote to my aunt to ask her opinion about whether Zvi and I were a good match, and expressed her anxiety about the wedding.

As long as she's not married I don't quite believe it . . .
The desperation will come as soon as I see her installed
in a different country. But I have to swallow my own
feelings and if I make a big sacrifice then I hope at least
she will be very happy . . .

Blissfully unaware that Mutti had any worries, I was happy.
I cheerfully headed back to Holland to start putting
together a basic trousseau.

On 19 July 1952 Zvi and I married in Amsterdam Town
Hall with my mother, my grandmother, Otto, a few friends,
and Frau Schloss by our side.

Zvi's mother had travelled over from Israel for the ceremony, and was staying with us in Merwedeplein while we
waited for Zvi to arrive. He had already told me that his
mother had not taken the news well, and that she believed
he was making a terrible mistake. My grandmother was
staying in the apartment too, and after she and Mutti had
gone to bed, I crept in to see Frau Schloss to say goodnight.

'I see that you've finally come to speak to me!' she said,
her eyes glittering with dislike as she launched into a long
list of reasons why I shouldn't part her from her beloved
son. It was a horribly uncomfortable moment. I was only
too aware that in agreeing to Mutti's request, Zvi had
created heartache for his own family, but of course I
couldn't help feeling that she was behaving insensitively.

On the day itself I saw my mother and grandmother
beaming at me with tears of happiness in their eyes, while
my new mother-in-law wept into her handkerchief. She
watched the ceremony with an expression that made her
look as if she was suffering from severe indigestion.

Unfortunately she had one more surprise in store.

'Look!' she said, flourishing her passport in front of us, 'I have my visa for Switzerland and I will be coming with you on your honeymoon. I am all packed.'

After a sharp intake of breath I marched Zvi off into another room and said, 'Your mother is not coming on our honeymoon! And you are the one who will have to tell her that she can't come!'

Poor Zvi. After a private, and very uncomfortable conversation with his mother, he returned and we all congregated for the wedding photograph, before he and I departed for a wedding night on the Dutch coast and the train ride to Switzerland.

The mountains had been a magical place for me since I was a little girl and I couldn't wait to share them with my new husband.

On the first morning of our trip I bounded off to the nearest chairlift, feeling ecstatically happy to be out enjoying the fresh air and alpine scenery. As the chairlift rose higher and higher, with the meadows falling away below us, I looked across and was surprised to see Zvi clutching the safety bar tightly. His eyes were closed and he was sweating.

'What's wrong?' I asked.

'I can't look down,' he said. 'When will we get there?'

We soon arrived and I jumped off, puzzled that Zvi was so afraid of heights. Ahead was a twisting mountain path, leading higher and higher up the trails that I had always liked to climb. I set off, feeling the hot sun on my face, and stopping to look at some of the alpine flowers that we had always collected as a family. Beside me the side of the mountain fell away, revealing glorious views across the valley. I felt truly in my element. Eventually I became aware that I could only hear the crunch of my own boots on the path, and I looked back. Where was Zvi?

'Eva . . . Eva . . .' I heard him cry out.

When I found him, his arms were wrapped around a huge rock; he looked like he was moulded to it with every fibre of his being, and he was trembling.

He held out his hand. 'I can't go on. I can't go forwards and I can't go back. You'll have to help me.'

Rather nonplussed, I reached out and took his hand, leading him slowly down the mountain path.

Later, to make Zvi's day even worse, he ate a heavy lamb stew and spent the night being violently sick in a small sink in our bedroom.

'I feel terrible,' he moaned, clutching his stomach, while I lay in the darkness on that hot summer night wondering about this strange man that I had married.

Unlike couples today that live together for years before they marry, we really did not know each other very well, and our relationship was very innocent. (Zvi believed that babies were born from the woman's belly button.) Marriage was a true, and sometimes disconcerting, voyage of discovery. I had assumed that Zvi was like my father because they looked slightly alike, and I assumed that all men had Pappy's active, energetic interests and personality. And I had believed Zvi was sporty because I once saw him cleaning a pair of hiking boots out of his bedroom window – what a basis on which to accept a proposal! Now it occurred to me that perhaps Zvi was not like my father at all.

22

An Unbroken Chain

The next marriage in our family was a year later between my mother and Otto. It was a quiet wedding and Mutti did not even tell us about it until after the ceremony. I immediately understood why: they married on 10 November 1953, the day before my father's birthday and Mutti knew how much that would upset me.

Otto had been living in Merwedeplein with my mother for some time, but they were both haunted by all their memories, so they decided to move to Switzerland to begin their married life as a fresh chapter, close to Otto's remaining family. Although he was completely driven to ensure that Anne's diary was published, and gained the recognition it deserved, the war and loss of his family had placed a terrible strain on Otto's emotional and mental well-being. He often cried and suffered terrible shaking fits, and deep depression. The truth was that however much Otto loved Amsterdam, he could not bear to live there any more.

I understood his feelings only too well; the war and its aftermath had placed a severe strain on my emotional well-being, too.

After our honeymoon Zvi and I moved into two rented rooms in a house on nearby Anson Road, but neither of us warmed to our new accommodation. Our landlady was a widow with two unmarried daughters who ran a well-known Jewish delicatessen called Green's. The house was always messy and sombre. We had a small bedroom and a living room with a cooking ring, but we had to wash up our plates and pots and pans in the shared bathroom that always had a greasy film of dirt in the sink, left by other lodgers.

I had given up my job at Woburn Studios when I got married, as was the convention at the time, but sitting around the house was making me depressed and Zvi agreed that I should apply for a new job, and take some courses to fill in time during the day.

I wrote out dozens of job applications and meanwhile, enrolled at a local polytechnic to learn weaving and glove making. My first day there was a disaster. By the end of the session I badly needed to go to the toilet, but I was too shy to ask anyone where it was. It's hard to understand how crippling shyness can be unless you suffer from it, but the trauma of my time in Auschwitz and losing Pappy and Heinz had rendered me practically incapable of speaking to people. I just couldn't bear the thought of asking anyone the way to the ladies' bathroom, so I clenched my muscles, and then ran to the bus stop. It wasn't a long journey, but it felt like an eternity as the bus stopped and started and trundled slowly along. Eventually we reached my stop and I jumped off and shot down Anson Road, feeling the agony of each step. I reached our house just in time, but to my horror the coal men had arrived with their delivery, and in those days the coal was stored in the bathroom.

'Sorry, ducky,' the coal man said, holding his hand up. 'We're busy here, you'll have to wait.'

Wait? I couldn't wait another second. I sat down on the low garden wall and, much as I tried, I just couldn't hold it any longer. I wet myself, and when the coal men left I ran upstairs in my sopping skirt to get clean.

Later that night I told Zvi all about my ordeal and, although he was very sympathetic, I could see that he was somewhat mystified by his wife, who was so self-conscious in public but usually quite outspoken in private with him. Back in the camps I'd sworn that I would never be a victim, but nearly ten years on, that was how I appeared, in public at least – a cowed shell of the outgoing girl I used to be.

Soon after this incident I was offered a two-week probationary period for a job with a photographic studio in Victoria. The trial went well, and I was offered the job on a full-time basis, but I knew that I hated it and I didn't want to accept a position there. You might think that the solution was clear cut – I could say, 'No thank you, this job is not for me.' I could tell them that my personal circumstances had changed. I could make up a lie, and decline. But I couldn't say any of those things; all I knew was that I couldn't tell them I didn't want the job. After much agonising, I asked Zvi to ring up the office and tell them that he was being sent to work in Manchester, and we were leaving London. This was untrue, and a very elaborate deception to solve an easy problem.

My weaving and glove making didn't amount to much, either. I managed to make one single glove, and weave one purple and pink scarf that I sent to my mother-in-law in Israel. In her indomitable fashion she wrote to say, 'The thing that I dislike *most* about the scarf is the colours . . .'

'I am never doing anything for your mother again,' I

227

told Zvi indignantly, although to be honest she may have had a point.

By now Zvi was doing well at work with the stockbrokers Strauss Turnbull, and we were looking for our first proper home together. As soon as we could we bought a small ground-floor flat in Olive Road, and we even started work on our first garden, planting an apple tree that we took with us to our next house where it is still producing a wonderful crop today.

On the outside, life looked perfect – we were a young couple making our way in the world – but in reality I was still struggling with the emotional and physical after-effects of Auschwitz.

We hadn't been living in Olive Road long when I developed a temperature. It wasn't a particularly high temperature, but no matter how much I rested, it wouldn't go away. I felt unwell almost all of the time. Eventually my doctor sent me for more tests and they told me that I had scarring on my lungs and a form of TB in my bones. This was terrible news as, at the time, TB was a disease that took people months, or even years, to recover from.

I was sent to the famous Royal National Orthopaedic Hospital in Stanmore, and spent three miserable weeks being X-rayed and examined, before a doctor appeared at my bedside one morning and said, 'You don't have TB, Mrs Schloss, you are free to go.' I was delighted to be leaving that cold and draughty hospital, which seemed very primitive compared to some European hospitals I had seen, but the doctor also told me that the scarring on my lungs indicated I had suffered from a serious disease at one time – probably while I was in the camp.

It wasn't the end of my medical problems. Soon after I returned home I discovered that Auschwitz was responsible for something with potentially even more profound consequences.

One rainy London afternoon I decided to go to a lecture on geology at the Natural History Museum. When I came out I shivered in the damp miserable weather and decided to cross the road and have a cup of tea in a café. I sat down and ordered my tea, and noticed that an older man at a nearby table was looking at me. He leaned over and cleared his throat, and I wondered what he was going to say. But instead of trying to chat me up he asked if he could read my palm. I knew that it was foolish, but I was curious, and a bit taken aback. I turned over my hand to let him trace his fingers along my palm.

'Hmm, oh yes,' he said, while we both stared intently at my hand. 'I can see from this line that you're going to have a very long life.'

That certainly sounded like good news.

Then he paused. 'Wait, I can't see this clearly.' He frowned and peered more deeply into my palm. 'This is the line that shows whether or not you will have children, but it's not easy to trace – I just can't tell if you will have a family or not.'

Until that moment I had never considered that I might not be able to have children. I snatched my hand back in horror. Pappy's words about carrying on an unbroken chain through family had stayed with me, and suddenly I felt that if I couldn't have children with Zvi it would be unbearable.

I rushed home in tears and slammed the front door behind me. Zvi was sitting in the living room.

'Forget about waiting until we are more settled,' I said. 'We have to make a baby right now.'

'All right,' he replied, looking confused, 'but I thought you wanted to wait until we have a bigger place to live?'

'No, we have to start trying immediately!'

But for a while it looked like the palm reader's prediction might be true. We tried for a year, but there was no sign of a baby.

Eventually we made an appointment at the Elizabeth Garrett Anderson Hospital on the Euston Road and, as we sat in the waiting room, the possibility that we might never have children lay between us like a great unspoken weight.

The doctor confirmed my worst fears. The strain of Auschwitz had affected my hormones and my body was not functioning in the way that it should. I started to take a course of hormone treatment, and waited, and waited – but still no baby.

By now I was engulfed in a terrible sense of gloom, and so in the autumn of 1955 Zvi suggested we join my mother and Otto on a holiday in Norway to take my mind off things. In those days Norway was not an international tourist destination and we spent a memorable trip enjoying the beauty of the fjords and waterfalls, trying, and failing, to make ourselves understood in English, eating reindeer meat and travelling about on local buses. Even with all my problems I couldn't help but relax and enjoy myself, and when I returned to London I discovered that I had missed my period. At long last – I was pregnant.

Although I had undergone some terrible and nerve-shattering experiences in my life, I was still remarkably ignorant about pregnancy and childbirth.

For the first few months I was terribly sick, and threw up immediately at the slightest whiff of food. One evening I was dishing up some stew for Zvi, but as soon as I lifted the lid off the pan and the smell hit me, I vomited, right on the floor beside the table.

Zvi started screaming, 'What are you doing? You're being sick on my dinner!' I was so enraged with him, I lifted the heavy pan lid and brought it down across his head with a terrific crack – nearly knocking him out. Although I was a shy person in public I was never that way with him – and I had quite a temper, too.

After nine long months I was whisked off to a maternity hospital in the City of London, with little knowledge of how my baby would actually emerge into the world.

Mutti and Zvi were both with me in the ambulance but, in the style of the time, they were turned back at the door to the hospital.

In those days childbirth was still something that a woman went through alone, and I looked back at them with terror.

'Come back tomorrow,' the nurse told them briskly, leading me away with a steely grip on my elbow.

Mutti was very upset, and clutched Zvi's arm. 'She looks like a sheep being led to the slaughter.'

With little fuss, I was deposited in a room and told to lie down and wait. I did as I was told and wondered what was going to happen. Soon I was gripped by a terrible pain, and I let out a piercing shriek.

The door to my room opened and the nurse said, 'Be quiet, you've got hours to go yet,' and quickly shut the door again.

As the night wore on I shrieked some more and clutched my belly, convinced that this was the worst experience anyone could ever go through and I'd been an idiot to want it so badly. As soon as my baby did emerge though, I changed my mind. She was not the best-looking baby in the whole world at first, and she had jaundice, but as soon as I held her little body in my arms I knew that this was the moment I'd been waiting for.

'I think I'm ready to have my second baby straight away,' I told the nurse, who must have thought I was delirious.

We decided to call her Caroline Ann and over the next few months she blossomed into a beautiful baby, with bright alert eyes and a head of dark hair. Zvi told me that he believed having Caroline changed me fundamentally. It was true: I could feel nothing other than joy about this new, perfect little person. There is something about a newborn baby that symbolises all the optimism in the world – no matter how bleak the past.

A new chapter in my life had begun, and I was soon preoccupied with all the tasks facing a new mother. We realised almost immediately that our little flat wouldn't be big enough for the three of us and we found a big house that we loved in the London suburb of Edgware. The house needed quite a lot of renovation as it had been requisitioned by the army during the war, but Otto helped us with a loan for the down payment and we moved in and started doing it up.

All my initial fears about getting married had proved to be groundless. Zvi was not only a supportive and loving husband, but also a hands-on father; he adored his new daughter and spent hours playing with her and changing her nappies. He even made a full cooked breakfast every morning for our lodger so that I could breastfeed Caroline in peace. Thank goodness I had accepted his marriage proposal, I can't imagine how my life would have been without him.

In those days Edgware was still more like a leafy English village than a London suburb, and although I loved its calm tranquility, I was also feeling lonely. Our house was empty and silent in the daytime, and the streets were usually quiet and deserted. Zvi suggested that I start working as a photographer again, but I was far too timid to get any clients.

When Mutti and Otto arrived to stay I told her about my plan, and she took matters into her own hands. Back then, women left their babies outside in prams on the front lawn to get fresh air, and my mother went door to door every time she spotted a pram, asking other new mothers if they wanted to have some baby pictures taken. Soon I had my first commissions and I started a promising business taking photos of babies and nursery-aged children, developing the photos in a downstairs cupboard that I turned into a darkroom. I was a very good photographer, with a lot of professional experience, but I still lacked confidence in my own abilities.

It was when I branched into wedding photography that disaster struck. I was delighted to accept a commission to photograph a wedding for a local teacher, and I laboured away all day long making sure that I had exactly the right shots. In the 1950s a wedding was the most important occasion in a couple's life, and so you cannot imagine my horror when I finally got into the darkroom to develop the film, and discovered that I had not captured a single photo. The film was entirely blank.

My mind whirled, I literally shook with nerves and I lay awake that night, but I just couldn't think of any solution. After three weeks the newly married bride rang me up to inquire about when her photos might be delivered.

'Actually, I don't really know how to tell you this . . .' I stalled, then took a deep breath. 'I'm sorry but there has been a terrible accident and none of the photos have come out . . .'

I clutched the phone tightly in my hand, waiting for the explosion, but there was a deathly hush. Seconds passed, and I wondered if she had misheard me. Eventually, in a strained voice, she said politely, 'Oh dear, well that is a shame . . . But there's nothing we can do about it, so never mind.'

Later, still stunned, I sat down with Zvi and said, 'Can you imagine if that had been a Jewish wedding?' We both raised our eyebrows thinking of the explosion of emotion that would surely have occurred, followed by much shouting and yelling. These English people were a strange, if pleasant, breed – and they certainly knew how to keep their feelings to themselves.

I liked the English for their quirky individuality, their good manners and patience, and what seemed to me a rather quiet but deeply held dislike of authority and being told what to do. (In this they were the opposite of everything German.) But I still found the British sense of reserve hard to understand.

For as long as I remained crippled by shyness it was apparent that no English woman would run up and befriend me. By now I had given birth to my second daughter, Jacky, and I spent many solitary hours taking the children out to the park, and the local lake. During these outings I spotted one lady on a regular basis, and I hoped she might like to talk to me. It took me a long time to screw up my courage, and however much I prepared myself in advance, I always lost my nerve at the last moment and left without speaking to her.

One day I'd arranged for a babysitter so that I could go into town and, as I left the house, I saw that my neighbour was leaving too. I followed her to the bus stop, planning how I would start the conversation, but as soon I saw the bus rumble in the distance I was gripped with terror. I joined the queue behind her. The bus pulled up, the door opened, and I saw my potential friend step on board. If I was going to speak to her it was now or never, but I couldn't summon up the courage to get on board. Instead, I slid behind a tree and hid there until the bus had gone. It was hopeless.

Thankfully I had managed to make one good friend. Soon after Caroline was born I met a lady called Anita who also had a baby, and we are still friends today. We spent many hours together sitting by the lake in Edgware, rocking our prams and talking about our lives and children. We were close, but I certainly didn't expect Anita to join me for part of a new chapter in my life – in Switzerland. For a time, however, she did join us.

Zvi had been offered a new job working for an Israeli bank in Zurich. It was quite a promotion for him, but I was reluctant to move and start my life again in yet another new country. He promised that we would rent our house and return after a few years, and in the end, I agreed. I was sad to turn my back on Edgware and return to the Continent (even with the enticement of weekend skiing). My one, big, consolation was that I'd be close to Mutti and Otto again – even though I knew that they were fully occupied with their work on *The Diary of Anne Frank*.

23
Otto and Fritzi

I once asked my mother how she could be so happy and in love with Otto, when she had also seemed to be so happy with my father. I didn't want my mother to spend her life alone but, if I'd thought about it, I would have assumed that nothing could replicate the happiness of our family unit, and that no one could take the place of Pappy, who was such a dominant figure.

Mutti told me that they were two different men, each for very different times in her life.

'Evi, when I was a young woman your father was the perfect husband for me,' she explained. 'He was dashing and exciting, and he made all the decisions for us. I never knew what was going to happen the next day, and it was all a big adventure. But I have a different relationship with Otto, it's more equal. We discuss everything and we share everything together and make decisions. Your father was the right husband for me when I was a young woman, and Otto is the right husband for me now that I am older.' Quietly she added, 'We both have suffered so much, and we understand each other perfectly.'

Her explanation made perfect sense, but it still hurt me a little to see how much Mutti and Otto loved each other. No one could ever take Pappy's place in my heart, but I must say that Otto was a wonderful stepfather to me and a loving grandfather to my children. He carried their photos with him in his wallet and would often show them to people, and delight in what they were getting up to.

By now Zvi and I had three girls, Caroline, Jacky and Sylvia, who was born during our time in Switzerland. Every year Mutti and Otto would take one of them away on their own to get to know them as individuals. We always spent our family holidays and Christmas together, too.

I was a fanatical skier and couldn't wait to get to the Alps for winter holidays – but even I liked a lie in sometimes so I didn't welcome Mutti and Otto arriving in our bedroom at the crack of dawn to thump on the end of the bed with a walking stick. Otto would cheerfully shout, 'Time to get up! Everybody up!'

Otto remained a true German in his manner and enthusiasms, and never liked anyone lounging around in bed. 'You can tell he was in the German army,' Zvi would groan, referring to Otto's service in World War One. (He also hated my messiness; when he stayed at our house in London, after we moved back from Switzerland, he would put on overalls and go out and clean the garage, or tidy the garden.)

In the summer Otto and Mutti came with us on family holidays to the beach, first in Cornwall and then in later years, in Tuscany. Otto would pull funny faces and practise gymnastics with the girls on the sand, and we would all go swimming in the sea.

Marrying Mutti had given him a new life, as he once explained to a young woman who wrote to him as she imagined him to be, based on what she knew of his life during and immediately after the war.

All you know about me has happened twenty-six years ago and, though this period was an important part of my life leaving unforgettable marks on my soul, I had to go on, living a new life . . . think of me not only as Anne's father as you know me from the book and play, but also as a man enjoying a new family life and loving his grandchildren.

He certainly did enjoy his family life, and he adored Caroline, Jacky and Sylvia – teaching them to ice skate in Switzerland, organising New Year's games and presents for all the children in the resort, and buying our girls a bike on holiday in Italy so that he could run after them down the dusty roads while they learned to ride.

My daughter Jacky remembers how she used to run into their room in Edgware, 'jump into bed with them, cuddle and listen to Otto tell me stories. He made up wonderful stories and I always wanted to hear the next part.'

Nevertheless, his remarks above strike me as being only part of a more complicated truth. Our new lives always included the ghosts of the people from our original families, and the success of *The Diary of Anne Frank* meant that Anne in particular was to play an important, and sometimes all-consuming, role in our lives.

Otto and Mutti spent practically every waking moment for more than thirty years dealing with issues relating to the publication, or staging, of the diary, and later the administration of Anne Frank Stichting (House and Museum) in Amsterdam and the Anne Frank Foundation in Switzerland – as well as answering a never-ending volume of correspondence from around the world.

First in a little attic flat in Otto's sister's house in Basel, and then in their own house in Birfselden, Otto and my mother would sit down together every day and discuss how to respond to each letter. *The Diary of Anne Frank* struck a deep chord, particularly with the young people who read it, and Otto was determined to answer every one of them. He would pace up and down the floor of their work room, reading out a letter from a seventeen-year-old girl in California who had written to say her parents didn't understand her. 'Now, how do you think we should respond to this?' he'd ask my mother. She would sit, fingers poised over the typewriter, and give such matters a more womanly sense of consideration.

In 1963 Otto and a group of supporters managed to save 263 Prinsengracht from demolition, buying the building and setting up the Anne Frank House in Amsterdam. He was deeply involved in the administration and complicated management of the organisation, even taking a view on the performance of various members of staff. He and Mutti visited the Netherlands at least once a month to oversee everything.

Then there were the various matters arising from the publication of the diary in many countries, and an ongoing battle over the rights for the play with an American writer called Meyer Levin, all of which took their toll on Otto's fragile nerves.

Meyer Levin had met Otto shortly after reading an early edition of the diary, and had written a version of the play that Otto liked. It was a serious and truthful account of the diary, that stressed Anne's Jewish heritage – but theatre producers feared that it would be too sad and sombre for audiences. Meyer Levin failed to find a top theatre producer who would stage his version of the play, and another (much lighter, and less Jewish) version was commissioned by Frances Goodrich and Albert Hackett who had written *The Thin Man*, *Father of the Bride* and *Seven Brides for Seven Brothers*.

Otto's initially friendly relationship with Meyer Levin soured, and Levin pursued Otto through the courts for many years. The case embroiled everyone with whom either Meyer or Otto had dealings, even Eleanor Roosevelt, in a dispute that turned into an insane vendetta. Levin would write angry accusations to newspapers in countries that he knew Otto was about to visit.

In January 1960 Levin wrote to Otto, 'Your behaviour will forever remain a ghastly example of evil returned for good, and of a father's betrayal of a daughter's words.'

The saga of the play had ruined Meyer Levin's life, and left him a broken man. After his death, Levin's daughter wrote that she believed her father had 'lost his moral bearings' in his dispute with Otto, but I had some sympathy for Meyer Levin, despite what he put Otto through. His version of the play was much better, and I thought that there was some truth in his accusation that a plot by the Hacketts and Lillian Hellman had prevented producers from staging it. Overall, the case was a glaring example of the deep feelings, and even madness, that the legacy of Anne Frank would draw out in people – and it was one that would affect my life too, especially after I began to talk about my own experiences.

In addition to the very unpleasant series of court battles with Meyer Levin, Otto was also embroiled in a series of legal cases against anti-Semites and Holocaust deniers who challenged the veracity of the diary, claiming that it was a fake written by either Otto or Meyer Levin.

In 1959, Otto and two publishing houses brought a case to court in Germany against two men, Lothar Stielau and Heinrich Buddeberg, who claimed the diary was a forgery. Three experts were sent to Basel to examine the diary, which they declared was genuine. The case continued until October 1961 when Stielau's lawyers announced that he had changed his mind, as there were 'no grounds for claiming that the diary was a forgery'.

Over the years, however, Otto was forced to defend the diary in court repeatedly, including a well-known battle, starting in 1976, with the Holocaust denier Robert Faurisson. This resulted in a ban on Faurisson's publisher, Heinz Roth of Frankfurt, publishing the pamphlets that claimed the diary was a fake.

These long-running legal battles exhausted Otto, and they were usually accompanied by an increase in anti-Semitic hate mail and personal attacks on his character. The last case had further, unforeseen, consequences when Otto was informed that another team of experts would be arriving from Germany to examine all the material he had in his possession relating to Anne.

Otto, who was already ageing and quite ill by that stage, took this instruction literally and gave one of his best friends, Cor Suijk, some extra unpublished pages from the diary. I think Otto felt these pages were very private, and that by giving them to Suijk he could honestly tell the German authorities that he had handed over to them everything he had in his possession but also keep them a secret.

I'm not sure it was his intention to give these pages to Suijk permanently. Otto was involved in every minute detail of the diary's publication, and liked to keep strict control of it. My view is that he would not have wanted these pages published to the world at large even if the sale proceeds could fund charitable activities on behalf of promoting the diary in the US.

These five pages contained Anne's reflections on her parents' marriage, as well as Anne's belief that Otto never truly loved her mother. They also contained some remarks about her own sexual awareness, and some statements that Otto believed unfairly tarnished all Germans as being Nazis. In total, I believe these passages changed nothing of substance in the diary, and Mutti and I bitterly regretted that they were published, with all the subsequent furore.

The success of the diary brought many wonderful people and events into our lives, too. Otto and Mutti loved to travel and meet the people who had been so touched by Anne's legacy, across the world. Many of these were ordinary young boys and girls, but there were also notable world figures, including John F. Kennedy, then an up-and-coming US senator, who helped organise a benefit performance of the play in New York. Later, as President, he asked his Secretary of Labor to lay a wreath at the house in Amsterdam.

There is also a lovely photo of Otto and Mutti with Audrey Hepburn, who was considered for the part of Anne in the film. Audrey Hepburn grew up in Holland during World War Two and had been deeply affected by seeing the deportation of the Jews, but in the end she couldn't bear to play Anne, saying it would have been an overwhelming experience for her. She was always very moved by Anne's diary and years later, she took part in a musical performance at the Barbican Theatre in London, reading sections of the diary. I met her backstage and we both broke down in tears. We embraced, and I said to her, 'You have brought Anne back to life.'

The Diary of Anne Frank brought with it a tremendous sense of responsibility, and both Otto and my mother were completely dedicated to ensuring that Anne's legacy was protected, and conveyed in an appropriate way. They lived frugally, never taking taxis and eating the simplest of meals. 'The money we make is Anne's money,' Otto would say – and he was determined that no one ever spent lavishly at the expense of the diary. Sometimes I felt that he took this too far. If we went out to dinner with some Anne Frank supporters Otto would pay for their meal, but never for Zvi and me. But Otto was determined to be correct.

There was one issue, however, where Otto admitted he was unfair. In his appointment books and correspondence from before the diary was published he talks frequently about both of his children, making no distinction between Anne and Margot. Perhaps he favoured one over the other, as many parents do, but there is no evidence of it. He often writes about Margot, and her interests and personality. After the success of the diary, however, his thoughts turned almost exclusively to Anne – and he rarely mentioned Margot, or his first wife Edith, except in relation to Anne.

The diary, and Anne's legacy, became his life and – although he was pleasant to everyone – he had little interest in people who were not interested in 'Anne Frank'.

In our own house he often used Anne as an example when he was talking to my children, saying, 'Anne would not have done that . . .' if they had done something wrong, or if he thought they could have behaved differently. I can understand how much he wanted to keep Anne alive by making sure that Caroline, Jacky and Sylvia knew all about her, but sometimes they found this unnerving. Occasionally he would even call one of the girls 'Anne'.

Our youngest daughter, Sylvia, always wanted me to sleep in bed with her when we visited Mutti and Otto's apartment because she felt that it was haunted with a 'spooky' presence.

'For weeks beforehand I dreaded the thought of having to stay in that flat,' she says. 'It was like a museum, and I even called Basel a "ghost town".'

As far as the girls were concerned, Otto was their grandfather, but sometimes they wished they could have him to themselves.

'He did teach us to ice skate and ride a bike,' Sylvia says, 'but I felt that there was a barrier between us. We always knew that somehow our lives took second place to Mutti and Otto's life with Anne Frank. Maybe I was the one who put up that barrier, but I felt that we always had to live up to his expectations of Anne.'

As an adult I could see how much we benefitted from having Otto in our lives. He helped me in so many ways when I was feeling lost in my life, gently steering me in a new direction. I often thought that he must mind that I was alive when his own daughters were not – but I can honestly say that he never conveyed that in all the time that I knew him. He treated me with all the care and attention that he would have done if I were his own flesh and blood.

If I felt any resentment it was sometimes directed at Mutti, not Otto. When Otto helped us with the deposit for our house in Edgware, he asked that he and Mutti could use our front room as their bedroom and study when they visited London. They spent three months of every year with us, and I looked forward to their arrival, eagerly making plans to go out shopping or have lunch with Mutti. Inevitably, though, I was annoyed when these plans were put on hold or cancelled, because they decided to continue working on answering letters or some other issue relating to the diary. I would book a lunch and shopping trip into town and then anxiously watch the morning tick past as Otto and Mutti discussed first one letter then another.

'Are you ready?' I'd ask Mutti, seeing our lunch date slipping away.

'Just one more letter,' she'd say. 'We can still make it to the shops.'

More time would pass, lunch would come and go, and I'd interrupt them again. 'We really have to start making a move,' I'd tell her.

But she would look across the table at Otto, and he'd gesture helplessly at the pile of unanswered letters – and another trip would be cancelled.

Mutti always put her relationship with Otto first, and sometimes I wished I could claim more of her attention.

In 1968, much to my surprise, I discovered that I was pregnant with my fourth child, but the pregnancy was difficult from the start. I had been suffering from colitis, and had gone to see a doctor who subjected me to a horribly painful internal examination.

Later that night I miscarried the baby, and was rushed off to hospital while my friend Anita came round to look after the children. Zvi was away in Israel on business for several weeks – but Mutti and Otto were due to arrive in a few days from a trip to Denmark. I was kept in hospital for a few days, and I was feeling tired, emotional and worried about the girls. It was one of those moments when you want your mother.

'Mutti, please come now and stay with me,' I asked her, over a crackling phone line to Denmark. 'I want you to come, I need you.'

'It's just so difficult,' she told me. 'You know we're supposed to be here for a few more days, and they have the schedule all planned . . . and what would Otto do if I wasn't here . . .'

She arrived three days later, after finishing her visit to Denmark, and on that occasion I really wished that Mutti had put me first.

Despite my resentment over that incident, we had many wonderful times together. We always celebrated my birthday, Otto's birthday (the next day, on 12 May) and Aunt Sylvi's husband Otto's birthday all together at one big party. The children wrote and performed skits, telling lots of jokes to the accompaniment of Mutti's deep, raucous laugh.

Otto remained in remarkably good health until after his ninetieth birthday but by 1980 there were signs that something was wrong. 'I'm not ill,' he told people, 'I'm just tired.'

He didn't know that a doctor had told Mutti months

earlier that he was suffering from a serious case of cancer, and wouldn't survive long.

I visited them during the spring and summer of 1980, and saw how quickly Otto was deteriorating. He still enjoyed company but now only wanted to see one person at a time, and he was becoming very weak. He looked almost hollowed out, with his skin turning a ghastly shade of grey. He struggled on, but in the last few weeks he couldn't get out of bed, and Mutti carried him around the flat. Friends urged her to send him to hospital – but she wouldn't hear of it, insisting that she would look after him at home. As the end neared, his lungs started to fill with water and he had to be admitted for treatment.

With Mutti at his bedside, he died on 20 August.

Otto Frank had become something of a father figure to many of the people who read the diary, and was a great humanitarian who spread a genuine message of tolerance and understanding. His death brought in a flood of condolences, and the Anne Frank Stichting in Holland even considered chartering a plane to fly in the many mourners who wanted to attend the funeral.

Otto was cremated in a simple service, which was unlike Jewish tradition but according to his wishes, and we convened afterwards for a memorial where Mutti played some of Otto's own words that had been recorded for an interview. His calm voice echoed throughout their small home like an otherworldly presence that already knew the role he would play in history.

In his last visit to the Netherlands to commemorate Anne's birthday on 12 June, he had been delighted when Queen Beatrix presented him with the country's highest honour – the *Orde van Oranje-Nassau*. It was a fitting tribute to all of his public endeavours, but his friends and family would also be mourning Otto, the private man. Zvi and I and the children missed him terribly, but my mother was truly lost without him. 'My life is over,' she would say, looking at his portrait hanging in their living room. 'Oh Otto, why did you have to leave me?'

He had managed to preserve the legacy of the past, but also to live in the present. 'I never retrace my steps,' he told one young Anne Frank fan on her way home from a visit, walking her briskly forwards to the next tram stop without looking back.

24

New Beginnings

There is nothing like turning fifty for making you reflect upon your life. Even if this milestone birthday isn't a catalyst for great personal change, you can't help but look back on where you came from, and assess the person you've become. On 11 May 1979 I turned fifty, and when my family gathered to celebrate, Mutti stood up and read a speech.

In a loving and very moving account, she touched on my childhood, largely skimmed over our experiences in the war (which would not have livened up the party) and wrote a paragraph or two that I've already discussed, claiming that I had adjusted well to life in post-war Amsterdam. Then she reflected on the fact that I'd married Zvi, raised three daughters, lived in Switzerland and England, and was now running my own antique shop.

One of my great joys, the births of my grandchildren, still lay ahead but, as Mutti correctly summarised, I had already lived a full life. I had many of the things that women of my generation wanted – my marriage was a very happy one that had stood the test of time (unlike many others that I had seen disintegrate), my daughters were bright and healthy, we had a comfortable income and had built a lovely home, and I had carved out my own identity and profession, first as a photographer and then as an antique dealer.

Yet the thread of the Holocaust, the trauma of Auschwitz and the loss of Pappy and Heinz, was silently woven into all aspects of my life. It had loomed over me in public, reducing me to a shadow of myself; it had trapped me at night in terrible nightmares. It had even come between me and Mutti – we who had been through it together but could never talk about it, or comfort each other. It was part of the fabric of my being, I came to realise, and I began to wonder if I could change.

Living in Switzerland for six years had made me realise how much I disliked authoritarianism, and rules of any kind. We had moved there in 1958 so that Zvi could take up a position with the Israeli bank, Leumi, and we found a nice house in the small village of Pfaffhausen outside Zurich. The children could run around in the open air, sledge every day and ski every weekend, and generally enjoy what could have been an idyllic upbringing.

Despite the beautiful scenery, however, I found that for me, life was not idyllic. The strict bureaucracy that governed all aspects of public life, and the narrow-mindedness of the people themselves, grated on me. We found that, despite being native German speakers, we gravitated towards the expat Americans who lived in our village, and made few Swiss friends.

Rules and regimentation brought out the rebel in me. I parked at will in the old quarter of Zurich and enraged a policeman by ignoring his commands to move my car. What was the worst thing he could do to me? I had already been in a concentration camp. When Jacky was being kept in hospital for an unnecessarily long stay because she refused to eat the only food they would give her – polenta – I gobbled it up and took her home with me. (The renowned Zurich children's hospital only allowed two visiting days per week. It was much more hygienic than England's hospitals, but much less humane.)

Much to everyone's horror, I held up a train by taking the signal board out of the conductor's hand and refused to give it back until Zvi had clambered up the steps to the platform with the luggage, and we were ready to leave. Although I would never deliberately steal anything, I took a relaxed attitude if my small children ate a piece of cheese from the shelf as we were going around a shop, without paying for it. Being stripped of every penny and possession we owned by the Nazis, and fighting for financial restitution for decades afterwards, had left me with a somewhat different view about the sanctity of 'ownership' and private property.

These are not qualities that I would necessarily recommend to other people – especially if you want to stay out of trouble! But this is how I was, and even today, arbitrary man-made rules mean very little to me. It was the 'rules' that made us stitch yellow stars on our coats and sent us off on cattle trucks to our deaths. Where were the 'rules' about compassion, humanity and not killing people, when we needed them?

These were some of my thoughts and feelings but, aged fifty, they remained buried within me, unspoken.

When we returned to our house in Edgware I realised that it was full of signposts to the past but they were somehow never discussed. Paintings by Pappy and Heinz hung on the walls, Mutti and Otto frequently occupied the front room, where Otto even gave talks about Anne to small groups of children. All three of us had our concentration camp numbers tattooed on our arms. Yet I never talked about the Holocaust, and none of my daughters ever asked me.

I was deeply shocked one day when I was taking one of the girls to the doctor and he saw the Auschwitz number on my arm and blurted out, 'May I ask you something personal? Are you normal?'

'What do you mean?' I replied, suddenly struck by anxiety and the self-conscious urge to cover up my arm.

'I mean, how can you be a normal person after all that you've been through?'

I walked out of the surgery in a daze. Maybe I wasn't normal. How could I even tell what normal people were like? I hadn't gone mad, like some Holocaust survivors, but I knew that I felt wrong in myself. It was like a loose wire that was swinging around inside me, and couldn't connect. The only way I knew how to explain it was to say that I wasn't my true self.

On top of this, Zvi had his own traumas to come to terms with. He was such a clever and hard-working man, who had studied and worked his way up from being a poor refugee to become a successful banker, but he still carried with him the anxiety and insecurity of his childhood. One manifestation of this was that he hated crumbs. In Edgware this fixation was so strong that we had a vacuum cleaner plugged into the wall at all times and Zvi would stop almost every meal midway through, and make the girls lift their plates off the dining table so that he could hoover up the crumbs underneath.

Growing up in a house with so much unspoken sadness

and anxiety cannot have been easy for my children, and I think it affected them in different ways.

My middle daughter, Jacky, says she remembers the past as being sort of 'a taboo' but that she thought little about it, other than knowing that Pappy and Heinz had been killed in the war (which was common in a lot of families of our generation).

For her, our family was warm and loving and happy, but another of my daughters told me that in some ways she felt that I was not there for them. I was very hurt to hear this because I always tried to do everything with them, whether that was taking them to school, teaching them to drive (perhaps not to be recommended – Jacky once abandoned the car in the middle of a roundabout and walked home in tears), encouraging Caroline to become the founder of the Jackson Five fan club, or travelling across Europe to be at their bedside if they broke a leg skiing.

My children were the most important people in my life, I loved them dearly and I tried to make their lives as happy as possible – although I was quite strict and I wanted to prepare them for a life that might not always be easy. I knew that Holocaust survivors often spoiled their children with all the love and attention they could give them; sometimes they were too protective. In Israel we knew one woman who would even climb up a tree after her son to feed him a banana.

Zvi worked long hours at the bank during these years, and I really was the glue that held the family together, but perhaps it is true that emotionally, a part of me was absent. Looking back I can see that I was absent from myself.

Luckily I did have help in these years, with visits from

Mutti, Otto and Grandma Helen, before she died in 1963. We also had a series of au pairs, the most successful of whom was a young Swiss girl called Elizabeth Ravasio who arrived in our home aged eighteen and lived with us for many years. She remains a neighbour, close friend and co-worker today. I discovered that Elizabeth was talented at almost anything she turned her hand to, whether that was child rearing, decorating or becoming an excellent sales woman in my antique shop.

My interest in antiques was another development that Otto played a big part in. His sister Leni owned a beautiful antique shop in Basel, and she encouraged me to help her find pieces to sell. She took me round the silver vaults in London, and, as my interest grew, taught me about running a business of my own.

Edgware Antiques opened its doors in 1972 and Elizabeth and I made a formidable team. I had always been good at mending things, and I took extra classes in wood and porcelain restoration. Our trade became bigger and more organised, and I became well known as Edgware's only antique dealer. We sold mostly to other dealers, and while Elizabeth worked with the customers, I hit the road and scoured the Home Counties around London for many of the historic and fascinating items that were being cleared out in house clearances. I prided myself on being able to repair a wooden writing desk, source twenty grandfather clocks or sort through a filthy house until I found a hidden gem. Once, I unearthed a series of valuable Victorian porcelain dolls wrapped up in old towels and hidden in a corner. On occasion a dealer would turn up and buy every piece in the shop, and we would have to start again from scratch.

I'd been a good photographer, but antiques were my passion and I became knowledgeable and astute. The shop flourished for many years and, as the business changed, we moved into antique fairs, too. My best buy was a Dutch Jacob Israel tile that I found in a junk shop on Harrow Road. I paid nine pounds for it, and the very next day I had a phone call from an Oxford professor who'd also had his eye on it. He offered me one hundred, two hundred – up to two thousands pounds to sell it to him, but I liked it and I wanted to keep it for myself.

I'd found the perfect career. I'd always liked a bit of a gamble, and I think I inherited some of Pappy's flair for business. I was certainly never short of ideas, and had the same initiative that Mutti and Grandma Helen had shown when they started their own businesses in Amsterdam and Darwen, after the war. They too had once been quiet young women, under the thumb of other people in the household, but once they had to go out and show what they were made of, they never looked back. I'm sure neither of them had the time or inclination to wonder whether they were feminists, but boy, were they two tough, enterprising ladies!

By the early 1980s I had matured into a successful woman who ran my own business and was immensely proud of my likeable and accomplished daughters, each fulfilling their own talents. Inside though, I was still the same traumatised teenager who had been liberated from Auschwitz in 1945. By now, Zvi was the manager of Bank Leumi in London, and we often entertained, throwing big dinner parties and drinks receptions. I wondered if any of those people realised how terrified and insecure I felt while I smiled and chatted? Deep down I wrestled with the question: would I ever be able confront my fears and come to terms with the past? As I entered my fifties I had no idea that a new stage in my life was starting, or the magnitude of the change that was about to come.

25
One Day in Spring

The day that changed my life nearly didn't happen.

In 1985 the Anne Frank House in Amsterdam staged three hugely successful exhibitions about Anne's life and legacy in New York, Frankfurt and Amsterdam. Two young members of staff, Jan Eric Dubbelman and historian Dienke Hondius, working under director Cor Suijk, were enthusiastic about spreading the scope of the exhibit further, but the trustees of the Anne Frank House were not so sure. The exhibition was expensive, and, forty years after liberation, they felt that there might be 'insufficient interest'.

Fortunately Jan Eric and Dienke were passionate about their mission. The exhibition had already been translated into English for the American visit, and a dual language version in Amsterdam – so the UK seemed like the obvious next port of call. Short of funds but full of determination, Jan Eric arrived in London, and set up a temporary home in an Islington squat. Riding around London like a fiend on his lady's bicycle, he started to spread the word, identifying Labour Party-controlled councils that he thought might be sympathetic to the meaning of the exhibit.

'I quickly found out that there was more than "sufficient interest" in holding the exhibition,' Jan Eric says. Soon he had a list of about ten councils across the UK that would be keen to host the exhibit – starting with the GLC in London.

The card inviting me to the opening dropped through my letterbox at 49 Dorset Drive, looking small and innocuous. I thought the exhibition was an excellent idea: *The Diary of Anne Frank* had sold millions of copies in some countries and spawned Anne Frank clubs, Anne Frank libraries, Anne Frank streets, and even, in the 1960s, an Anne Frank village for displaced persons near Wuppertal in Germany. The diary had sold less well in other countries, though, including the UK, and I felt that people were still reluctant to hear about the Holocaust. I also believed that the lessons of the Holocaust continued to be relevant: by the mid-1980s the Cold War, Apartheid and conflicts from Central America to Northern Ireland, were raging. It seemed like a good time to continue a discussion about tolerance and human understanding.

Even so, I woke up on the morning of 12 February 1986 with no idea that it would be a turning point in my life. Zvi brought me a cup of tea in bed, as he did every morning, and then left for work. I put on my dressing gown, went downstairs, turned on the radio and poured out bowls of cereal for Mutti and myself. Soon she appeared in the kitchen too, and we sat down and started chatting about what we would wear. I was blissfully unaware that I would return to Edgware that evening deeply shaken – and profoundly changed.

I remember very little about speaking at that first Anne Frank Exhibition – only the shock of Ken Livingstone ushering me to my feet and onto a small stage, and then looking out into the crowd and seeing Mutti, Jacky and Caroline, who had come with a big group of her friends, watching me with nervous anticipation. The next hour or so was a blur, but after I'd finished speaking they gathered around me. Mutti eagerly patted my shoulder, saying, 'Well done, well done!' Strangers approached to thank me or comment on what I'd said and I answered them in a heady daze of relief and adrenalin, not even knowing what I'd told them.

I left feeling that I was walking on a precipice between my present life and the one I had left behind. Suddenly my mind was full of memories of Pappy and Heinz, our life in Amsterdam, the terrible train journey to Auschwitz and then saying goodbye on the ramp. I could remember how cold and dirty it had been in Birkenau, the frostbite cutting into my toes and the pain of starvation. I felt the shock and terror on turning around and seeing Mutti being led away to what we believed was her death in the gas chambers. I hadn't thought about these memories for years, I had pushed them away – I hoped – for ever. Now I had let my story tumble out, and I couldn't stop the memories even if I wanted to.

'Today was an amazing day,' I told Zvi later. We'd climbed into bed, exhausted; the house was finally quiet. 'I was terrified when they asked me to talk, I don't even know where the words came from. Then people asked me questions – I never really thought that anyone was interested. Now I have to do it all over again, though; the exhibition is going around the country, and they want me to be there.'

I was lying in my own bed, surrounded by everything familiar – the antique chest of drawers that I loved, the grey curtains with the small pink roses that glowed when the sun shone through them in the morning – but now it all looked different. Telling my story had terrified me, excited me and left me drained. I couldn't imagine having to repeat the experience. What would I say?

'I'll help you,' Zvi said. 'We'll work out what you're going to say, and I'll type it up for you.'

And that was what we did. Just as Mutti and Otto had worked together on their letters, Zvi pulled out our old typewriter and started to piece together my story.

'But there isn't any feeling in it!' I protested, waving the first draft in Zvi's face. 'This is too factual. What about how scared I was, how lonely I felt? How devastated we were when we said goodbye?'

'I'm a factual person!' Zvi replied, shrugging.

I had to agree that it wasn't his fault that he couldn't convey the depth, or range, of emotions I'd been through, especially since I'd hadn't explored them myself. I tried to work a bit more feeling into the typed words in front of me, and approached the forthcoming exhibitions with great apprehension.

We took the exhibition to several towns and cities, but two openings stick in my mind. Leeds was a city I knew well as Sylvia had studied there. Back then, the Thatcher years of high unemployment and the miners' strike had both taken a heavy toll on Yorkshire, and the city was looking like it had seen better days.

I stayed in the home of one of the local organising committee members. It reminded me of the northern semi-detached house that my grandparents and aunt and uncle had moved to in Darwen, and I could feel the damp chill of an English spring seeping through the bedroom wall.

Many Jewish people came to the event, but a lot of ordinary local, working-class people came, too. Back then the Holocaust wasn't as widely discussed as today, and it was a very emotional afternoon for all of us.

I also remember visiting Aberdeen, a solid stone city that I had never been to before, and where the thick Scottish brogue meant that I sometimes found it difficult to understand the questions! Despite the chilly northern climate, the people of Aberdeen supported the event wholeheartedly, and I particularly remember a young girl who had composed some music and a poem. She performed it very movingly, and we kept in touch and wrote to each other for many years.

As I travelled across the UK I made many new friends. I had never encountered anti-Semitism in Britain (although I know that it exists, just as it does elsewhere) but I had been hurt over the years by comments about 'bloody foreigners', which used to be directed at anyone with a different skin colour or accent. Now I felt that I really connected with the British people, who were so willing to find out about the Holocaust. I was touched that they responded with such genuine feeling to my experiences.

Of course many of the people who came were Jewish, but as word of the exhibition spread, all sorts of different groups including women's groups, army organisations and churches asked me to speak to them.

Even using Zvi's typed speeches, these first events were a torture for me – and possibly for the audience, too. I've always found it difficult to read from a sheet of paper, and I sounded stilted and far removed from my own personal story. I found it impossible to speak freely, to look people in the eye and relax, knowing that my story would unfold in a natural way, just as it should. I realised that if I was going to continue speaking I was going to have find out what it was I really had to say – and so I began to use Zvi's words less, and my own words more.

In those early days it wasn't just the ordeal of public speaking that I found so difficult, it was reliving the events themselves. After I'd spoken, people asked me all kinds of questions, and I tried to think about them and answer each one properly. There were personal questions, as well as moral and philosophical ones. Did I wish that I had not been Jewish? Did I still believe in God? Could I ever forgive the Nazis or Germany? Had the guards at Auschwitz ever raped women prisoners? How had I managed to survive my ordeal without going mad?

Every night I would lie in bed, gripped in a sleepless turmoil brought on by these questions and my memories of the past.

One evening, while Zvi and I were out for dinner with friends, a way forward appeared.

'We don't know anything about your story,' my friend Anita said. 'Please tell us about it, we'd like to know.'

Hesitantly I started to talk in a more personal way about what had happened to me, and Zvi and Anita and her husband sat transfixed. At the end, I took a gulp of my drink, and Anita said, 'Eva, I think you should write all that down.'

At the time there were only a few books available from people who had survived the Holocaust, and I had never thought that my story would be amongst them. Would anyone really think I had something worthwhile to say? I approached a well-known London literary agent called Andrew Nurnberg, and after he'd listened to me for a few minutes he assured me that he thought we could find a publisher for my story.

I knew that it was going to be hard enough recounting all my painful memories, and I was not a writer, so I approached the mother of one of Jacky's school friends, a teacher called Evelyn Kent. I wasn't sure if she'd be interested in helping me write a book, but as soon as I asked her, rather awkwardly, she said, 'Eva, I've been waiting for years for you to ask me to write your story.'

So we began. Evelyn bought one of the first computers and every evening, at about eight o'clock, I would go over to her house and talk and talk – and she would type and type. We would work to an exhausted conclusion by about midnight and then I would leave, walking home in the cold black night full of a strange elation from talking about things I'd kept trapped inside me for so long. It was terrifying, and wonderful – and sad.

After two years we finally finished the manuscript for *Eva's Story* and Andrew Nurnburg secured a publishing deal in the UK with W.H. Allen. The book was a gritty, raw account of the details of my time in Auschwitz, and I wasn't sure how people would react to it. Would they want to know what it was like to have a bucket of faeces thrown over you, or how it felt to wake up in your bunk next to a stiff, dead body?

Having witnessed Otto's lengthy problems over the years, first with Meyer Levin, then with Holocaust deniers and even people who claimed that he wrote the diary himself, I knew that taking a more high-profile role in the world of 'Anne Frank' would be difficult. Of course, I had known Anne before we went into hiding, and Otto later became my stepfather – making me Anne's posthumous stepsister, but, despite this, I knew that I would be attacked by people claiming that I wanted to jump on the 'Anne Frank bandwagon'.

Otto had often been (very unfairly) accused of profiting from his daughter's death. I knew that this was completely untrue, and not at all his motivation, but people had said the most vile and hideous things about him. It had made me question even further whether human beings had any fundamental decency.

As I feared, some people said the same about me. One woman claimed I had not even known Anne as a child, pointing out that I had got the colour of Anne's cat wrong. Otto's friends, and testimony from Otto himself when he was alive, proved that I had known Anne and that the basis of this claim was complete nonsense – but I admitted that I had got the colour of the cat wrong. When we were writing about it I told Evelyn that I couldn't remember what colour the cat was. She had a big tabby cat herself and said, 'Well, could it have been tabby?' I shrugged and said that it could have been. We later learned that the cat was black. Such are the kind of details that have often been bitterly fought over in the legacy of Anne Frank.

Despite such claims, the publication of *Eva's Story* was a huge success, and I was whisked around the country in a sports car by a young man from the publishing company. The media were particularly interested in the fact that I'd survived Auschwitz with Mutti, and we appeared together on breakfast television with Selina Scott (then a big celebrity). I also spoke on BBC Radio 4 *Woman's Hour*, talked to countless local newspapers and signed copies in bookshops across Britain.

Reading the book was a personal, and painful, experience

for my family. I'd talked to my mother about the details of each chapter while I was writing it, and she was very proud of the final story – even contributing two chapters herself about her selection for the gas chamber in Auschwitz and then her separation from me on the train to Russia. We'd lived it together. Zvi was moved, and sometimes amazed by the details I revealed, seeing a deeper side to the woman he'd married.

I think it was my children who struggled most with the book, particularly reading about a past I'd never discussed with them. One of my daughters told me that she didn't want to read *Eva's Story*, but later I saw a copy open, midway through, on her bedside table. She didn't want me to realise that she knew what I'd been through.

For me the book was a fitting conclusion to an outpouring of painful memories that had taken me on a difficult and emotional journey. Some of the grim details of life in Auschwitz had previously been harshly imprinted on my brain, and I found that I could now let go of them. They never vanished completely, but they seemed less vivid. They were the past. What never diminished, however, was the sense of grief I felt over the displacement of my family – and the loss of Pappy and Heinz. Those feelings have remained with me for my whole life.

After writing *Eva's Story* I realised that I really wanted to tell the world something about Heinz. 'Everyone remembers Anne,' Mutti would say, 'but Heinz was a talented young man too – and his life was cut short. It's as if no one remembers it.' It took a long time for this hope to come to fruition, but many years after the publication of *Eva's Story* I set about writing a book for young people called *The Promise* with my friend Barbara Powers. *The Promise* told many stories about Heinz and included his poetry and paintings. An Ohio playwright and theatre director Jack Ballantyne liked the book so much he decided that he wanted to write a new play called *A Light in the Darkness* inspired by the story.

Now that I was speaking more, and writing, I began to lose interest in the antique business. I wanted my new experiences to be meaningful, though, not just an emotional release for me.

I have to report that there were some notable disasters along the way. After the American edition of my book was published by St Martin's Press, a group from St Petersburg, Florida, invited me over to speak to them. It was my first speaking engagement in America and I was incredibly excited and nervous.

I flew over with Elizabeth Ravasio and we waited anxiously at our hotel to find out what was going to happen. I think I expected someone to arrive in person, tell me all about what the evening would entail and calm my nerves – but no one appeared. Eventually someone drove over and left a note for us about when we'd be picked up – but nothing about the evening itself. Two days passed and my anxiety grew. On the night of the speech we arrived at the venue and our host told us that I was a 'surprise speaker' – guiding me towards what seemed like a cupboard, where I had to wait until I was announced.

I reassured myself by imagining that a small group of friendly people was waiting on the other side of the door. Then the host returned and ushered me into a packed auditorium full of hundreds of people eagerly waiting to hear what this lady, who'd flown all the way from England, had to tell them.

My mind went totally blank and my throat dried up. I took a deep breath and hurried through a brief version of my story. A very brief version. Then I ran out of things to say. I looked at the clock. Although it felt as if hours had passed, I had only been speaking for ten minutes!

'Well, that is my story. Thank you very much,' I concluded, and walked off – leaving the audience watching me speechlessly.

After that I took advice and tried noting down the main points of what I wanted to say – but that didn't work either as when I stood up to speak I could never remember what had connected the points, or how to get from one point to another.

The only option was to continue to slowly try and piece together my own story, as I wanted to tell it, with some hiccups along the way – and trust the audience to under-stand that we were having an experience together. Now I never write down what I'm going to say in advance, so I can never repeat it, and I've found that this leaves me room for my story to develop. I can tell people how my reflections on the past are changing, and I've found that they really connect with me when I talk to them, almost as friends, and explain to them what my story means to me at that very moment.

Telling my story was one way of spreading a message about prejudice and tolerance, but I also wanted to work with other people to build something that would hopefully outlast the memories of individual survivors themselves.

One area in which I knew that I could put my experience

to good use was the foundation of the Anne Frank Trust in the UK. Running a touring exhibition from Amsterdam was proving expensive and complicated, especially as it was now so much in demand. Jan Eric brought together a small group of us in the UK to run the exhibition, but at first we couldn't find the right people to help expand our operation. It wasn't until we took the exhibition to Bournemouth in April 1989 that I met three people who would form the core of the Anne Frank Trust for many years.

Bee Klug, an acquaintance of mine, became Honorary Life President. Rabbi David Soetendorp (the son of the Rabbi who presided over the synagogue Mutti and Otto had attended in Amsterdam) took on the role of founding Chair. He also introduced us to an enthusiastic young woman called Gillian Walnes, who agreed to be our first Secretary, and then became the founding Executive Director. Gillian set about running the trust with enormous energy and dedication and she is still in her post today. Together we have seen the work of the Anne Frank Trust spread across the country, from cathedrals to prisons – reaching millions of people.

Establishing the Trust in the UK and touring the country to talk about my experiences gave me an immense sense of purpose and satisfaction. I could hardly imagine more – but a new, and completely unexpected, element of my story was about to emerge: a play about my life.

26
The Play

This is a play about questions. Some of the questions seem unspeakable. Admittedly many of the questions are unanswerable. Even so, that doesn't diminish the importance of asking the questions.

James Still, author of *And Then They Came For Me: Remembering the World of Anne Frank*

Watching an actress play you on stage can be an unsettling experience: will she look like you, talk like you, embody something essential about your personality? Can you connect with this person; will she even reveal a side of your own personality that you hadn't been aware of? Or will she be a stranger? Just a woman on stage acting out a character that you don't recognise.

Despite his long-standing commitment to staging a play, and then a film of *The Diary of Anne Frank*, Otto never watched a single performance. He couldn't bear the thought that actresses would be saying the words he once heard Anne and Margot speak, pretending to be the children that he would never see again. I wondered if I would have the same reaction when I was approached to be involved in a new production about friends of Anne Frank and the legacy of the Holocaust.

As the Resident Director at the George Street Playhouse in New Brunswick, New Jersey, Susan Kerner saw the deep impact that her 1994 production of *The Diary of Anne Frank* had on its young audiences. She started to wonder if a new piece of theatre would place the Holocaust in a broader context. She initiated the project with Kristen Golden and Stephen Mosel of Young Audiences New Jersey, and they commissioned a well-known playwright called James Still to start working on it.

Susan asked me if I would like my family's story to feature in the play, along with that of another friend of Anne's, Ed Silverberg (who appeared in the diary as 'Hello' Silberberg). She also asked Barbara Lederman, Susanne Lederman's sister, but she did not want to be involved.

After thinking it over and discussing it with Zvi and Mutti, I decided that this sounded like a very exciting and worthwhile project. 'A lot of the young people I meet through the exhibition really don't know much about the Holocaust,' I told Zvi. 'Maybe a play like this would help them understand more, and even give them a feeling of connection to it. After all, although they think it is ancient history, we know that it wasn't so very long ago.'

Soon after I agreed to take part, James Still flew to London and we met for long afternoon sessions, talking about the past and my experiences. He explained that this wasn't going to be an ordinary play. Although actors and actresses would play our characters from the 1940s, the scenes would also be intercut with projections of real-life interviews with Ed and me.

James worked on the script for two years, sending new drafts back to me for my comments. At one point he told me he had seven hours of material that he had to condense down into one hour. He also had to rework the script around our filmed interviews. James didn't want us to read from a script but to answer the questions naturally. Of course, we always managed to answer them in ways that took him by surprise, and so he constantly had to rewrite the draft.

Finally, in 1996, we had a script and production that we were all happy with. *And Then They Came For Me: Remembering the World of Anne Frank* was first produced at the Indiana Repertory Theater in October 1996, and then premièred at the George Street Playhouse in New Brunswick in November 1996.

Susan Kerner had asked me to fly over to see a final rehearsal and Zvi and I arrived in New Jersey the day before, anxiously wondering what the final production would be like.

Ed Silverberg, Susan and James were there too, as well as a cameraman who was recording the rehearsal. We sat down, silently, and the actors and actresses appeared on stage. For the whole hour it felt like we were collectively holding our breath as we were transported back to the terrible tension and drama of those days. My heart thudded loudly when I heard the words I'd once listened to from Pappy and Heinz.

None of the characters looked anything like we did in real life – it was a colour-blind casting in which the actress playing Anne Frank was of Korean descent and Pappy was played by an African-American actor. No one had told me about this in advance, and I was very surprised at first. It worked wonderfully well in emphasising the essential message of humanity however, as within moments I'd forgotten the ethnic background of the actors and was totally absorbed in the characters and the story.

I found it terribly difficult to sit through some of the scenes featuring my own family's story, and if James Still hadn't created a perfect balance between the tension of those scenes with lighter moments – and scenes with Ed – I might have found it unbearable.

When the play finished I let out a deep breath, relieved that James and Susan had crafted such a beautiful, perfectly balanced piece of theatre. I was crying, and when I looked around I saw that Zvi, James, Susan and Ed were all crying, too. Even the cameraman was sobbing. I understood then the power of theatre. It can be unpredictable, it can fail; but only theatre can bring people together in such a way to share a live experience.

After the try-out in Indiana I returned to New Brunswick with Elizabeth Ravasio for the play's six-week run. I was grateful to be involved with such a successful production and moved to be meeting and talking with so many Americans who opened their hearts to me.

Over the next few years I travelled widely across the US, taking part in many different productions of *And Then They Came For Me*. The play was staged in some exciting locations, like the Kennedy Center in Washington DC, but it was the people I met in the small towns, church halls and school gymnasiums across the country that have touched me most.

In Atlanta, the Georgia Ensemble Theater have staged the play for many years. I visited often, receiving an honour in the State Senate and taking part in a statewide tour of Georgia.

Walking up the steps to speak in the State Senate was an experience I will never forget. Trumpeters heralded my arrival and I entered a packed chamber where hundreds of politicians were waiting to listen to me. I had a typed speech in my hand, but as soon as I saw them I knew that I couldn't deliver it. I put the speech to one side and looked them in the eye as I told them, speaking directly from my heart, about my experiences. Later Elizabeth Ravasio, who was travelling with me, said, 'Eva, that was your best speech – you should always speak like that.' And my typed speeches were finally relegated to history.

In the South, many white people came up to me and told me about their bitterness at losing the Civil War and their hatred towards the 'Yankees'. 'But it was so long ago,' I would reply, confused. 'Surely it must have been before even your grandparents' lifetimes.' Even so, they couldn't forgive, they told me. I also met many African-American people in the South who told me about how much *they* had suffered – and how deeply they understood my message about discrimination and prejudice.

The meaning of the play seemed to affect anyone touched by war or discrimination. I met a Vietnam veteran who approached me after one performance and told me about the horrors he had seen, and how he couldn't forget them. I told him that these things do fade over time. I also met families who had adopted Vietnamese and Cambodian children who had come to America as refugees after that war, and helped those children rebuild new, loving homes.

As I travelled I realised what an important role drama plays in US high schools, with even rural schools having large well-equipped theatres capable of staging professional productions.

I sat in some of these schools and tried to explain the Holocaust to teenagers who struggled to comprehend what I was telling them.

'Were you allowed to take your cat or dog with you?' one boy asked, while a girl put up her hand and said, 'What did you do on a Sunday?'

I had to carefully explain that a concentration camp was in no way similar to their own experiences of going to summer camp, telling them that when I arrived at Auschwitz I was not supposed to leave alive.

My time in America brought me into contact with people of every background and race, from small church groups in Texas to a large fundraiser for the Dallas Children's Theater at the famous Petroleum Club, and Oklahoma Native Americans who told me they believed their people had been through the same experience of discrimination and genocide as mine.

In Boston the play was staged at the same time as a Broadway try-out for a new, hotly anticipated Wendy Kasselman version of *The Diary of Anne Frank*. Many preferred *And Then They Came For Me*. Judith Klein wrote in Boston's *Jewish Journal*, 'The stark reality struck me as no production of *The Diary of Anne Frank* ever has. It was stunning and brought tears to my eyes, and those of others around me.'

One young girl with a terminal disease was stretchered into the theatre to see a performance as her last wish, and her family said it made the last two weeks of her life more bearable.

On another night a young German woman stood up and started crying. She said her grandfather had been a Nazi, and his brother had been in the Resistance. Her grandfather had shot and killed his brother – and the family had never come to terms with it. She had left Germany to get away from her family past, and until that night she had never spoken about it to anyone.

In Philadelphia I was delighted when we staged the play at the Arden Children's Theater and the National Liberty Museum asked to complement the performance with an exhibition of Heinz's paintings. This also happened in other cities, including Dallas and California. To see Heinz's paintings on display after fifty years brought a lump to my throat. I'm glad that people let me look at them quietly on my own, because I don't think I could have spoken to anyone. I thought, 'You see, Heinz, I haven't forgotten you. You were frightened that you wouldn't make your mark on the world – but you are still with us. You have made your debut.'

In San Francisco, *And Then They Came For Me* has been staged successfully for many years by the New Conservatory Theater, and it has always received huge support from the gay community. Gay people were of course persecuted by the Nazis, too, and have suffered so much discrimination since. One of the directors, Andrew, has often put us up in the home he shares with his partner, James – which I have to say is the most beautifully decorated house I've ever visited! I fell in love with San Francisco's tolerant *joie de vivre*, and once sent Zvi packing to a bookstore so that I could enjoy myself at Gay Pride and a 'leather fest' without his grumbling.

In Hailey, Idaho, we staged the play for two weeks in 2001 with the help of a Hollywood celebrity – Demi Moore.

Demi and Bruce Willis had taken a prominent role in the life of Hailey after buying a large ranch nearby. They had also bought and restored the Liberty Theater, setting up a permanent theatre company called the Company of Fools. We stayed in Demi's house in town, which Bruce Willis had built to house her doll collection. It looked like a traditional nineteenth-century American home, and it was delightful – apart from the rather disconcerting life-size model of a naked Demi holding her pregnant belly, just as she did in the famous *Vanity Fair* cover shoot.

We met Demi almost every day, with her three daughters, and she took an active role in staging the play and helping out with the costumes. In breaks we would talk about my experiences, and how hard she found her own upbringing. I liked her tremendously, and our experience was only slightly marred by an argument at the final after-show party. Demi and Bruce (who by then were separated, and both had new partners) hosted a lavish party for us at their house in town, and I brought a friend of mine who lived in Idaho. I'd told her that there was a strict rule against taking photos in the house, but my friend ignored this and started snapping away. Soon Demi got wind of this and confronted her, demanding that she hand over the film.

It was all very awkward. I was mortified that Demi was upset and felt that we had abused her trust, especially as I greatly appreciated her efforts on behalf of the play. We managed to resolve things, though, and we parted good friends.

One night, during our stay in Idaho, we drove to Boise so that I could give a talk at the Egyptian Theater. When I arrived I was amazed to see my name up in lights, proclaiming

'*The Eva Schloss Story*' and I felt a flutter of nerves as I walked in to a full auditorium with more than 800 people. As we sat waiting, even more people arrived, standing in the gangways and out on the fire escape – until finally the police and fire service arrived to make sure that the evening went off safely.

I was touched and surprised that the people of a rural state in the western part of the US would be interested in the Holocaust. When local people raised money to build the Idaho Anne Frank Human Rights Memorial Park in Boise I was delighted to plant a tree, as did Miep Gies.

Travelling with *And Then They Came For Me: Remembering the World of Anne Frank* has truly been a gift to me. I've met so many new people, and hearing about their moving experiences in response, has made me reflect on my own. In particular, it's enabled me to connect to a younger generation. Most recently, I've worked with a British Muslim anti-hate campaigner, Nic Careem, who has taken the play to school groups in the UK, as well countries as far away as China.

Everywhere I travelled I met young people willing to engage with the issues and the emotion of the play, and this often had quite a profound impact on their thoughts about the world. This was particularly true in countries where people had experienced oppressive government, or where they had not come to terms with their own experiences of the Holocaust.

Jenny Culank was the first British producer of the play. Jenny was the artistic director of the Classworks Theatre in Cambridge. She'd been keen to stage *And Then They Came For Me* ever since seeing the first production at the Gatehouse Theatre in London, organised by Susan Kerner. We worked together on some fantastic productions with young people in Britain, and then in spring 2000 the call came from the Anne Frank House in Amsterdam: they'd received funding from the EU and wanted to know if we could stage the play in Latvia, with the aim of improving the relationship between ethnic Latvians and Russians.

After breaking free of Soviet occupation in 1991, Latvia was beginning a very tentative discussion about its role in the Holocaust. The Nazis had invaded and occupied Latvia for four years between 1941 and 1945, and almost all Latvian Jews had been murdered immediately. In addition, tens of thousands of Jews from Germany and Austria were brought to Latvia to be murdered – including Zvi's grandmother. The Nazi death squads that roamed the Baltic countries were particularly vicious. In fact, some SS soldiers were so traumatised by carrying out the killings that top Nazi leaders were inspired to introduce gassing as a less personal method of murder. But local anti-Semitism was also very strong and many Latvian people actively supported the genocide.

Forty-five years later a debate about the Holocaust in the Baltics had barely begun. The International Department of the Anne Frank House decided that Latvia would be a good location for their programme to encourage talking about the Holocaust in communities where it was not widely discussed.

It was tough. At first the young cast, made up of six Latvian girls and six Russian boys, were barely aware that the Holocaust had taken place.

For Jenny it was a particularly poignant experience – some of her own family had immigrated to Britain from the Latvian Jewish community.

'I showed them a photo of my Latvian grandmother, and they just couldn't comprehend it. How had this English woman got Latvian relatives? They had been shut away in the Soviet Union and had no sense of the wider world.'

The young people spent several weeks staying in a remote farmhouse with Jenny, preparing for the production. 'I wasn't sure at first if they would be able to get into the play, or if they would be able to immerse themselves in the process. I asked them to keep a diary, like Anne, and they all did.'

I was due to fly out and join them for the production, but midway through their rehearsals Jenny called and asked me if I would speak to them on the phone. I wasn't sure what we would find to say, but they all lined up to talk to me and each of them asked questions, shared stories and took the time to get to know me.

By the time I flew out in August, Jenny had told me that she was sure this was going to be one of the most meaningful productions she'd ever staged. Latvia was still a country that was very unwilling to confront its past, and what had happened to the Jews. Each of the young people taking part in the play was deeply affected by having to learn the truth.

We arrived at the Jewish Centre in Riga for the first performance, which was being attended by the Latvian President. The evening began with the Russian and Latvian parents giving each other bunches of flowers – quite a gesture in a country where that ethnic divide is very strong.

James Still, the playwright, had arrived too, and we all sat through the play – not understanding a word of the language, but feeling deeply connected to what was happening on stage. At the end I spoke to the audience, as I always do, with my usual sense of amazement that bringing people together to talk and share can change hearts and minds.

I knew that some of the older people looking back at me would have known people who killed Jews – or had perhaps even been involved in killing Jews themselves. More than anything I was struck by meeting one boy in the group who couldn't bring himself to admit to me that he was Jewish, too. The stigma was still too strong. I hope that he heard me tell him how proud I am to be Jewish, and felt my support for him.

After that first show in Riga, Jenny and I travelled to the south-eastern city of Daugavpils where the play was staged in a huge derelict factory, once used to manufacture Russian cigarettes. I remember there was high unemployment at the time and they suffered from social problems. Then I left the young cast and wished them well. The play would continue to tour across Latvia for a year, with performances taking place every weekend in different towns.

Before I left Latvia I indulged my old hobby, and visited some of Riga's antique shops. In one I found a perfectly preserved porcelain plate from Hitler's Berlin Olympics in 1936. Turning the cold china over in my hand I chatted with the German man who was selling it to me – and remembered all the hate and turmoil that had consumed Europe back then. I imagined my own family – still at home in our apartment in Vienna and unaware of what the future would bring. I paid for the plate and left with a strong sense of how far we have come in the world in a few short years – and how far we still have to go.

Jenny also staged a memorable production of *And Then They Came For Me* in Northern Ireland in 1999, bringing Catholic and Protestant children together to see the play – which was highly unusual. They sat apart, in their own groups, but it was a big step forward that they were even in the same room.

Everywhere we went, the play was staged in front of packed audiences who were often moved to tears by the performance. Only one person didn't understand *And Then They Came For Me* – Mutti.

I had returned from the first run in New Brunswick with a video of the show. Back home in Edgware, I pushed it into the video recorder and settled down, expecting to have a long chat with her about the performance. Almost immediately, though, she started frowning with confusion. 'But that's not Heinz,' she said. 'And that's not Pappy. That's not us.'

As the play went on she became agitated, and upset. By that stage of her life she was becoming increasingly confused, and she couldn't understand that I'd told her it would be our family – and yet it wasn't our family at all. With great sadness I realised that although Mutti and I had been inseparable for our long, lifetime's journey together, old age was parting us and I would soon be taking the next steps without her.

27
Mutti

S tarting to speak out undoubtedly transformed my life, and freed me to reclaim my true self – but it also changed how other people in my life saw me. Especially Mutti.

As I spoke to groups of people, Mutti would often sit in the front row, or just behind me, looking on with an expression of awe and adoration. I could tell that she was immensely proud of me, and I felt that at last she appreciated that I had gifts, too. I was not only 'practical' and 'handy'. Now she could see who I really was.

Apart from that turbulent time immediately after the war in Amsterdam and my resentment that she wasn't with me after my miscarriage, Mutti and I had the closest relationship, but she still saw me as her 'little Evi'.

When you have more than one child it's almost inevitable that, as you watch them grow up, you label them the 'rebellious one', or the 'sporty one'. And quite often, as children, we come to dislike or disagree with the labels that our parents have assigned us.

In our family, Heinz was the 'clever one', as well as the sensitive and artistic one. I was the athletic, tough little girl who was good with my hands. Of course Heinz *was* very intelligent, sensitive and artistic – but as I got older I started to believe that there was more to me than Mutti sometimes appreciated.

When we first visited my grandparents in Darwen after the war I heard Mutti tell Grandma Helen, 'I think Eva will be a dressmaker when she grows up, she's good with her hands.' I was horrified. I thought, 'I don't want to be a dressmaker!' Later she agreed with Otto, and steered me in the direction of photography. It turned out to be a career I enjoyed very much, but I still bristled when I heard Mutti tell people that I wasn't very intellectual.

For the first few years after Otto passed away I worried that Mutti seemed very lost and depressed, but eventually she started to recover. She spent more time with us, but she wanted to keep her main home in Switzerland. Otto had bought a bungalow for her just around the corner from our house in Edgware, but Mutti didn't want to live there. She'd made her home in Switzerland and she had lots of friends there. During the day she went to talks and events hosted by the University of the Third Age (U3A) and she also took arts trips to Italy.

She continued to be very involved in the work of the Anne Frank House in Amsterdam, and the Anne Frank Fund in Switzerland that controlled the rights to the diary. As time passed she sometimes disagreed with the direction of the Swiss-based Foundation. Mutti felt strongly about sticking to Otto's core beliefs about prudent spending, and keeping Anne's legacy as something simple and tangible – in line with the spirit of the diary. After Otto died, Mutti increasingly felt that her contributions in trustees' meetings were not always valued, and she was gradually marginalised.

Despite this she kept up an active correspondence with the hundreds of people who continued to write to her about Anne and Otto. There was still a flood of letters to be answered, and Mutti went about this with the same care and attention that she had devoted to them in Otto's lifetime.

The truth was that Mutti took a very active and minute interest in all of us – and even in people she didn't know very well. And if she didn't agree with what you were doing she would certainly tell you!

'If you wanted to talk to someone who would listen quietly – and not venture any opinion – then Fritzi was definitely not the person for you,' says my cousin Tom.

Tom was recently divorced and living in Switzerland at the time. He spent a lot of time with Mutti, having long conversations and, so he tells me, listening to her tell him what he should be doing with his life.

'I was wondering what direction my life should take, and though Fritzi was very interested in the arts, she definitely thought I should have a profession that was well paid and had good prospects.'

That sounds like my mother. She had seen enough of life's hardships to be very practical when it came to earning a living and making life as comfortable as possible.

She was outspoken, but she also cared about people – and asked very detailed questions. As her daughter I sometimes felt that she asked too many. Mutti wrote me long letters, telling me everything that she had been doing – and wanting to know exactly what was going on in my life. I had three girls living at home, I was running the antique shop – and I spoke to Mutti on the telephone all the time, in between our frequent visits. In other words, I didn't have time to write long letters – but try telling that to Mutti.

'I wish you would write me longer letters,' she would complain, making me feel guilty as only a mother can, 'and you never answer all my questions. What I would like is for you to answer each question I ask, in order . . .'

Otto once wrote that Mutti and I were very close. 'Eva discussing everything: her business, her interests, her private and social life. Mother wanting to know every detail, asking and asking and giving advice when needed. The only struggle is over correspondence . . .'

He described how Mutti would wait anxiously for a letter, 'looking at the mailbox whenever the postman is coming, getting very nervous until finally a letter arrives.' Then she would worry about how a letter from London took six days to come, when one from America only took three. 'Anyhow, a letter in hand and all the anger is over.'

My mother was quite obsessed with letter writing, as her volumes of correspondence show.

I don't regret not answering all of her questions – a lot of them were about things like what I was eating for dinner – but I do regret that I didn't sit down with her and talk about the important experiences we'd shared.

Given everything we'd been through it might seem strange that we never talked about it afterwards. At first I think we were concentrating on getting through those first dark days after the war, rebuilding our lives without much enthusiasm. Then I moved to England and got married, and Mutti married Otto – and after that it never seemed to be the right time. I looked at her from the outside and I saw that she was happy and contented with Otto. She must have seen the same with me. Neither of us dug beneath the surface and talked about the pain that we still felt.

By far the biggest shock of writing this book was discovering that my cousin Tom had kept a large stash of my parents' letters to my grandparents from both before the war and afterwards. I'd never read those letters, I don't think I even really knew that they existed – but when I told Tom that I was writing this book he gradually started sending them to me – at first posting them to my email, and then bringing them in person in a large shoe box.

I literally trembled with emotion to find my parents coming back to life in my hands. You believe that you will always remember clearly the people you love – but as time passes you start to remember only the memory of your memories. Now, vividly, I found Pappy and Mutti back with me again – speaking in their own voices – sometimes in a thick cursive scrawl, sometimes in almost indecipherable old gothic German lettering, sometimes neatly typed on the very thinnest shiny paper. I was excited, tearful and sometimes shocked to see that: yes, this is how they really were. I had forgotten.

I've already woven the substance of these letters into the book but, taken as a whole, they challenged some of my assumptions about our lives. I could see, for example, how happy we had been living in Amsterdam, even after the Occupation. Of course there were a lot of things my parents couldn't write about because of censorship, but even so there is a strong sense that we were living a normal family life. The only time my mother alludes to the Nazi invasion is when she says that my father would love to have more children, but 'that is the one thing that I can't give him,' because the situation is so precarious.

Later, after we return to Amsterdam from Auschwitz, she often writes to Grandma Helen about her own sadness and loss – about Pappy and 'Heinzerl' (her little Heinz) and about how she has to try not to cry, and to keep up a brave face for me.

In one sad aside she writes about going to the synagogue in Amsterdam with Otto and Henk, my former boyfriend, and how she couldn't help but wish that it was her own son sitting next to her.

Reading these letters left me feeling bereft and heartbroken – why did we never talk about how we felt? Why couldn't I see how much my mother was suffering too? I always thought that she didn't realise how devastated I was, but in her letters she tells Grandma Helen that she knows I am distraught, and angry with her, but that she has to try and be my father, mother and brother all rolled up in one.

How I wish I could talk to Mutti about all of this now. I can't turn back time and have that conversation with her, but I can get some comfort from knowing that, as we got older, she particularly enjoyed spending time with my children, and then my grandchildren – her great-grandchildren. They were a huge joy in her life.

In the 1980s Zvi and I bought a holiday home beside the walled town of Mougins in the south of France. We'd first fallen in love with the area after visiting on the recommendation of Mrs Hirsch – the owner of the boarding house on Chichele Road where we met. We bought two rooms converted from a chicken shed, and over time we extended to make a further two rooms. This became our holiday base, and we spent many summers there.

By now our family was expanding. In 1985 Jacky gave birth to our first grandchild – Lisa, who is beautiful and smart, and still the apple of my eye. When Lisa got married recently she asked Zvi to give her away, and when we saw them emerge together to walk down the aisle we were all in tears.

Three years after Lisa was born she was joined by a brother. After three daughters and one granddaughter we were excited about having a new baby boy in the family, and I told Jacky that I hoped she would call him Eric after my father.

'I was thinking about calling him Robert actually,' she told me, much to my disappointment.

Jacky must have seen my face fall. I was with her in the delivery room, and when he emerged she held him for a while and we all looked at him.

'Well, now that he's here I can see that he doesn't really look like a Robert,' she said. 'I think he looks like an Eric.'

Eric was a blond-haired little boy with a sunny temperament, who used to run around winning over every female he came across. Now he's a handsome, fair-haired young man – and he still has many admirers.

A few years after he arrived, in 1992, my eldest daughter Caroline gave birth to our second grandson – Alexander. Alex is tall and brainy, with a sweet and sensitive personality. He's studying pure mathematics at the University of Oxford and I'm sure that one day he will solve a complicated equation and change the world!

Then Sylvia's two daughters, Sophie and Ella, joined the family in 1993 and 1996. They are both still teenagers but we can already see that they have inherited our love of the arts. They often come to spend a day and tell us all about their latest achievements. Sophie loves to practise her German with us and Ella recites her latest poems.

When the children were little we'd spend every summer splashing about in the pool at Mougins together, going on boat trips, eating ice cream and playing on the beach. In the morning we would start the day with a cup of tea in bed, and Zvi would make us each eat a carrot as he believed it was good for the gums. Then I would take part in all of their games, Zvi would smile and wave from the side – sometimes holding one of the children on his knee while reading the *Financial Times* or the *Economist*, and Mutti would watch from a deckchair, enjoying having her family around her. After lunch we'd have a nap in the shade, and then I would feed the children a biscuit from my famous orange biscuit box – which they would often complain was stale and yucky. (It's true that, after Auschwitz, I hate wasting food and I never throw anything away. When you've once eaten a speck of sugar off the ground, you don't turn your nose up at leftovers.) Then in the evening I'd make fish soup for a family dinner.

Of course, like all families, we had our ups and downs, but I'm happy that Mutti was able to live long enough to see Pappy's prophecy of an unbroken chain fulfilled.

Mutti must have had a cast-iron constitution. Aside from having a hysterectomy in Amsterdam soon after the end of the war she was rarely in ill health. On one trip to Mougins she had a nasty accident, trapping her hand in her deckchair. It was terrible – she screamed and screamed in pain, but we couldn't extricate her. Eventually when we got her free and took her to hospital, we discovered that she had broken three fingers, but she still insisted on leaving on her own for her return journey to Switzerland as planned.

Some time later, she was walking down the street one day near her home in Birsfelden, when she stepped, face forward, into a tram. It was a near-fatal accident, but Mutti was tough. She pulled through. It made us think seriously about her future though – and I asked her to come and live with us in London.

Mutti came for a while, but she really couldn't settle – she'd lived in Switzerland for decades and she missed her flat and friends. 'I was so happy in my apartment with Otto,' she told me. 'When I'm there I feel like he's still with me.'

We agreed that she would return, but found her a Polish lady to care for her. That worked for a while, but then Mutti said, 'Why must I live here with a stranger looking after me when all my family is in England?' She came back to stay with us again, but still couldn't settle and went back to Switzerland once more.

For a few years Mutti travelled back and forth; sometimes living with us, sometimes living in Switzerland while I flew over and visited her every weekend.

Eventually I realised that she was starting to have problems with her memory, and that she really couldn't look after herself.

In 1995 Mutti moved over to England for good, and lived with us in Edgware. Soon after I started travelling a lot with the play, *And Then They Came For Me*, and Elizabeth Ravasio came to stay with Mutti when I was away. Eventually Elizabeth suggested that it would be easier if Mutti lived with her, in Elizabeth's house, which was just around the corner.

Elizabeth was a devoted companion and carer to my mother in her later years. By then her memory was failing and she was becoming easily confused. When someone came to interview Mutti about Otto she searched her memory for what seemed like hours but all she could remember about him was that 'he had a very small head'.

Those of us who knew just how much she loved Otto, and how important they were to each other, found that painful to listen to.

Then, one night Elizabeth and Mutti decided to go to the cinema to watch *Titanic* with Leonardo di Caprio and Kate Winslet. I think the concept of an old lady looking back on painful memories of catastrophe and death was too poignant for Mutti. She became incredibly upset and restless, and returned home very disturbed. She had taken sleeping pills for many years, and that night I think she took too many. When she woke up later to go to the toilet she was groggy and she slipped on the cord of her dressing gown, falling over and breaking her leg. It was a horrible break – her femur bone was sticking through her skin and the paramedics had to carry her out to the ambulance in terrible pain.

At the hospital she recovered slightly, but then the strain of the fall brought on a series of small strokes. The doctors told me that when old people have a stroke they often withhold food and liquid to let them die. I was well aware that Mutti was nearing the ending of her life – but I was outraged by this suggestion.

'No way!' I shouted at them. 'My mother survived Auschwitz. I am not going to starve her to death now. She will go in her own time.'

I would not allow my mother, who had lived through the Holocaust, to be killed by the NHS. I still find the idea of starving people to death deeply disturbing and I am never convinced by medical claims that the patients do not realise what is happening to them. I'm sure that it is cheaper and more convenient for the hospitals, however.

Contrary to the doctors' opinions, Mutti did recover enough to be sent to a very dirty local convalescence hospital where the staff didn't seem to pay any attention to their patients. Elizabeth and I decided that we certainly did not want her to end her days there – and we took her home.

For a few months we cared for her, feeding her and lifting her in a hoist and, although she was clearly fading, she lived out her last few days fully conscious, with her family around her. Although Mutti could hardly speak, and was curled on her bed like a foetus, I remember the way her eyes lit up one day when we brought Ella – her youngest great-grandchild – to see her, and Ella crawled up Mutti's bed to say hello.

In 1998 Mutti died, at the age of ninety-three. Her life spanned the full horror and history of the twentieth century. She was born, in the midst of a large and lively family, when the Hapsburg Empire ruled much of Europe, and then lived through World War One and the Holocaust. Her life and circumstances changed in ways few of us can imagine but she remained an immensely kind, thoughtful – and feisty – woman. Above all, she was determined that I should go on and live a happy and full life, and she devoted all of her energies to that. She was the best mother anyone could have asked for. I couldn't have made it without her.

A few months after Mutti's death I set off with Elizabeth on a trip to Japan, where there had always been huge interest in Anne Frank. I spoke to many groups who were interested in the diary, and large numbers of people turned out to see the Anne Frank Exhibition, with a lot of Frank family possessions that we'd had shipped over for the occasion. I was very pleased that, because Mutti was Otto's wife, the story of my family was also included in the exhibition – alongside some of Heinz's paintings.

We stayed in Japan for more than a month, and as I travelled across that beautiful country I often thought about Otto and Mutti, and the meaning of what they had tried to accomplish with their lives. Neither of them believed in the afterlife, but they were both true humanitarians who dedicated much of their time to encouraging people towards a world that had some tolerance and compassion. I know that they would both have liked to see the Anne Frank rose that is grown in Japan. It has fragile petals that, before they curl up and die, change colour from pink to orange.

28
Reaching Out

'What I learned from the story of Anne Frank is what happens when you grass someone up . . .'

Oh well, maybe everyone gets something different from stories about the Holocaust. The man I was speaking to was serving a sentence in Wormwood Scrubs prison – one of Britain's most notorious jails. He'd been taking part in a two-week project organised by the Anne Frank Trust, and was explaining what he'd got out of it.

The Anne Frank Trust was first invited into prisons in 2002 by the then governor of Reading Prison in an effort to tackle racism and hate crime. In tense enclosed communities, racial and religious differences, and homophobia, can quickly get out of hand. Since then more than 22,000 prisoners have been through the education programme, and in 2011 the exhibit took place in fourteen prisons and young offenders' institutions.

A large part of the programme is training a group of prisoners who volunteer to help show people around the Anne Frank Travelling Exhibition – but these men and woman also come together every day to talk about hate and intolerance, and to write about their own experiences. Very little is done to help people in prison, and I've been involved in this fantastic and unique programme since the beginning. The project coordinator, Steve Gadd, usually arranges for me to join the group at the end of the two weeks to talk about my own experiences. I can't speak at every exhibit, but without a doubt, it's the most satisfying part of my work and I benefit from it just as the much as the rest of the group.

Prisons are difficult places to think about – and most people prefer not to. In my years of speaking at different institutions I've had to challenge my own preconceptions about how we should treat the people who end up incarcerated. I've met so many men and women whose lives were hopeless long before they committed any criminal act – and it has made me wish that we could intervene earlier to help them, sparing society the consequences of the crime itself and the cost of locking them up. I've come to realise that you can understand a person who has committed a terrible crime, without forgiving the crime itself.

Now I'm used to the clanging gates, jangling keys and high walls that make a prison visit so unique, but to begin with I was nervous, and daunted.

The high stone walls of Durham Prison hold some of the most serious criminals in Britain. It was impossible not to feel hundreds of eyes watching me from the narrow windows as a prison officer shut and locked a succession of heavy metal gates, and led me across the courtyard and onto one of the wings.

The first time I went to Durham, a three-hour train journey from London carried me north through some of England's most beautiful scenery. As we pulled into the station I saw the most stunning view of Durham Cathedral, but even that could not take my mind off the fact that I was about to meet some of the most dangerous women in the country. I wondered what they would think of my story, and whether we would understand each other.

Security was tight and, even after so many years, I felt uneasy being searched and patted down by a uniformed guard. Of course, I reminded myself, this time they were making sure that we weren't taking prohibited items, like keys or drugs inside the prison – not locking me up in a concentration camp.

Gillian Walnes, the Executive Director of the Anne Frank Trust, had been very unsure about whether to ask me to visit the prison – what if the barbed wire and guards reminded me of Auschwitz? I had assured her that I would be fine, but actually it was only in this moment that I realised the two experiences had almost nothing in common. Not only are the physical surroundings very different, but people in prison are there as punishment for a crime, whereas my family had done nothing wrong.

The guard led us into a large, brightly lit gymnasium, where an audience of women dressed in casual clothes and trainers was waiting. Along the way I saw Rosemary West, who was serving a life sentence for her role in some of the country's most notorious serial killings. I knew that she'd taken part in acts of horrible torture as well as murder, and I was certainly pleased that she was heading towards the library and not coming to listen to me. How would I cope, I wondered, if I was confronted by someone who had been incarcerated for acts of violent sadism?

Nervously I settled into my seat in the gym and listened to the introduction. In my mind I ran through several possibilities about how to start my talk – but I decided to get straight to the point.

'Some of you are full of hate,' I told them. 'I was full of hate, too, and I think I have a message for you.'

I began to tell them something about our family and life in Vienna. 'We were a very happy family, but it didn't last long . . .' before I moved on to our time in Amsterdam and then deportation to Auschwitz.

At first the women had looked bored or mildly curious – weighing me up to see if I had anything worthwhile to tell them. Now the gym was completely silent, and you could hear a pin drop.

'I don't know how I survived,' I said. 'I look back and I still wonder. And I don't know *why* I survived. My brother was much more talented than me. But I did . . .'

I realised that this was the crux of my message to these women – I was a survivor, and they could survive, too.

'There is always hope,' I told them, 'even when life seems bleak. You must have the will and strength to change your life – and achieve what you want to achieve.'

Then the Anne Frank Exhibition caught my eye and I remembered that day in 1986 when Ken Livingstone had, unwittingly, sent my life hurtling in a new direction. 'This exhibition has changed my life,' I concluded, 'and I hope that it will change yours.'

I sat back, sipped from a glass of water, and waited for questions. For a moment I wondered what would happen if no one spoke – but hands shot up and soon these women were asking me everything about my life, my beliefs and how I found the strength to go on.

Had I ever wanted to meet a Nazi for a face-to-face reconciliation? 'No, but none has ever asked me,' I replied. Did I believe in God? Had I ever had counselling? 'I haven't but it would have been very useful,' I admitted. Did I think that the Exhibition does any good?

'Yes,' I said. 'You see here how dangerous it is to have discrimination. You need courage to speak up when you see injustice. You do have a voice. Later in your life you might even think about it, and make different choices.'

These women were no longer nameless prisoners to me – they were individuals, each with their own story to tell. Some were serving sentences connected to drug crime. Many were victims of a lifetime of abuse and were serving time for retaliating against men who had subjected them to years of violence.

'I killed my darling husband,' said one well-spoken lady called Evelyn who I met on a visit to a London prison. I was rather taken aback to hear such a bald statement, but her plight was a common one. She and I corresponded for years.

Other women I've met have been victims of a miscarriage of justice. When I returned from my visit to Durham I received a letter from a woman convicted, and then later freed on appeal, in a well known case. She wrote me a very moving two-page letter thanking me for my talk, and telling me that, 'I have learnt from you that no matter how tough life gets, if you have the will to survive, that will keep you going . . . Although I am in prison I hope one day to be released. I am holding on because of that light at the end of the tunnel. Listening to you has brought me more hope and strength to carry on.'

Each of the women I've met has engaged with my story in a different way. At a recent visit to Downview prison in Surrey I got a cheer of support from a gay woman when I talked about how the Nazis had persecuted the gay community, followed by a heartfelt and very moving thank you from an Irish Traveller when I spoke about how I had been sent to Auschwitz with a train full of Gypsies. I knew that one of the women in the audience had survived the Rwandan genocide, and lost members of her family. She sat and listened to me quietly, and didn't ask any questions – but I hope that she felt my solidarity with her.

Speaking in men's prisons is a different experience, but I find that the impact of the Anne Frank Exhibition is just as powerful. During my visit to Wormwood Scrubs in December 2011 one man called Mark told me, 'I wasn't interested at the start, to be honest, but now I can see it's relevant because it's like slavery, and what black people went through.'

Another man called Paul, who was serving a sentence for knife crime but claimed to be innocent, said, 'I was thinking a lot about my own case and what has happened in my own life. But this puts it all in a different perspective.'

At the end of my talk the Deputy Governor, David Redhouse, got up and spoke. 'We are a rainbow prison,' he said. More than half the inmates at Wormwood Scrubs are black, and there are a high proportion of Muslim prisoners and other religious groups. He cautioned us all against taking the easy route of 'ignorance towards others' way of life,' and looking for scapegoats, especially in difficult economic times.

You may read all of this and think – that's nice, but does it really do any good?

Whenever I wonder about that, I think of Faith, who

trained as a guide on the exhibit while in prison and now works for the Anne Frank Trust.

'When you are in prison you do feel despair,' she says. 'You wonder how you can go on. How will you ever be able to rebuild your life on the outside? You reflect on what you have done in the past, and you wonder what you can do in the future – and if you will get another chance.' It's about responsibility, she says. Thinking about your values, feeling empathy towards people who are different to you, and being humane.

Alongside my work in prisons I also speak to a very different constituency: schoolchildren. Unlike prisoners, their course in life has not yet been set, but I find that despite the huge difference in our ages, we can often identify with each other's problems.

Young people worry a lot, of course, about being different and not fitting in. They understand how dangerous and harmful bullying is – and my story highlights how bad the consequences can be. They struggle with authority, fight with their parents and feel that life is black and hopeless – just as I did.

I tailor my story according to their background and how old they are. I try to spare the younger children the horrific details of the camps, but they are usually the ones who want to know all the gory details. 'But how did the guards not get killed too when they gassed people in the gas chambers and then opened the doors? Where did the gas go?' asked one very persistent eight-year-old boy.

In classes with large numbers of Muslim pupils I often have to explain a lot of the background to the Holocaust, but they always listen very attentively.

Sometimes they want to talk about the Middle East, and ask me, 'Why do Israeli soldiers kill Palestinian children?' I try to answer them with as much information as I can, and explain my own point of view, which is that there is a war there, and although it is wrong to kill civilians and children, the soldiers are often trying to find terrorists who hide out in ordinary homes.

In large inner-city comprehensive schools I talk more about finding your purpose, and being able to overcome problems and still have a good life.

I speak at state schools, private schools, religious schools and international schools. The children look very dissimilar from one another and act very differently, but wherever I go I find young people who are open to me, my history and my message to them – and this gives me hope for the future of the world.

29

Going Back

The Auschwitz I returned to in January 1995 was every bit as cold, foggy and bleak as I remembered.

It wasn't the first time I'd been asked to return, but I'd always said no. Now a Dutch documentary crew had asked me to accompany them to make a short film about my experiences, before the camp was opened to the world in a big international ceremony to commemorate the fifty years since liberation. My first reaction was to refuse again.

'We thought you'd say that – but will you take a few days to think it over?' they asked.

I put the phone down and discussed it with Zvi. I remembered that Mutti had never wanted to return, saying that she couldn't see what you would get out of it but more horrible memories. I also knew of other survivors, however, who had gone back, and had found a sense of what was popularly known as 'closure'.

Perhaps going back to Auschwitz would bring me a sense of resolution. Perhaps if I could see it again as a real place, not just in my nightmares, it would cease to haunt me to the same extent. I agreed to go, and set off for Poland with Zvi.

As soon as we arrived at the main gate of Birkenau I felt the horror closing in on me. The main towers and the railway track were still there, the towers looming over us in the cold grey morning, and we walked silently through the deep snow, into the camp.

Almost from the moment we arrived, Zvi started quietly crying – it was really an overwhelming experience for him. I didn't cry. All I could think was, 'This is every bit as bad as I remember.'

The perimeter fence was still standing, with the barbed wire sagging in places, no longer electrified. Otherwise the camp was now an open expanse, stretching for what seemed like miles into the distance. It hadn't looked that way in 1944, back then each area had been fenced off and patrolled by guards.

A few barracks were still intact but a lot of the wooden buildings had gone, perhaps tumbled down in the years of decay. I showed Zvi the long central walkway and the wooden pallets on either side where we slept. It was dark and dank inside, just as it had been, and I told Zvi about the rat that chewed my toes one night.

Then I went over to see the toilet block, and the long row of open holes. I felt my stomach turn over to remember how much I hated bending over those holes, hearing the boots of the Kapos marching up and down behind me, and I laughed a little to think of Pappy warning me not to sit down in case of germs.

We walked the length of the camp, following the railway line that eventually ran almost up to the gas chambers. At the back were the collapsed brick buildings where the gas chambers and crematoria had been. The Nazis had blown them up before leaving, hoping to hide their crimes. All of this looked unfamiliar to me – the gas chambers and crematoria were always kept carefully screened from the rest of the camp, although we could never deny the reality of those smoking chimneys, raining ash down on us day and night and filling the camp with that unmistakable smell.

We stopped for a few moments, and I read something from my book, *Eva's Story*. Then we left.

I felt no resolution. I had found no closure. The weight of all of those people – millions of families of grandparents, parents, children and babies, who had died in this quiet Polish field, pressed down on me. They had been murdered, day after day, year after year, for four years – and I couldn't even believe that they had gone to heaven. Once they had been people with lives, but many of them had gone to their deaths anonymously – we don't even know their names.

On the way out we saw some of the renovations to the camp that were being carried out before the memorial ceremony. For years Auschwitz-Birkenau had languished behind the Iron Curtain and few people had visited. Now it was being prepared as an international tourist site. Signs were being erected to tell people the locations of specific horrors – a gas chamber, a barrack for Hungarian Jews, the hospital. I was aghast, and speechless, when we reached a newly constructed cafeteria. Workmen were sitting at the tables, laughing and chatting and drinking hot chocolate. Zvi winced when someone offered him something to eat. 'No, I couldn't,' he said, clutching his throat with revulsion. 'I think I would be sick!'

To me it seemed like a bizarre dream.

Later I watched the memorial ceremony on television, and I heard Elie Wiesel say, 'Although we know that God is merciful, please God, do not have mercy for those people who created this place.'

Wiesel survived Auschwitz to become a writer and Nobel laureate, and I agreed wholeheartedly with his next comment. 'Remember the nocturnal procession of children, of more children, and more children, so frightened, so quiet, so beautiful,' he said. 'If we could simply look at one, our heart would break. But it did not break the hearts of the murderers.'

Then I saw world leaders laying wreaths and making remarks about how such things could never be allowed to happen again.

'But it has happened again,' I said to Zvi. 'It is happening in different parts of the world right now.'

Millions visit Auschwitz every year, and I've heard that there is a huge crush of people pushing in through the entrance and then making their way around the camp wearing headsets that deliver a guided tour. I've even met people, some of them Jewish, who visit many concentration camp sites, getting some kind of thrill from the horrible sensation of being in the midst of terror and death. The idea gives me goose bumps, although I'm very much in favour of young people visiting as part of an educational trip.

The shoes and suitcases and hair from the victims that are displayed in the museum at Auschwitz can always be preserved, but eventually everything the Nazis built will be worn down by nature, and Auschwitz will revert to a flat, fetid landscape where the flies swarm, the sun beats down harshly in summer, and the snow is feet deep in winter. Who knows what people will remember of that spot in a hundred years' time? It is only a place. If I want to pass on my experience, and my hopes for the future, I can better do it through people.

For many years I also stayed away from Austria and Amsterdam, not wanting to be reminded of a happier past with Mutti and Pappy and Heinz. But eventually I did return, going back to Vienna with Zvi and our daughter Sylvia in the late 1970s. Austria was much as I remembered it, and I couldn't help but be charmed by the smiling easygoing people, the food and drink, and the sunny days we spent in the countryside. We explored the city of Vienna and I took Sylvia to Schönbrunn Palace, where I had once run around and played. I would have liked to take Zvi and Sylvia to see the house where Heinz and I had grown up, but my memory suddenly went blank – I just couldn't remember the address. No matter how much I tried, it wouldn't come back to me, although of course I knew the way to Lautensackgasse off by heart. When I got home I remembered it straight away. My psyche had been protecting me, and I have never seen that house again.

Since that visit we have been to Austria several times and we even once thought about buying a holiday apartment there, but the warmth of some of my childhood memories can never overcome the deep unease, and fear, of what happened.

I think I can now admit that I was born an Austrian, but for many years I denied any link to my homeland. When people asked me where I came from I told them I was Dutch.

The place I feel the deepest connection to is Amsterdam. I didn't go back very often during Otto's lifetime, but after he died and I took a more active role in the Anne Frank

House, I started to visit again. Arriving in the city is always very emotional for me; my eyes fill with tears when I land at the airport, and I think about how much Heinz would have loved to come home to Amsterdam, and never had the chance. It is a city of many mixed memories, but I love my Dutch friends and, if it wasn't for my family in London, I would live out the rest of my life there. Aside from the work of the Anne Frank House, I've also enjoyed becoming involved in the work of the Dutch Resistance Museum. I've donated some items, including Heinz's paintings, his and my father's passport and the Russian uniform I was given after being liberated from Auschwitz, to their permanent collection.

That uniform very nearly ended up back in Russia. In January 2012 I visited Moscow to be reunited with some of the soldiers who had liberated Auschwitz-Birkenau in 1945. At a press conference I held up the uniform and told them all about how the soldiers had given it to me, and how I had worn it all the way through the Ukraine, across the sea to Marseille and back to Amsterdam.

'Ah, that's wonderful,' a Russian organiser told me, with a glint in his eye. 'I think it should be on display here in Moscow.'

'Oh, I think you've got enough old Soviet uniforms,' I told him. 'I'm going to hang on to it.'

Joking aside, I was so grateful to be able to thank those soldiers. I remember them as strapping young men, tall and bear-like in their winter uniforms. Now they are white-haired, hunched and elderly, wearing glasses and displaying their war medals proudly on their blazers.

I asked them what it had been like to discover Auschwitz,

and if they had expected to find such camps, containing the few straggling, starving survivors.

'No, it was terrible,' one told me. 'We were just boys. I was only eighteen. We found other places like this. But we had already seen so many horrors.'

As they advanced across Russia and Poland they had encountered some terrible scenes – and Auschwitz-Birkenau had been one among many.

When I left Moscow I thought about what he had said. Was the Holocaust unique, or one horror among many? Through Otto, and then through the work of the Anne Frank House and the Anne Frank Trust, I had come to know of many cases of genocide, killing and discrimination, and each one must seem equally terrible to the people who lived through it. Despite that, I believe the Nazis' determination to wipe every Jew off the face of the earth – and the willingness of so many ordinary people to let it happen – is without any historical parallel. But, of course, I did not experience it as a historical event. I can only tell you about something very personal that happened to me, and how I survived it.

30
Epilogue

Last night I lay awake and wondered what the ending of my story should be. In thirty years there will be no survivors of the Holocaust, and so this book is my letter to the future.

My dream is that someone will pick it up, long after I am dead, and be shocked and astonished to discover that this was once how the world was. Persecuting people because they are Jewish – or because they are black, or because they are Gypsies, or Muslims, or gay – will seem as ridiculous, inhuman and outrageous as the slave trade appears to us now.

That is a far-fetched dream, you might think. Just look at all the horrors taking place in the world right now. Just look at all the uncertainty we face, and the conflict between different religions.

I am a pragmatist, but I am also an optimist. When I climb on board my local bus in north London I notice that families are as often as not made up of people from different ethnic backgrounds. I even had to change my way of thinking about my own family, and realised that it was not as it used to be. I would never have married a man who wasn't a Jew, and when one of my daughters married a non-Jewish man we were disappointed. But times have changed and we have all become more integrated, and that is a good thing.

Now when I visit schools I notice that the children rarely pay any attention to where their classmates come from. They might like or dislike them as individuals, but that does not seem to be based on the colour of their skin or their religion.

Living in a world where everyone can 'belong' is not some high-minded ideal for me – it has been one of the biggest questions that has plagued my life.

On 14 February 2012 I walked across the courtyard of Buckingham Palace and received an MBE for my work with the Anne Frank Trust and other Holocaust charities. My award meant that I was now a 'Member of the British Empire'. Even after sixty years of living in London it still made me wonder, where did I belong in the world, and where could I call home?

I'd started my life in Austria, become a stateless refugee and then been reduced to a number painfully tattooed on my forearm. After the war the Allies decided that Jews were not to be treated as a separate group, and we were designated 'Austrians' again (bizarrely, lumped together with the same Nazis who had persecuted us and considered us 'enemy aliens'). I never got Dutch citizenship and then I ended up, a few years later, living in the UK, where I'd never imagined I'd marry and have a family.

I'd lived through the era when the whole of Europe was consumed in a battle between Fascism, Communism and freedom – smashing any last vestige of that old Imperial age. And yet here I was accepting an archaic honour from an Empire that didn't exist any more.

It makes me smile when I hear people talk about the endless conflicts that rage in other parts of the world, like

Africa, compared to the 'civilised' way we go about things in Europe. I can tell you that not so long ago Europe was not very 'civilised' at all.

This book has told you some of my memories of that time, but remembering should have a smaller place in the world than changing things for the better.

I was struck by this thought particularly, when I visited Argentina a couple of years ago for the first anniversary of the Anne Frank House in Buenos Aires. I knew, of course, of Argentina's history of sheltering Nazis after the war, and of the many ordinary people who had lost their families because of the country's most recent military dictatorship. It was a history I couldn't help but reflect on as I was honoured in a room in parliament in front of Eva Peron's desk. (A much more controversial Eva than me.) So it was with great feeling that I spoke to a group that included some of the Mothers of the Plaza de Mayo who had bravely campaigned for justice after losing their children to the military junta, but it was meaningful that I also spoke to 100 senior army, navy and air force officers who came to listen to me. They signed an agreement that all cadets should visit the Anne Frank House when they joined up.

Above all, my hopes rest with the young, which is why the final highlight of my trip to Argentina was seeing the education minister sign a commitment to teach the Holocaust as part of the school curriculum.

This summer both my grandsons visited Africa to work with charitable organisations. I think a sense of doing things for other people, and for humanity, has been passed down in our family from Otto Frank, although I know that wanting to contribute to the world is something widely shared by young people today.

So yes, there should always be memorials and days of commemoration, but life only moves forwards and I have always been an active person. Life goes on.

Writing this story was completed for me, in a way, when many of the people you have read about came together in London to celebrate the sixtieth anniversary of my wedding to Zvi. It was a beautiful sunny day in early September and Zvi and I walked into the room to hear our granddaughter Lisa playing a version of 'What A Wonderful World'.

My life had come full circle. I was overwhelmed to be sitting there with our daughters; our grandchildren; my cousin Tom, who as a ten-year-old tucked up in his bed in Darwen had heard about my horrors; Jan Rosenbaum, the baby who had brightened up my bleak life in post-war Amsterdam; Anita, my first real friend in London; Elizabeth, who had been by my side as a young au pair, then as a business partner and finally caring for Mutti; Dienke and Jan Eric who had first brought the Anne Frank Exhibition to the UK; Jenny Culank and Nic Careem who produced *And Then They Came For Me*; Erika and Teresin from the Anne Frank House in Amsterdam; Zvi's family from Israel – and even Harold, a friend from America, who told stories about taking me to casinos and pig racing, reminding everyone that I am not a paragon of virtue who philoso-phises about life from on high!

I grew up in what was far from a wonderful world, but I have still found a life with much joy and love in it, and my deepest regret is only that Pappy and Heinz could not share it with me.

After speaking about my experiences for more than twenty-five years I can anticipate most of the questions that people ask me, but that does not mean that I have all the answers.

A few months ago I finished speaking, and looked down at a class of schoolchildren. A Somali girl with dark eyes hesitantly put her hand up and asked, 'Do you think it will happen again?'

I can't answer that, but maybe you can. Will it? I hope not.

Acknowledgments

Although many people offered us moral support in writing this book, we would especially like to thank those who advised us in our research, particularly Karen Tessel at the Dutch Resistance Museum, Professor Dienke Hondious from the University of Amsterdam, and Teresien da Silva and Erika Prins at the Anne Frank House in Amsterdam.

We're also particularly grateful to Tom Greenwood who unearthed many family letters and sent them to us to be used in the book – and shared his own memories with us.

For their immediate belief in this book, and much practical help along the way, thanks also to Gaia Banks at Sheil Land and Fenella Bates at Hodder & Stoughton.

We would also like to thank Zvi Schloss for his patience and help, sitting through every meeting about this book and reading every draft – and for all the unstinting support he has provided on so many other projects over the years.

Eva Schloss-Geiringer and Karen Bartlett

Picture Acknowledgements

Most of the photographs are from the author's personal collection. Additional photographs: © AFF, Basle, CH/AFS Amsterdam, NL: 5 (top left and middle left, bottom left and right)/ photos Anne Frank House, (top right and middle right)/ photos Getty Images. © Corbis: 6 (bottom). © Getty Images: 7 (bottom). © Press Association Images: 6 (top), 16 (bottom)/ photo Lewis Whyld. © TopFoto: 7 (top).

Every reasonable effort has been made to contact the copyright holders, but if there are any errors or omissions, Hodder & Stoughton will be pleased to insert the appropriate acknowledgement in any subsequent printing of this publication.

childbirth 231–2
childhood
　in Amsterdam 52–97
　in Belgium 41–51
　betrayal, and capture by the
　　Nazis 91–7
　flight to Holland 39–40
　in hiding 80–92
　in Vienna 15–27, 31–9
　see also schooling
Christian Socialism 30
Churchill, Winston 67
concentration camps 76, 77, 106–7
　Auschwitz *see* Auschwitz-
　　Birkenau concentration camp
　deportations to 99–103
　gypsies in 103, 116
　and tourism 305, 306
Culank, Jenny 278–9, 280, 282, 313
Cyprus, displaced persons camps
　214
Czechoslovakia 11, 50
Czernowitz 158–60
Czopp, Ninni 97, 112, 182
Czopp, Rusha 182

da Silva, Teresin 313
Dachau 106, 210, 211
Darwen 184–6, 221
Dekker, Mrs 83
Dekker family 82, 84
Denmark 59, 247
Deutsch, Herr and Frau 47
Diary of Anne Frank, The 61,
　172–3, 188, 219, 236, 239–40,
　244, 259
　inquiries concerning veracity of
　　242–3
　originally unpublished pages
　　given to Suijk 242–3
　productions 240–41, 243–4,
　　270–71

Dias, Vaz 179, 180
Dijk, Ans van 196
discrimination 4, 30, 274, 275,
　276, 299, 309
　see also anti-Semitism; prejudice
displaced persons 164
　Anne Frank village for 259
　camps in Cyprus 214
Dollfuss, Engelbert 30
Downview Prison 300
du Bus de Warnaffe, Charles 41–2
Dubbelman, Jan Eric 258, 269, 313
Dubois, Mr 43–6
Durham Prison 296–9
Dutch Resistance Museum 308
dysentery 112

Edgware Antiques 255–6
Ella (granddaughter, Ella Yaron,
　daughter of Sylvia) 289–90, 293
Ellen (girlfriend of Heinz
　Geiringer) 64, 183
Eric (grandson, Eric Hovelsen, son
　of Jacky) 289
Eternal Jew, The 72
ethnic displacement 164
Eva's Story 263–6, 305
evil 106, 150–51
　see also Holocaust

false identities 82, 83
family background 7–14
Faurisson, Robert 242
France 163–4, 288, 290–91
Frank, Anne 106, 150, 172, 173,
　264–5
　childhood friendship with 2,
　　61–5
　diary of *see Diary of Anne
　　Frank*, The
　photos of 2, 61
Frank, Edith 63, 150, 156, 244

Frank, Elfriede (Fritzi, previously
    Mrs Geiringer) 225, 237–49,
    249, 250, 283, 284–5, 290–93
Frank, Herbert 188
Frank, Leni 255
Frank, Margot 2, 63, 73, 78, 150,
    172, 244
Frank, Otto 2, 61, 63, 148–9, 150,
    156–7, 163, 169, 172–3, 174–5,
    188, 189, 191, 193, 195, 201,
    237–49, 255, 264, 265, 270, 284,
    286, 292
    and Anne's diary 172–3, 188,
        219, 236, 240–43, 244
    cancer 247–8
    death 248
    marriage to Fritzi 218–19, 225,
        237–48
    Orde van Oranje-Nassau 249
Franz Josef I of Austria 8, 17, 29,
    160
Freud, Anna 16
Freud, Sigmund 7

Gaby (cousin) 22, 24, 34
Gadd, Steve 295–6
gay community 276, 300
Geiringer, Blanca (paternal aunt)
    22, 24
Geiringer, David (paternal grand-
    father) 9, 10, 13
Geiringer, Elfriede (Fritzi), née
    Markovits (mother) 2, 10, 104,
    189, 190–91, 282–94
    after Otto's death 249, 250,
        283, 284–5, 290–93
    in Amsterdam 55–6, 57–8, 60,
        70, 71, 73–4, 76, 80, 81, 82–3,
        85, 86–9, 92, 94, 95–7, 165,
        168, 169–76, 178–82, 186–8,
        192–3, 197–9, 200–201, 256,
        287–8

in Birkenau 108, 109, 112,
    113–14, 118, 119–20, 121,
    125, 126, 127, 129, 131–3,
    136, 137–8, 141, 143, 146,
    147, 149, 150–51, 152–3
in Brussels 42, 43, 45–7, 48
death 293
and Eva's marriage 218, 221–2
and *Eva's Story* 266
final months 292–3
journey back from Birkenau to
    Amsterdam 154, 155, 156–9,
    160, 162–5
letter writing 159, 184–5, 187,
    190–91, 246, 284–8
in London 231, 233, 246, 247,
    255, 259, 260, 282
marriage to Otto Frank 218–19,
    225, 237–48
in Vienna 15, 17, 19, 24–5, 26,
    31, 33, 35, 36–9
in Westerbork 98–9, 101–2,
    103
in Zandvoort 69
Geiringer, Erich (father) 5, 10, 48,
    104
    in Amsterdam 53–4, 55, 56,
        57–8, 60, 63–4, 67, 70–71, 74,
        76–7, 78, 80–81, 89–90, 93,
        94–5, 96
    in and around Vienna 6, 11–14,
        19, 22–5, 26, 35–6, 37
    in Auschwitz 107–8, 110,
        131–2, 134–6, 148
    in Belgium 40
    death 173
    paintings 177
    in Westerbork 98–9, 101, 102,
        103
Geiringer, Heinz (brother) 4, 5,
    104, 105, 114, 283
    in Amsterdam 52, 60, 64–5, 71,

72–3, 74–5, 76–7, 81, 88,
  89–90, 93, 95
in Auschwitz 107, 109, 110,
  131, 148
in Belgium 40, 42–3, 47, 48
death 173
paintings 90, 105, 175–7, 276
and *The Promise* 266–7
in Vienna 6, 15–16, 17, 18–19,
  23, 25–6, 31, 36, 38–9
in Westerbork 98–9, 102–3
Geiringer, Hermine (paternal
  grandmother) 9, 10
Geiringer & Brown 9, 13, 26, 71
Gemmeker, Albert Konrad 100
Georgia 273–4
Gestapo 83, 91, 92–8, 118, 195,
  196
ghettos 50, 72, 117
Gies, Miep 172, 278
Gino (boyfriend of Fritzi Geiringer)
  24
Goebbels, Josef 32
gold 123
Goodrich, Frances 241
Great Depression 26, 54
Greenwood, Otto (uncle) 22, 34,
  35, 247
Greenwood, Sylvi (aunt, née
  Markovits) 22, 34, 35, 247
Greenwood, Tom (cousin) 22, 34,
  184–5, 186, 285, 287, 313
Gunning, Dr 172
gypsies 103, 116, 300

Haan, Jannes 196
Hackett, Albert 241
Haganah 214
Haifa 211–15
Hailey, Idaho 276–7
Hapsburg Empire *see* Austro-
  Hungarian empire

Harold (friend) 313
Hassel, Elisabeth 100
Heiler, Lisa (granddaughter,
  daughter of Jacky) 289, 310–11,
  313
Heinemann, Truda 171
Hellman, Lillian 241
Henk (boyfriend) 192, 201, 206,
  288
Henneicke, Wim 194
Hepburn, Audrey 243–4
Heydrich, Reinhard 75
Hilda (maid) 20, 185
Himmler, Heinrich 107, 139
Hirsch, George 101
Hirsch, Mrs (landlady) 202, 203–4,
  288
Hitler, Adolf 28, 53, 141–2, 162,
  210
background 29–30
failure to gain entry to Vienna
  Academy of Fine Arts 17–18
oath of allegiance to 33–4
rise to power 27, 30–32
War tactics 59
Holland *see* Netherlands/Holland
Holocaust 4, 309
in the Baltics 279–82
concentration camps *see* concen-
  tration camps
deniers 241–2
educating people about 259–82,
  294–302 *see also And Then
  They Came For Me*; Anne
  Frank Travelling Exhibition;
  Anne Frank Trust; *Diary of
  Anne Frank, The*; *Eva's Story*;
  prison work; school speaking
  engagements
and gypsies 103
unveiling and start of 'Final
  Solution' 75–7

Hondius, Dienke 258, 313
honeymoon 223–4
hormone treatment 230
Höss, Mrs Rudolf 128
Höss, Rudolf 67–8, 123–4, 130
Houthuijs, Wim 196–7
Hovelsen, Eric (grandson, son of
    Jacky) 289
Hungarian Jews 111, 124, 130–31,
    132
Hungary 11

Idaho 276–8
IG Farben 107, 143
Ingolstadt 208–11
International Bank of Settlements
    123
Israel, State of 215, 220, 302
Israeli Defense Force 215

Jaap (studio boss) 192
Japan 294
Jews
    anti-Semitism *see* anti-Semitism
    and concentration camps *see*
        Auschwitz-Birkenau concen-
        tration camp; concentration
        camps
    converting to Christianity
        19–20, 34
    flight abroad from the Nazis 5,
        34–40
    and the Holocaust *see*
        Holocaust
    Hungarian 111, 124, 130–31,
        132
    Latvian 279, 280, 281
    marriage to non-Jews 310–11
    and Palestine/State of Israel
        213–15, 220
    Polish 117, 154
    and the Red Cross 162

refugees in Amsterdam 54, 63,
    67, 72–97, 171, 183–4
refugees in Belgium 41–2, 47–8
Soviet 155
stigma of being Jewish 281
of Vienna 7–14, 18–20, 29, 31–7
Johnny and Jones 99
Juliana, Princess 68

Kapos 112–13, 118, 119–20, 127,
    129, 133, 134, 304
Kasselman, Wendy 275
Katee-Walda, Gerada 89, 90, 94,
    95, 176, 195
Katowice 154, 155–6
Kennedy, John F. 243
Kent, Evelyn 264, 265
Kerner, Susan 271, 272, 279
Klein, Judith 275
Klompe, Miss 83, 84, 85–6, 87, 88,
    91, 93
Kloss, Litty 35
Klug, Bee 269
Koord, Janny 56–7, 65, 150
Koord, Rudi 150
Kristallnacht 50
Kuroczkin, Pawel 146

Latvia 279–82
Le Blanc, Jacky 43–4
Le Blanc, Madame 46
Lederman, Barbara 65, 271
Lederman, Susanne 64–5, 149
Leeds 261
Leumi bank 251, 254, 256
Levie, Herman de 64, 150
Levin, Meyer 240–41
Light in the Darkness, A 267
Lindberg-Salomon, Paula 198
Lisa (granddaughter, Lisa Heiler,
    daughter of Jacky) 289, 310–11,
    313

Livingstone, Ken 1, 3, 259, 298
London 1–3, 188–9, 193, 200–207,
    215–16, 218–21, 225–36, 239,
    246, 252–7, 258–64, 282, 290,
    291, 310
Lueger, Karl 28–9

Mahler, Gustav 7
Margolis, Alexander (grandson,
    son of Caroline) 289
Markovits, Elfriede (Fritzi), later
    Mrs Geiringer, then Mrs Frank
    2, 10, 11–13
Markovits, Helen (maternal grand-
    mother) 10, 11–12, 20, 35, 39,
    42, 49–50, 185, 222, 255, 256,
    284
Markovits, Rudolf (maternal
    grandfather) 10–11, 20, 21, 31,
    35, 39, 42, 49–50, 59, 185
Markovits, Sylvi (maiden name of
    Aunt Sylvi) 22, 34, 35, 247
marriage
    honeymoon 223–4
    married life 225–36, 238, 251–7,
        259–61, 288–90, 303–5, 307,
        313 *see also* Schloss, Zvi
        (husband)
    proposal and consideration
        217–21
    wedding day 217, 222–3
Martin (childhood friend) 22
Mauthausen concentration camp
    173
MBE 311
Mendoza, Mr 73
Mengele, Josef 109–10, 133, 137
Minni (cousin) 125, 127, 133, 136,
    137, 141, 150, 182–3
miscarriage 247
mob rule 39
Monowai, HMS 163

Moore, Demi 276–7
Moscow 308
Mougins 288, 290–91
music 24–5, 56, 71, 74, 116, 160
Mussert, Anton 58

National Liberty Museum,
    Philadelphia 276
National Socialists, Netherlands
    (NSB) 58, 68–9, 194
Native Americans, Oklahoma 275
Nazi informers/agents 85, 95,
    194–9
Nazis 4, 6
    anti-Semitism *see* anti-Semitism;
        Holocaust
    arrival in Vienna 31–4
    assassination of Dollfuss 30
    Austrian 30, 32, 33
    and concentration camps *see*
        concentration camps
    Gestapo 83, 91, 92–8, 118, 195,
        196
    in Latvia 279
    and the Middle East 213
    occupation of Holland 66–103,
        287
    SS guards/soldiers 105, 108,
        109, 111, 113, 116, 118, 121,
        124, 127–9, 139–40, 144, 146,
        279
    torture 93–4
Nederlandse Unie (NU) 69
Netherlands/Holland 2, 36, 164–7
    Amsterdam *see* Amsterdam
    Dutch government-in-exile 68
    early response to World War II
        53, 59–60
    Hunger Winter 166–7
    Nazi-imposed anti-Semitism
        70–103
    Nazi invasion 6, 66–7

Nazi occupation 66–103, 287
neutrality 36, 53
NSB party 58, 68–9, 194
Political Investigation
    Department 197
prejudice 162–3
resistance 71, 83–9, 91, 94–5,
    166
Special Justice Act 197
New Brunswick 271, 272, 273
Nicholas, St 20
Northern Ireland 282
Norway 59, 230
NSB (National Socialists,
    Netherlands) 58, 68–9, 194
NU (Nederlandse Unie) 69
Nurnberg, Andrew 263, 264

Odessa 160–63
Oklahoma Native Americans 275
Olga (Birkenau Polish prisoner)
    142, 146, 147
Opekta 63
Osram 11
Oświęcim 110
Otto (uncle) *see* Greenwood, Otto
    (uncle)

Pact of Steel 50
Palestine 211–15, 302
Peck, Mr 205–6
Pfaffhausen 251
Philadelphia 276
Poland 11, 50
    anti-Semitism 111
    Auschwitz *see* Auschwitz-
        Birkenau concentration camp
    devastation of 154–5
    Polish Jews 117, 154
post-traumatic stress 178–82,
    186–8, 192, 226–7, 256–7
Powers, Barbara 267

pregnancy
    Eva's 230–32, 246–7
    pregnant women in Birkenau
        117
prejudice 4, 9, 162–3, 274
    see also anti-Semitism; discrimi-
        nation
Presser, Jacob 99
Prins, Erika 313
prison work 295–301
Promise, The 266–7

rape *see* sexual abuse/rape
Ravasio, Elizabeth 255, 267, 273,
    274, 291–2, 294, 313
Reading Prison 295
Red Cross 162, 172, 173, 174, 179
Redhouse, David 300
Reitsma, Floris 91, 92, 168
Reitsma, Mr 91, 94, 95, 96, 168
Reitsma, Mrs 91, 94, 95, 96, 168
religion 18–20, 199
Roma *see* gypsies
Rommel, Erwin 89
Roosevelt, Eleonor 241
Rose, Alma 116
Rosenbaum, Jan 167, 183, 313
Rosenbaum, Martin 56, 167, 171,
    183
Rosenbaum, Rosi 56, 167
Roth, Heinz 242
Rotterdam 66, 68

Sam (friend) 201, 206–7
San Francisco 276
Schaap, Pieter 196
Schiele, Egon 7–8
Schloss, Caroline Ann (daughter)
    232–3, 239, 245, 254, 259
    son, Alexander Margolis 289
Schloss, Frau 208, 217, 222–3
Schloss, Jacky (daughter, later

Jaqueline Hovelsen) 3, 235,
239, 245, 251–2, 254, 259, 289
daughter, Lisa Heiler 289,
310–11, 313
son, Eric Hovelsen 289
Schloss, Meier 208–12, 213
Schloss, Shlomo 208, 209
Schloss, Sylvia (daughter) 238,
239, 245, 261, 307
daughter, Ella Yaron 289–90,
293
daughter, Sophie Yaron 289–90
Schloss, Zvi (husband) 3, 204,
207–24, 225–6, 227–8, 229–30,
231, 232–3, 235–6, 238, 251,
252, 253, 254, 259, 260–61, 263,
273, 288, 289, 290, 303–5, 307,
313
Schloss family background 208–13
Schnitzler, Arthur 7
Schönbrunn Palace 17, 22, 160,
307
Schönerer, Georg von 29
school speaking engagements
301–2, 311
schooling 18–19, 22, 43, 48, 72–3,
171–2, 181, 182, 191
Schuschnigg, Kurt von 30
Scott, Selina 265
sexual abuse/rape
in Birkenau 127–9
childhood non-parental abuse
45–7, 88
of German women 145
Seyss-Inquart, Arthur 69, 71–2
shyness 189, 226, 234–5
Silva, Teresin da 313
Silverberg, Ed 271, 272, 273
Simons, Branca 196–7
Sobibor death camp 100–101, 106
Soetendorp, David 269
Sophie (granddaughter, Sophie

Yaron, daughter of Sylvia)
289–90
Soviet Union
Jews 155
losses in World War II 161
Russian uniform 308
Soviet soldiers 138, 140, 143,
144–6, 153, 154, 155, 159,
308–9
Ukraine 158–63
Special Justice Act 197
Stalin, Joseph 155
Star of David 76, 82
Stielau, Lothar 242
Still, James 270, 271–2, 273, 281
Strauss Turnbull stockbrokers 228
stress, post-traumatic 178–82,
186–8, 192, 226–7, 256–7
Suijk, Cor 242–3, 258
swastikas 33
Switzerland 189–90, 223–4, 225,
239, 251–2, 284, 285, 291
Sylvi *see* Greenwood, Sylvi (aunt,
née Markovits)
synagogues 50
Szaynok, Wanda 122

Theresienstadt 150
Tom *see* Greenwood, Tom (cousin)
tonsillectomy 78–9
Treblinka death camp 106
Trotsky, Leon 7
typhus 112, 119–21, 172

Ukraine 158–63
United States of America 78, 80
speaking engagements in 267–8
and *And Then They Came For
Me* 271–8

Versailles, Treaty of 11
Vienna 7–39, 307

anti-Semitism in 31–4
Hietzing 7, 17–18, 20
internationalism 28–30
Jews of 7–14, 18–20, 29, 31–7
Nazi arrival in 31–4
Schönbrunn Palace 17, 22, 160, 307
socialist 'Red Vienna' 30

Wagner, Otto 17
Walnes, Gillian 269, 297
Wannsee Conference 75, 106
wedding 222–3
wedding photography 233–4
West, Rosemary 297
Westerbork transit camp 97–103, 106
Wiesel, Elie 305–6
Wilhelmina, Queen of the Netherlands 68
Willis, Bruce 277
Winter, Rootje De 156
Woburn Studios 205–6, 218, 221
Woman's Hour 265
World War I 9, 11, 36, 53
World War II
  and the Americans 78, 80
  BBC bulletins 89
  bombing raids 58–9, 152
  devastation 154–5
  displacement from 164, 214, 259
  end of 162
  final months of 152
  German invasion of Denmark and Norway 59
  German occupation of Holland 66–103, 287
  Holland's early response to 53, 59–60
  outbreak 50–51
  'phony war' ends 67
  Soviets *see* Soviet Union
Wormwood Scrubs 295, 300

Yaron, Ella (granddaughter, daughter of Sylvia) 289–90, 293
Yaron, Sophie (granddaughter, daughter of Sylvia) 289–90
Yugoslavia 11
Yvette (Birkenau French prisoner) 146, 147, 148, 149

Zandvoort 69
Zionism 213–15
Zita of Bourbon-Parma, Empress 14
Zyklon B 107, 143, 150